Rethinking European Social Democracy and Socialism

With a combined focus on social democrats in Northern and Southern Europe, this book crucially broadens our understanding of the transformation of European social democracy from the mid-1970s to the early-1990s.

In doing so, it revisits the transformation of this ideological family at the end of the Cold War, and before the launch of Third Way politics, and examines the dynamics and power relations at play among European social democratic parties in a context of nascent globalisation. The chronological, methodological and geographical approaches adopted allow for a more nuanced narrative of change for European social democracy than the hitherto dominant centric perspective.

This book will be of key interest to scholars and students of social democracy, the European Centre-left, political parties, ideologies and more broadly comparative politics and European politics and history.

Alan Granadino is Postdoctoral Research Fellow in the Faculty of Social Sciences at Tampere University, Finland.

Stefan Nygård is Senior Researcher in the Department of Philosophy, History and Art Studies at the University of Helsinki, Finland.

Peter Stadius is Professor in Nordic Studies and Director of the Centre for Nordic Studies, CENS, University of Helsinki, Finland.

Routledge Advances in European Politics

Linguistic Claims and Political Conflicts
Spanish Labyrinths in the European Context
Andrea C. Bianculli, Jacint Jordana and Mónica Ferrín Pereira

EU-Korea Security Relations
Edited by Nicola Casarini

European Futures
Challenges and Crossroads for the European Union of 2050
Edited by Chad Damro, Elke Heins and Drew Scott

Poland and Germany in the European Union
The Multi-dimensional Dynamics of Bilateral Relations
Edited by Elżbieta Opiłowska and Monika Sus

Electoral Politics in Crisis After the Great Recession
Change, Fluctuations and Stability in Iceland
Eva H. Önnudóttir, Agnar Freyr Helgason, Olafur Th. Hardarson and Hulda Thórisdóttir

The Pandemic Crisis and the European Union
COVID-19 and Crisis Management
Paulo Vila Maior and Isabel Camisão

Belgian Exceptionalism
Belgian Politics between Realism and Surrealism
Edited by Didier Caluwaerts and Min Reuchamps

Rethinking European Social Democracy and Socialism
The History of the Centre-Left in Northern and Southern Europe in the Late 20th Century
Edited by Alan Granadino, Stefan Nygård and Peter Stadius

For more information about this series, please visit: www.routledge.com/Routledge-Advances-in-European-Politics/book-series/AEP

Rethinking European Social Democracy and Socialism

The History of the Centre-Left in Northern and Southern Europe in the Late 20th Century

Edited by Alan Granadino, Stefan Nygård and Peter Stadius

LONDON AND NEW YORK

First published 2022
by Routledge
4 Park Square, Milton Park, Abingdon, Oxon OX14 4RN

and by Routledge
605 Third Avenue, New York, NY 10158

Routledge is an imprint of the Taylor & Francis Group, an informa business

© 2022 selection and editorial matter, Alan Granadino, Stefan Nygård and Peter Stadius; individual chapters, the contributors

The right of Alan Granadino, Stefan Nygård and Peter Stadius to be identified as the authors of the editorial material, and of the authors for their individual chapters, has been asserted in accordance with sections 77 and 78 of the Copyright, Designs and Patents Act 1988.

With the exception of the Introduction chapter, no part of this book may be reprinted or reproduced or utilised in any form or by any electronic, mechanical, or other means, now known or hereafter invented, including photocopying and recording, or in any information storage or retrieval system, without permission in writing from the publishers.

The Introduction chapter of this book is available for free in PDF format as Open Access from the individual product page at www.routledge.com. It has been made available under a Creative Commons Attribution-Non Commercial-No Derivatives 4.0 license.

Trademark notice: Product or corporate names may be trademarks or registered trademarks, and are used only for identification and explanation without intent to infringe.

British Library Cataloguing-in-Publication Data
A catalogue record for this book is available from the British Library

Library of Congress Cataloging-in-Publication Data
Names: Granadino, Alan, editor. | Nygård, Stefan, editor. | Stadius, Peter, editor.
Title: Rethinking European social democracy and socialism: the history of the centre-left in Northern and Southern Europe in the late 20th century/edited by Alan Granadino, Stefan Nygård and Peter Stadius.
Description: Milton Park, Abingdon, Oxon; New York, NY: Routledge, 2022. | Includes bibliographical references and index.
Identifiers: LCCN 2021040379 (print) | LCCN 2021040380 (ebook) | ISBN 9781032020020 (hardback) | ISBN 9781032020099 (paperback) | ISBN 9781003181439 (ebook)
Subjects: LCSH: Socialism–Europe–History–20th century. | Political parties–Europe–History–20th century. | Right and left (Political science)–Europe–History–20th century.
Classification: LCC HX238.5 .R48 2022 (print) | LCC HX238.5 (ebook) | DDC 335.5094–dc23
LC record available at https://lccn.loc.gov/2021040379
LC ebook record available at https://lccn.loc.gov/2021040380

ISBN: 978-1-032-02002-0 (hbk)
ISBN: 978-1-032-02009-9 (pbk)
ISBN: 978-1-003-18143-9 (ebk)

DOI: 10.4324/9781003181439

Typeset in Times New Roman
by Deanta Global Publishing Services, Chennai, India

Contents

List of Contributors	vii
Acknowledgements	x
Introduction: North and South in European and global social democracy ALAN GRANADINO, STEFAN NYGÅRD AND PETER STADIUS	1
1 The Socialist International as a transnational political actor, 1950–1970 KRISTIAN STEINNES	9
2 From democratic socialism to neoliberalisation: Political and ideological evolution of Nordic Social Democrats and Portuguese Socialists after the economic crisis of the 1970s SAMI OUTINEN, ILKKA KÄRRYLÄ AND ALAN GRANADINO	29
3 Put (Southern) Europe to work: The Nordic Turn of European Socialists in the early 1990s MATHIEU FULLA	48
4 Social democracy, globalisation and the ambiguities of "Europeanisation": Revisiting the Southern European crises of the 1970s MICHELE DI DONATO	67
5 Logics of influence: European Social Democrats and the Iberian transitions to democracy STINE BONSAKSEN	84
6 Radicalism and reformism in Post-war Italian socialism: A comparative view PAOLO BORIONI	105

7 Cultural affinity and small-state solidarity: Sweden and Global
  North–South relations in the 1970s   124
  ANDREAS MØRKVED HELLENES AND CARL MARKLUND

8 Looking South: The role of Portuguese democratisation
  in the Socialist International's initiatives towards Latin America
  in the 1970s   142
  ANA MONICA FONSECA

9 Contribution to the critique of "Social Democracy in One
  Country": The case of Sweden   155
  OLLE TÖRNQUIST

10 Defining progress in post-war Mediterranean: Communist
   Movements and their influence in Algeria and Egypt after 1945   176
   RINNA KULLAA

   Epilogue: North-South and Social Democratic transformations in
   Europe and beyond   194
   BERND ROTHER

   Index   203

Contributors

Ana Mónica Fonseca is Assistant Professor at the History Department and researcher at the Centre for International Studies (CEI) at ISCTE-University Institute Lisbon (ISCTE-IUL). Between 2006 and 2015, she was also a researcher at the New University of Lisbon's Portuguese Institute for International Relations (IPRI-UNL). Her main research areas are Southern Europe democratic transitions, Portuguese-German relations during the Cold War, transatlantic relations, German History, democracy promotion and transnational history. She has published in several national and international academic journals (*Journal of European Integration History*, *Portuguese Journal of Social Sciences*, *Ler História*, *Relações Internacionais*) and contributed to various edited volumes.

Andreas Mørkved Hellenes (b. 1986) works as a postdoc at Aarhus University on the research project Nordic model(s) in the global circulation of ideas, 1970–2020. He holds a PhD in history from Sciences Po Paris and the University of Oslo, and his main research interests include diplomacy, socialist internationalism, transport history and Nordic-European relations.

Ilkka Kärrylä is Postdoctoral Researcher at the Centre for Nordic Studies, University of Helsinki, Finland. He specialises in the political and intellectual history of Europe and the Nordic countries, especially the history of economic thought and policy.

Mathieu Fulla is Faculty Member at the Centre for History at Sciences Po, France (Paris). His research focuses on the history of labour movements in Western Europe and the political and economic history of Europe from 1945 to the present. He recently co-edited with Marc Lazar *European Socialists and the State in the Twentieth and Twenty-First Centuries* (Palgrave Macmillan, 2020).

Michele Di Donato is Assistant Professor of Contemporary History at the University of Pisa, Italy. His research focuses on the international history of the European Left, the Cold War and late 20th-century globalisation. Among his publications are "Landslides, Shocks, and New Global Rules: The US and Western Europe in the New International History of the 1970s", *Journal of Contemporary History*, 55:1 (2020), 182–205; "Reform Communism" (with Silvio Pons), in Juliane Fürst, Silvio Pons and Mark Selden, eds., *The

viii   *Contributors*

Cambridge History of Communism, vol. III (Cambridge: Cambridge University Press, 2017), 178–202; and *I comunisti italiani e la sinistra europea. Il PCI e i rapporti con le socialdemocrazie (1964-1984)*, (Rome: Carocci, 2015).

Sami Outinen, DrSocSc, is a researcher of contemporary history, currently a visiting scholar in the Faculty of Social Sciences at the University of Helsinki and a coordinator in the research project "Finns in Russia 1917–1964" at the National Archives of Finland. His research interests include political ideologies, economic policy, Nordic labour market, global economic regulation, employment issues, migration and the approaches of conceptual, comparative and transnational history.

Paolo Borioni is Associate Professor at Rome University La Sapienza. His fields of research are history of political theories and institutions, Nordic history, social democracy and welfare state history. He has previously taught Italian history and European politics at Temple University. He is member of the Scientific Advisory Board of Fondazione Instituto Gramsci and Fondazione Giacomo Brodolini. Among his last publications: "Socialdemocrazia e capitalismo: dalla parità del lavoro col capitale alla sua rimercificazione", *Studi Storici*, 1, 2021; "Libertà di stampa e accesso agli atti nella Svezia del Settecento: una riforma luminosa in un contest ambivalente", *Le Carte e la Storia*, 2, dicembre 2020; "Governo locale, finanze e welfare: il caso danese" in M. Degni (a cura di), *Rapporto Ca Foscari sui comuni 2020, Il governo locale: Modelli ed esperienze in Italia e in Europa*; "The Nordic model in ordo-liberal Europe: from welfare parity to social hierarchy?" in S. Hänninen, K-M Lehtelä, P. Saikkonen, *The relational Nordic welfare state. Between utopia and ideology*, EE Elgar, Cheltenham UK-Northampton MA.

Stefan Nygård is an intellectual historian and senior researcher at the Department of Philosophy, History and Art at the University of Helsinki. He has recently edited *The Politics of Debt and Europe's Relations with the "South"* (Edinburgh University Press, 2020) and co-edited *Decentering European Intellectual Space* (Brill, 2018).

Bernd Rother is Senior Fellow with the Bundeskanzler-Willy-Brandt Foundation (Berlin) and co-chairperson of the SPD's forum on history.

Rother's recent publications include: Sozialdemokratie global. Willy Brandt und die Sozialistische Internationale in Lateinamerika, Frankfurt/Main (Campus) 2021 (English edition forthcoming in 2022: Global Social Democracy. Willy Brandt and the Socialist International in Latin America); Willy Brandt and International Relations, London (Bloomsbury) 2019 (Ed. with Klaus Larres); Willy Brandts Außenpolitik, Wiesbaden (Springer VS) 2014.

Peter Stadius holds a PhD in history and is professor in Nordic Studies and research director of the Centre for Nordic Studies at the University of Helsinki. His research interests include the image of Scandinavia and the Nordic region throughout history, and especially the dynamics between north and south in a European setting.

Olle Törnquist is a Swedish global historian and Professor Emeritus of Politics and Development at the University of Oslo. He has written widely on radical politics, development and democratisation, focusing on Indonesia, India and the Philippines, with Scandinavia and South Africa and Brazil as reference cases. His most recent book is *In Search of New Social Democracy* (Zed-Bloomsbury).

Kristian Steinnes is Professor of modern European history at the Norwegian University of Science and Technology (NTNU), Norway. His research includes modern trans- and inter-national history focusing on subjects such as European social democracy, the European Union and British European policies. He supervises students and teaches courses connected to his expertise. He has been a visiting fellow at the University of Portsmouth, UK, and at the European University Institute, Firenze, Italy.

Alan Granadino is Postdoctoral Research Fellow in the Faculty of Social Sciences at Tampere University, working in the Academy of Finland project "Foreign Policy in Alliance or in Non-Alignment?". He holds a PhD in history and civilisation from the European University Institute. His research interests include the entangled political, social and intellectual history of contemporary Europe. Specifically, he is interested in the history of European integration, European social democracy, the Nordic model and the Spanish foreign policy during and after the transition to democracy.

Stine Bonsaksen has an MA in European studies and is currently a PhD candidate at the Norwegian University of Science and Technology. Her PhD project examines how the Scandinavian social democrats handled the issue of incorporating the young, unstable democracies on the Iberian Peninsula into the Western community of democracies. It explores the role of transnational networks and diverging views on how best to further democratisation. Other research interests include social democracy, European integration and Norway-EU relations.

Rinna Kullaa is Associate Professor at the Faculty of Social Sciences in Tampere University. She is a specialist in global history, international relations, European Union's foreign and security policy, the contemporary Mediterranean area and Russian foreign policy. She has been an Academy of Finland Research Fellow 2015–2020. Currently she is the project leader of the Academy of Finland NONHEGFP project (2019–2023).

Carl Marklund is Researcher Director at the Institute of Contemporary History at Södertörn University. His research examines the interfaces between Nordic social planning, geopolitics and nation branding and scientific knowledge production for the development of various policy fields. He has edited and co-edited several volumes and special issues, including *All Well in the Welfare State?* (Helsinki, 2013), *The Paradox of Openness* (Leiden, 2014) and *Baltic-Nordic Regionalism* (Tartu, 2015).

Acknowledgements

As editors of this volume, we wish to express our gratitude towards those people and institutions that have helped us on the way and made this book possible. The idea of focusing research on the North-South dichotomy in Europa, and more broadly, comes from way back in the identification of potential research themes at the Centre for Nordic Studies (CENS) at the University of Helsinki. Founding Research Director Henrik Stenius endorsed initiatives to pursue research on the topic right from the start in 2002, making it one of the research topics at CENS. Eventually a research network North and South in Europe (NASE) was established, receiving seed funding from the Faculty of Art's Future Fund in 2014. This book project was started at a workshop in Helsinki 2018, funded partially by Nordforsk and the Nordic Research Hub ReNEW, which also was the main funding partner for a follow-up workshop held at Södertörn University in April 2019. We are grateful to the Institute of Contemporary History for hosting us, and extend our gratitude to Director Ylva Waldemarsson, Professor Norbert Götz and Docent Carl Marklund. This book project is also closely linked to The HERA-financed project The Debt: Historicizing Europe's Relations with the "South" (project number 15.057), where Stefan Nygård, Bo Stråth and Henrik Stenius formed the Helsinki team. We are indebted to this project for contributing to the workshop expenses and for inspiring us to develop our research theme. We also wish to thank Rinna Kullaa, leader of the Tampere University–based project NONHEGFP, funded by the Academy of Finland (project number 322426), for showing sincere interest and providing insightful support to our ideas and initiatives. In preparing the book, Stefan Nygård has benefitted from the Academy of Finland (project number 297032).

# Introduction
North and South in European and global social democracy

Alan Granadino, Stefan Nygård and Peter Stadius

This book examines the political history of European social democracy with a particular emphasis on Northern and Southern European experiences in the period from the end of what is sometimes referred to as the golden age of capitalism in the 1970s, until the end of the Cold War and the early 1990s.[1] Focusing on the European North–South axis as our point of departure not only enables us to historicise a major division of contemporary European politics but also allows us to shed new light on the transformation of socialism and social democracy in the critical juncture that stretches from the international economic crises of the 1970s to the launch of third way politics in the 1990s. We especially wish to underline how political actors and parties have conceptualised social democracy across time and space, bring to the fore previously unexplored transnational networks and delve into the dynamics and power relations at play among European social democratic parties in the context of nascent globalisation. The geographical space of action is not only Europe but also a decolonising and decolonised Global South in the cold war–era context, and more recently the scene for the Arab Spring. The chronological, methodological and geographical scope of the book adds complexity to the conventional narrative of social democratic transformation, which is predominantly based on the British and German parties, and provides new knowledge on the often neglected role of socialist internationalism.[2]

Social democratic ideology, political practice and identity were significantly shaped by the entangled histories of the parties of Northern and Southern Europe as well as the transfers and lines of communication between them. In this book, these parties are analysed in the contexts of the Cold War, European integration and globalisation, and their relations are seen against the backdrop of the wider European and transatlantic international networks of the period. By turning the spotlight on such an overlooked spatial dimension and on transnational relations in the history of social democracy, the book aims at filling a historiographical lacuna. As Kristian Steinnes underlines in his orienting contribution, historical research on social democracy has long been tied to the framework of national welfare out of which the movement emerged. While this is understandable and to some extent justified, the long shadow of methodological nationalism has obscured crucial developments and platforms such as the regional, inter- and transnational arenas of European post-war socialism and social democracy

DOI: 10.4324/9781003181439-1

that we focus on in this volume. Making use of archival sources, the individual chapters of the book highlight conceptual and political transfers, as well as the negotiations, debates and power struggles that contributed to shaping projects for transnational solidarity. They offer new knowledge that we hope will be helpful for opening up fresh research perspectives and for identifying gaps or underrated aspects in the contemporary political history of Europe.

In the past three decades, academic literature on social democracy has been dominated by an interest in the crisis – and potential rejuvenation – of the so-called traditional social democratic ideas and policies. On the whole, they are associated with democratisation, the development of the welfare state, educational expansion and, above all, the Keynesian economic policies that were successful in generating rapid growth and high employment in post-war Western Europe. In the 1990s, political scientists were especially interested in explaining what they perceived as a paradox: while many European social democratic parties gained power in that decade, the social democratic ideas that had been predominant during the golden age (1945–1973) were in retreat. Later, the crisis of ideas was matched by a generalised political and electoral crisis. Scholars tried to understand the overall decline of social democracy, and the question of the end of social democracy emerged.[3] Most of them rejected gloomy predictions.[4] However, they coincided in pointing to the period between the mid-1970s and the early-1990s as the watershed decades in which the roots of social democracy's decline and transformation are to be found.

Already in its 1959 Godesberg programme, the Social Democratic Party of Germany (SPD) had formally rejected the goal of replacing capitalism. On the other hand, dismissing the opposition between revolution and reform, social democrats before and after were adamant in their insistence upon long-term transformative change. Social democracy was "more than a party charged to administer the society", as Olof Palme vowed in conversation with Willy Brandt and Bruno Kreisky in the early 1970s. Such beliefs were soon put to the test by changes in the international political economy (monetary depoliticisation and privatisation, empowered transnational financial markets), shifting electoral bases in post-industrialising societies and a growing gap between voters and their increasingly professionalised representatives.[5] What chances did social democracy have to remain on a *proactive* path towards societal change against these and other forces? Would its role be reduced to *reactively* mitigating the effects of the markets?

As many have argued, social democratic ideology was placed on the defensive because of the international oil and economic crises of the 1970s, which made redistribution of capitalist growth more difficult. In 1976, the Swedish social democrats that had been the standard-bearers of national and global new deal politics for over four decades ceded their leadership role in government to a non-socialist coalition. Together with their sister-parties across the world, they soon embarked upon a trajectory towards the post-Keynesian social democracy in the 1980s and 1990s. Through a substantial modification of the concept of "third-way politics", the revamped social democratic parties adapted to neoliberal economic paradigms and to the new international post–Cold War order, globalisation and the shrinking of the working class in Europe.[6]

This developmental narrative has provided a basis for understanding our current condition. Social democracy survived electorally, but it became incapable of transforming society in a more egalitarian sense.[7] Often evoked as one of the factors explaining the sharp rise of inequality and the recent emergence of right- and left-wing populism in Europe, this narrative emphasises structural, international, economic and social factors,[8] but it conceals many aspects of the evolution of European social democracy. For example, it obscures intra- and inter-party struggles and debates, it neglects alternative ideas proposed by European social democrats and it pays little attention to the relevance of intra-European collaborative networks, as well as tensions and hierarchies, in shaping the developmental paths.

Historians have touched upon the geo-cultural dimension of social democracy in both macroscopic works[9] and more narrowly focused case studies. They have demonstrated the relevance of the social democrats' transnational relations for explaining the development of this group,[10] notably during the transitions to democracy in Southern Europe in the 1970s, when the SPD and the French Socialist Party (PSF) promoted different understandings of social democracy and democratic socialism.[11] As for Northern Europe, scholars have explored connections between Nordic and British third ways mainly in the 1990s,[12] and they have concentrated on the parallels – more than the connections – between European social democrats.[13] Furthermore, it seems that the recent scholarly research on the transnational history of social democracy is missing an important element. While the Nordic parties, especially the Swedish SAP, have often been regarded as key representatives of social democracy during the Cold War, they are relatively absent from the transnational history of this group, which has tended to focus on the transitions to democracy in Southern Europe and on the development of social democracy within the European Community (EC).[14] This is a serious gap in view of the paradigmatic status of the "Swedish model" of social democracy globally and consequently also on the Iberian Peninsula in the 1970s and 1980s.[15]

It is against this background that the following contributions aim at a better understanding of the transformation of social democracy. It is worth recalling that the historical contribution of social democracy has been praised for a reason. Through struggle, planning and compromise, this form of politics succeeded in creating a society where the equality of opportunity was greater than before or since. At its peak in the 1970s, ambitious proposals were presented at the United Nations (UN) for a globalisation of the northern social democratic welfare model by extending it to the Third World, as it was called in Cold War parlance, in the context of a "New International Economic Order" (1974).[16] But while a certain nostalgia may be warranted, there is no return to the nationally confined welfare states of the past, whose strong reliance on gross domestic product (GDP) growth and unsustainable levels of energy use and resource extraction are incompatible with the current conditions of climate emergency. This is not to say that other paths of revising the model could not have been chosen over the neoliberal solution, as Mathieu Fulla demonstrates with his analysis of the partial survival and return of Keynesian alternatives in the 1980s and early 1990s within the Party of European Socialists (PES). This book therefore argues that we, instead of uncritically accepting the standard explanation of social democratic reinvention under the impact of oil shocks, debt crises and the economic downturn of the 1970s, and the ideological slogans from the Reagan-Thatcher era ("there is no society"; "there is no alternative" to free-market liberalism), should pay close attention to the choices and decisions made by historical actors at critical turning points, in the context of internal debates among politicians and policy makers, as exemplified by Fulla's discussion of the plans among European socialists for an alternative, less anti-Keynesian "third way" – before the European triumph of the Washington Consensus in the 1990s.

While there has been extensive research on the responses of social democracy to the challenges of the 1970s and beyond, political scientists have predominantly relied on national approaches. As a result, the narrative on the transformation of social democracy is heavily influenced by developments within the main parties, chiefly the British Labour Party (BLP) and the Social Democratic Party of Germany (SPD). Based on the experiences of these parties, scholars have often treated European social democrats as a homogenous group. As an example, in his influential book, Gerassimos Moschonas devotes special attention to the parties of Central and Northern Europe in order to achieve a "conceptual homogenisation" and to account for the logic and action of social democracy "in its entirety".[17] This perspective has overshadowed the experiences of social democratic parties that do not fit the ideal-typical model.

Macroscopically, this tendency is enforced by the way in which "Europe" is excessively treated as a monolithic entity by global and postcolonial historians. The substantial internal power geometries and North–South divisions that we examine in this book are too often airbrushed out of the picture.[18] One striking example of the insufficient attention devoted to internal North–South (not only East–West during the Cold War and beyond) hierarchies, also with respect to intra-European power relations, is the idea that an imposing hegemony of northern centrist and market revisionist Social Democracy went together with the support (and guide) given to the Iberian parties during the process of transition from the mid-1970s. As the other contexts where North–South is discussed in the book, this example underscores the extent to which the divide is social and spatial at the same time. The terms are embedded in a "rhetorical unconscious" that underpins the way in which ideas of progress and change since the Enlightenment have been imposed by the North upon the South.[19] Existing on multiple layers between the national, the regional and the global – as Bernd Rother reminds us in his concluding reflections – the North–South division is at the centre of present challenges within the European Union (EU), where it was transposed onto the older East–West divide during the Eurozone debt crisis in the early 2010s. Exposing one historical example of this European longue durée dichotomy also serves to understand the more visible present-day North–South cleavage within the EU. Furthermore, this frame of analysis offers a way of considering temporality as part of the story, since the various national processes are conducted with the idea of "catching up" or staying ahead. Attention to these synchronic temporalities adds to the understanding of the complexity of the historical development under study here.

North–South cleavages on a variety of topics certainly form a part of the history of European socialism and social democracy as well. As Kristian Steinnes observes in his chapter, in the immediate post-war period, before it faded towards the 1970s, there was a clear North–South division with regard to European integration. In part, because the northern social democratic parties in Scandinavia and England had established themselves more firmly in their respective national political systems, they also showed more reluctance and "needed" the European framework less than their southern counterparts. The North–South divide also manifests itself in the context of political cultures. In one specific area, pertaining to the relationship between unions, parties and the state, Italy provides a striking contrast to the Northern European Ghent system. Situating Italian socialism in a comparative framework, Paolo Borioni's chapter highlights the Italian absence of the kind of twofold parity (between capital and labour as well as unions and pro-labour parties) characteristic of Northern European social democracy. Divergent political cultures and structural economic imbalances are significant variables for understanding the comparatively poorer conditions for the Southern European left to adapt to post-Keynesian globalisation.

One pathway for coping with the multiple crises of the 1970s was provided by expanding transnational socialist networks. Initially, this entailed a revival of the left. At the beginning of the 1970s, several European socialist parties and labour unions adhered to the idea of transcending traditional social democratic policies by advocating workers' self-management (*autogestion*). The French socialists were pioneers adopting this idea from Yugoslavia to Western Europe. They adapted it to their own context and attempted to promote it internationally, chiefly among their Southern European counterparts. Actually, during a short period of time, self-management was a specific ideological goal for socialists in Southern Europe. It became an identity marker and, together with the issue of how to relate to the strong communist parties of the area, differentiated the Southern European socialist parties from their counterparts in the Socialist International.[20]

Self-management bears similarities to the idea of workplace democracy advocated by the Nordic social democrats at that time. However, a potentially different ideological development in the Socialist International (SI) was prevented.[21] In the second part of the 1970s, these projects were abandoned as a result of the fact that, in the context of international capitalist crises, leading social democrat parties such as the SPD promoted a more laissez-faire-oriented economic approach among their European partners,[22] while Southern European socialists prepared to integrate into the European Community. The expansion of transnational socialist networks favoured a dynamic exchange of ideas and practices between European parties, but it also increased the influence that social democrats of dominant European countries had over the socialists and social democrats of Southern and Northern Europe, as Alan Granadino, Ilkka Kärrylä and Sami Outinen point out in their comparative chapter.

In assessing specific developments in "Southern Europe" – increasingly conceptualised as such in this period – we should, as Michele Di Donato argues in his contribution, pay specific attention to the regionalist/internationalist responses to the "shock of the global" of that decade. Socialist internationalism contributed to reordering, challenging and overcoming lines of demarcation, in Europe and globally. Recent scholarship has notably re-evaluated the growing importance of the SI, at a time when social democratic politicians assumed leadership positions in their respective national governments, as well as the role of transnational collaboration in the European Community.

Several chapters in this volume contribute to this literature. With the European North–South framework as her point of departure, Ana Mónica Fonseca highlights the role of the SI as a catalyst for cross-border cooperation in the 1970s. She shows how the reinvigorated organisation – which at that time, as Steinnes reminds us, evolved well beyond its reputation as a powerless socialist discussion forum[23] – channelled international support from state and non-state actors alike. Among the key objects of this support were the Spanish and Portuguese socialist parties during the Southern European transitions to democracy and subsequently their sister-parties in Latin America, where Portuguese and Spanish socialists, chiefly Mário Soares and Felipe González, were important mediators. But, as Stine Bonsaksen notes in her contribution, the specific "impact" of the SI on the Iberian transformations can be assessed in different ways. Besides, the organisation itself was made up of voices and interests that were anything but uniform. Taken together, the chapters by Fonseca and Bonsaksen draw attention to the SI as a major forum for political transfers in and beyond Europe, which manifested themselves through agreement and collaboration as well as dissent and conflict over strategy. More often than not, the Scandinavian parties played the role of the third, mediating element, on this as on other international arenas.

In the momentous era of post-Bretton Woods globalisation, socialists and social democrats across Europe sought to make sense of their position with regard to the changing relation between national welfare, international cooperation and plans for a New International Economic Order beyond the Cold War division. In his chapter, Olle Törnquist highlights the unevenly successful strategies developed in this context by European social democrats facing insurmountable challenges not least in their ambitious plans for globalising the northern welfare model through platforms such as the SI and the UN. Sweden's strong commitment to this project can, as Andreas Hellenes and Carl Marklund propose in their chapter, be seen through the lens of "small-state solidarity" and "cultural affinity". These categories, they argue, can help us look beyond the common binary opposition between idealist and realist explanations for the global positioning strategies and the support for non-aligned world visions by neutral small-state Sweden.

Starting from the same historical constellation, Törnquist's discussion exceeds the framework of historical analysis and asks how the successes of Nordic social democrats in building broad alliances for inclusive democratic societies can be adapted for 21st-century conditions in the Global South. In different ways, both of these chapters underline how Swedish social democrats often saw the rise of the decolonised world as more of an opportunity than a threat, in contrast to the globally dominant great powers of the period. The challenges, but also popular desires, of adapting "Nordic social democratic" political reforms during the Arab Spring, as shown by Rinna Kullaa, bear similarity to the previously mentioned examples. In her chapter, she argues that some of the defining traits of the Nordic societies are highly valued by young generations in North Africa and the Middle East. While pointing out that the lack of social democratic movements characterises the history of the region, she wonders how its future would look like if approached from a different angle; one in which key aspects of Nordic social democratic societies, such as the state's protection of citizens' legal rights, education, health care and the environment, were at the centre. Both Törnquist and Kullaa focus in their chapters on failed outcomes and reflect on potentially missed paths of development.

Notes

1 The chapters originate in two workshops co-funded by the Nordforsk research hub ReNEW (Reimagining Norden in an Evolving World) and the HERA project "The Debt: Historicising Europe's Relations with the 'South'". The workshops brought together historians and political scientists interested in exploring new spatial angles and connections that would shine a light on the process of ideological and political transformation experienced by European social democracy in these decades.
2 Imlay, T., *The Practice of Socialist Internationalism: European Socialists and International Politics 1914–1960* (Oxford: Oxford University Press, 2018).
3 Lavelle, A., *The Death of Social Democracy. Political Consequences in the 21st Century* (Aldershot: Ashgate, 2008).
4 Egger de Campo, M. and Fleck, C. (eds.), "Editorial: End of Social Democracy?", special issue of *ÖZG Österreichische Zeitschrift für Geschichtswissenschaften – Austrian Journal of Historical Studies* 29, 1 (2018): 5–13; Callaghan, J., et al., *In Search of Social Democracy. Responses to Crises and Modernisation* (Manchester: Manchester University Press, 2009); Keating, M. and McCrone, D. (eds.), *The Crisis of Social Democracy in Europe* (Edinburgh: Edinburgh University Press, 2005); Giddens, A., *The Third Way: The Renewal of Social Democracy* (London: Polity, 1998).
5 For a recent discussion on this topic, citing also the quote by Palme, see: Przeworski, A., "Revolution, Reformism, and Resignation", in Maya Adereth (ed.), *Market Economy, Market Society. Interviews and Essays on the Decline of European Social Democracy*, New York: Phenomenal World Volumes, 2021, 16–31; Brandt, W., Kreisky, B., and Palme, O., *Briefe und Gespräche 1972 bis 1975* (Frankfurt am Main and Cologne: Europäische Verlags-Anstalt, 1975).
6 Bailey, D., *The Political Economy of European Social Democracy. A Critical Realist Approach* (Abingdon and New York: Routledge, 2009); Eley, G., *Forging Democracy: The History of the Left in Europe, 1850–2000* (Oxford and New York: Oxford University Press, 2002). In his latest book, Thomas Piketty points to crucial changes in voting patterns in this period, highlighting the role of education in political alignment. As the new "Brahmin left" ("*Gauche brahmane*") was increasingly transformed into the domain of the well-educated professionals, it was cut off from its traditional working-class base. Piketty, T., *Capital et idéologie* (Paris: Seuil, 2019), ch. 15.
7 Plehwe, D., "Introduction", in Mirowski, P. and Plehwe, D. (eds.), *The Road from Mont Pèlerin. The Making of the Neoliberal Thought Collective* (Cambridg, Mass.

and London: Harvard University Press, 2009), 1–42; Scharpf, F., *Crisis and Choice in European Social Democracy* (Ithaca: Cornell University Press, 1991).
8 Schmidtke, O. (ed.), *The Third Way Transformation of Social Democracy: Normative Claims and Policy Initiatives in the 21st Century* (Aldershot: Ashgate, 2002).
9 Sassoon, D., *One Hundred Years of Socialism. The West European Left in the Twentieth Century* (London: I.B. Tauris, 1996); Droz, J., *Histoire générale du socialisme* (Paris: Presses Universitaires de France, 1977).
10 Imlay, T., *The Practice of Socialist Internationalism: European Socialists and International Politics, 1914–1960* (Oxford: Oxford University Press, 2018).
11 Muñoz, A., *El amigo alemán. El SPD y el PSOE de la dictadura a la democracia* (Barcelona: RBA, 2012); Granadino, A., "Possibilities and Limits of Southern European Socialism in the Iberian Peninsula: French, Portuguese and Spanish Socialists in the Mid-1970s", *Contemporary European History* 28, 3 (August 2019): 390–408; Salm, C., *Transnational Socialist Networks in the 1970s: European Community Development Aid and Southern Enlargement* (Basingstoke: Palgrave Macmillan, 2016); Fonseca, A. M., "Apoio da social-democracia alemã à democratização portuguesa (1974–1975)", Transição Democrática em Portugal. *Leer Historia*, 63 (2012): 93–108.
12 Evans, B., "Introduction", in Evans, B. and Schmidt, I. (eds.), *Social Democracy after the Cold War* (Edmonton, Alberta: AU Press, 2012), 1–11; Cronin, J., et al. (eds.) *What's Left of the Left. Democrats and Social Democrats in Challenging Times* (Durham, NC: Duke University Press, 2011).
13 Andersson, J., *The Library and the Workshop. Social Democracy and Capitalism in the Knowledge Age* (Stanford: Stanford University Press, 2010).
14 Andry, A., "Was There an Alternative? European Socialists Facing Capitalism in the Long 1970s", *European Review of History: Revue européenne d'histoire* 26, 4 (2019): 553–572.
15 Granadino, A. and Stadius, P., "Adapting the Swedish Model. PSOE-SAP Relations during the Spanish Transition to Democracy", in Haldor Byrkjeflot, et al. (eds.), *The Making and Circulation of Nordic Models* (London and New York: Routledge, 2021), 102–123; Guillén, A. M. and Luque, D., "Evolving Social Policy Languages in Spain. What Did Democracy and EU Membership Change?", in Beland, D. and Petersen, K. (eds.), *Analysing Social Policy Concepts and Language. Comparative and Transnational Perspectives* (Bristol: Policy Press, 2014), 263–276.
16 Gilman, N., "The New International Economic Order: A Reintroduction", *Humanity: An International Journal of Human Rights, Humanitarianism, and Development* 6, 1 (Spring 2015): 1–16.
17 Moschonas, G., *In the Name of Social Democracy: The Great Transformation from 1945 to the Present* (London and New York: Verso, 2002).
18 The same divisions have also been overshadowed by the primacy of the East–West divide in Europe at the end of the Cold War.
19 Dainotto, R. H., *Europe (In Theory)* (Durham, NC: Duke University Press, 2006).
20 We are indebted here to the contribution of Frank Georgi to the workshops upon which this publication rests.
21 Flandre, C., Bergougnioux, A. & Peillon, V., *Socialisme ou social-démocratie? Regards croisés français allemands, 1971–1981* (Paris: L'Harmattan, 2006).
22 Bernardini, G., "Helmut Schmidt, the 'Renewal' of European Social Democracy, and the Roots of Neoliberal Globalization", in Knud Andresen and Stefan Müller (eds.), *Contesting Deregulation. Debates, Practices and Developments in the West since the 1970s* (New York: Berghahn, 2017), 111–124.
23 Sassoon, *One Hundred Years of Socialism.*

1 The Socialist International as a transnational political actor, 1950–1970

Kristian Steinnes

This is a study of the Socialist International (SI) in the 1950s and 1960s and its role as a political actor. In his mammoth volume on west European socialism, Donald Sassoon laconically claims the SI was a "Cold War organization which did little else besides formulate compromise resolutions which never had the slightest importance".[1] To what extent is this a sensible assessment? By highlighting an underestimated aspect of the SIs role in the post-war era, this chapter focuses on the power of transnational networks and socialisation. It explores how the SI was structured and operated, and it examines its potential and ability to influence individuals and policymaking and bring about policy change. Based on this analysis, the argument put forward is that the role of the Socialist International went far beyond that suggested by Sassoon.

Coinciding with the golden age of western capitalism, European social democracy was at its height in the post-1945 era. With an ambitious programme of managing the economy and building the welfare state, social democracy was a political and societal force that shaped Western Europe perhaps more than any political movement. After some challenging interwar years with tension between socialism in the form of communism and reformism, the latter gained the upper hand in post-war Western European politics, although at different speeds, strength and form. Not only did democratic socialism dominate national politics and government formation, social democratic and socialist parties and individuals also devoted ample time and resources to trans- and inter-national cooperation, eventually gaining momentum as a trans-European political force.

In transnational contexts, social democrats met in order to discuss and develop politics, which, in turn, is believed to have had repercussions for policy formation in national parties and polities. Yet despite acquiring a vital position in European politics, deficiencies exist in our knowledge about processes taking place in the transnational social democratic community. While a comprehensive body of literature deals with social democratic history, ideology and cooperation, analyses of the Socialist International's role at European level during the post-war period are scarce, although with a few exceptions.[2] Being a pivotal actor, the role and functions of the SI were defined by a range of factors: its history and post-war reconstruction, its structure and members, its stated aims and tasks, the context and arena in which it acted, the choices made, the knowledge and experience it

DOI: 10.4324/9781003181439-2

possessed, the contacts and cooperation it facilitated and its financial strength. In short, many factors have to be taken into account when analysing the Socialist International as a political actor.

A political actor is in this study defined as an individual, political party or organisation whose ultimate goal is to coordinate and bring about policy change according to their ideology or stated objectives. In the post-war era, the Socialist International established itself as an active and well-organised political actor in Europe fostering and facilitating social democratic cooperation. Because it consisted of national social democratic and socialist parties, it is best explained as an institutionalised transnational network whose aims, tasks and organisational structure were clearly defined.[3] A transnational network is in this context understood as regular cross-border interactions when at least one actor is a non-state agent or does not operate on behalf of a national government or an intergovernmental organisation. Not only did the SI act as a liaison between national political parties but it also cooperated and was in close contact with other transnational social democratic networks in Europe. As such the SI was a key body for organised transnational centre-left political cooperation and policy formation in post-war Europe.

In order to analyse and assess the functions of a transnational network and its ability to bring about policy change, constructivism, which focuses on intersubjective and social aspects of political systems, is taken into account. The constructivist take on interest formation in organisations is that they are flexible and changing. Broadly speaking, constructivism argues that discourse shapes how political actors define interests, and thus modify their behaviour.[4] Of course, no single theoretical approach can capture the complexity of socialisation, interest formation and politics, yet my proposition is that the Socialist International as a political actor during the 1950s and 1960s is better understood by bringing in constructivism and the concept of socialisation.

Transnational networks, socialisation and political behaviour

Approaches appropriate for the study of an institutional transnational network include concepts exploring mutual influence and socialisation. Socialisation and learning are embedded in concepts of institutionalism which is important because institutional configurations may impact political outcomes. Definitions of institutionalism differ substantially and do not constitute a single research programme.[5] Because institutions also may be defined as systems of norms and symbols, it gives the institutionalist approach a fairly wide remit.[6] An important point is the mutual constitutiveness of social structures and agents.[7] It is obvious that agents make structures, but actors are also subject to the behavioural modifications by those structures. From this point of view, interests and identities do not exist externally to a context of interaction between structures and agents.[8]

These observations encourage the application of constructivist and interpretative approaches, because an underlying theoretical foundation of transnational networks relies on the roles of ideas and culture in policy-formulating processes. The links between being part of a network and adaptation and internalisation of new or changed perceptions are the subject of socialisation theories.[9]

Schimmelfennig defines international socialisation as "the process of inducting actors into adopting the constitutive schemata and rules of an international community".[10] In line with this, Johnston suggests that "socialization aims at creating membership in a society where the intersubjective understandings of the society become taken for granted". When perception, values and ideas become internalised and take on "taken-for-grantedness", they are not only hard to change, but "the benefits of behaviour are calculated in abstract social terms rather than concrete consequential terms".[11] The degrees of internalisation also have to be taken into account because all actors are not always exposed to the same configuration of socialisation, nor do they enter into social interactions with similar prior identifications.[12] Hence, pro-social behaviour because of its "appropriateness" may be the norm, yet at the opposite end of the spectrum, one might find pro-social behaviour because of its material (dis)incentives.

Under which circumstances and to what extent are perceptions and policies transferred and internalised? Axelrod and Checkel have set out conditions or critical mechanisms for strengthening pro-norm behaviour, and listed preconditions as to why agents comply with norms embedded in regional and international institutions. The former lists identification (the degree of identification with the group), authority (the degree to which the norm is seen as legitimate), social proof (which applies to what people decide is correct behaviour) and voluntary membership in a group working together for a common end (defection from group norms carries costs in self-esteem).[13] The latter puts emphasis on five conditions under which agents should be especially inclined to comply by preference change: when an actor, first, is in a new and uncertain environment (generated by the newness of the issue, a crisis or serious policy failure); second, has few prior ingrained beliefs that are inconsistent with the group norm; third, acknowledges the authority of in-group members; fourth, interacts with group members who act out "principles of serious deliberative argument" instead of lecturing or demanding; finally, when interaction occurs in less politicised and more insulated, private settings.[14]

The speed, uniformity and effectiveness of socialisation and the transfer of values, ideas and norms in transnational networks thus largely depend on the kind of institutional and social environment to which actors are exposed. Generally, socialisation and compliance appear to be more likely to occur if an actor strongly identifies with the group or network norms, has common policy goals and subscribes to the authority of the institutional settings. Even though network concepts by and large are accepted as providing useful insights, they have also been criticised for their failing to specify the conditions under which specific ideas are selected, their limited ability to explain social and political change, and their metaphorical nature.

Social democracy – national priorities and international solidarity

Social democracy or democratic socialism is a composite and ill-defined concept, comprising a range of parties, ideas and individuals. Anthony Crosland once defined social democracy as a political ideology based on political liberalism, a mixed economy, the welfare state, Keynesian economic policy and commitment to equality.[15] This definition does not distinguish between political parties and different strands of electoral socialism and may be considered generic. Although dominant ideas of social democracy have evolved and changed and are put together by different strands, it is safe to suggest that they were made up of a particular *famiglia spirituale* with common yet not identical traits.

In reality, social democracy has varied according to national characteristics and history, as well as social, demographic and economic conditions. As such, the concept of socialism has been incessantly modified and adjusted to fit actual needs and challenges.[16] Consequently, an understanding of social democracy has to take account of social cleavages, including class, religion, language, territory and the urban-rural divides. Social democracy's expression in the form of political parties is diverse, and the balance among various elements differs from one place to another. Party composition may enlarge or reduce the political space for social democratic parties, given the presence of communist, socialist, agrarian, religious, communitarian, territorial, environmental and also populist parties. Based on these observations, it is obvious that social democracy had a strong national dimension.

Yet from the outset socialism contained an equally strong element of internationalism, which has been evident in its ideological tenets and manifested i.e., by the formation of internationals (the first 1864–1876, and the second 1889–1916). The former was set up even before the creation of most national political parties. However, with the consolidation of the nation-state and the advent of political parties and universal suffrage, the constituent bases of the emerging socialist parties increasingly were confined to and contingent upon the nation-state. This fortified a tension between a rhetorical, ideological and theoretical affinity to internationalism and international solidarity, and the political reality and pragmatism of being embedded to national constituencies and to a certain extent also gratifying nationalism and the nation-state.

Thus, rhetorically socialist and social democratic parties professed to a loose set of principles stressing internationalism, class consciousness and anti-militarism, while increasingly pursuing and applying a political strategy of bringing about societal objectives in a national context. This tension was evident in the second International during the late 19th century, for instance, in debates over imperialism, and later when many socialist and social democratic parties vigorously voted in favour of war credits at the outbreak of the First World War.

During the interwar years, tensions between a national and an international outlook continued, accentuated over time by deteriorating economic, societal and political conditions. At an organisational level, tensions were manifested by the intensified and widening gulf between socialist reformism and communism.[17] The reformist and democratic faction established the *Labour and Socialist International* as opposed to the *Communist International* (Comintern). However, with the economic depression, the emergence of fascism and Nazism, the rise of nationalism and isolationism, and the growing threat of war, cooperation among democratic socialist parties eventually was undermined during the 1930s, and large swathes of the parties directed focus towards national and domestic challenges.

Although the 1930s were difficult years for international socialism, it underwent a striking revival during the wartime and post-war years, paving the way for the golden age of social democracy, and the 1951 (re)creation of the Socialist International.[18] The setting up of the Socialist International created a structure in which transnational cooperation could come to its own as a transnational political actor. Yet the tension between a national outlook, represented by national parties and priorities, and the party organisations' stated internationalism, lingered in the re-established organisation.

The re-establishment of the SI did not only coincide with the golden age of social democracy. It also corresponded with a period of exceptional and stable economic growth and the building of the welfare state. At the time, whether they previously had been in power or not, many social democratic parties had matured into political and organisational bodies ready to take up governmental responsibilities. In a radicalised political era with an electorate generally leaning leftward, encouraged by the coming to power of the British Labour Party with its Beveridge report and welfare programme, social democratic parties represented a timely and powerful political alternative.

In parallel with the reestablishment of the SI, core Western European states ventured into closer cooperation by signing the Paris Agreement establishing the European Coal and Steel Community (ECSC), setting in motion the process of European integration eventually leading to the creation of the European Economic Community (EEC), the EC and in the early 1990s the European Union. As a major transnational political force at the time, the SI and social democratic parties were deeply involved in this process. The European integration issue figured prominently on the SIs agenda during the 1950s and 1960s.

The nature of the Socialist International

The Socialist International was an organisation with political aims, and implicitly with an ambition to carry out its stated policy objectives. It was put together by social democratic, socialist and labour parties. Because the prospective member parties were eager to ensure their autonomy and also regulate the scope and the ways in which they cooperated, it took six years of negotiations to re-establish the Socialist International after 1945.[19] The negotiations were held largely at the behest of the British Labour Party, who also provided the organisational framework. The way in which the SI was structured laid the foundation for its modus operandi, its activities and the eventual outcome of its undertakings.

The 1951 Frankfurt Declaration: *Aims and Tasks of Democratic Socialism* was an ideological statement significantly influenced by the British and Scandinavian labour parties.[20] It was based upon the principles of democratic socialism and included idealistic ambitions of establishing social justice within and between nations, and of ending all forms of oppression. It was headed by a statement on the principle of freedom and democracy – emphasising the commitment to parliamentary democracy, civil liberties and the defence of the West – and that socialists aimed at building a society in freedom by democratic means: "Without freedom there can be no Socialism. Socialism can be achieved only through democracy. Democracy can be fully realised only through Socialism".[21]

In Donald Sassoon's language, it was "capitalism with a caring and human face, and as few inequalities, as possible".[22] Braunthal claims that the promise held out by socialism and the Socialist International was no less than the creation of a new world.[23] Even though the Frankfurt declaration was built on the basic values that tie social democratic parties together, they never, as pointed out above, possessed an identical interpretation of socialism or an identical social model because of the traditions and socioeconomic conditions in their constituent countries.

The Socialist International was an association of national socialist parties that professed to democratic socialism. Although having a global ambition, it largely was a European organisation during the 1950 and 1960s. Until its 1976 Geneva Congress, it had few members outside Europe, and no formal contacts with Latin America. Its 1978 Vancouver Congress was the first congress arranged outside Europe. Moreover, all presidents and general secretaries during the period were European. During the 1950s, the SI comprised about 30 member parties. It has steadily grown, and in the mid-1980s, it approached 50. In 2020, it had 147 member parties and organisations from over 100 countries worldwide, yet by then an alternative organisation had been formed, the Progressive Alliance, due to internal disagreement and the apparent inclusion of non-democratic parties.[24]

Until the mid-1970s, when the majority of the member parties of the Socialist International and its ideologic roots emanated from Western Europe, it professed to a relatively coherent strand of democratic socialism.[25] Although broad swathes of the literature assume that social democracy was rather homogeneous in terms of its outlook, values, organisation and its strategy for acquiring power and changing the capitalist society – or at least ease the negative effects of a market economy – social democratic parties varied in their willingness and ability to modernise and adapt policies and strategies to changing social conditions.[26] During the post-war decades, it also meant disposing of Marxist features. For example, it was not until its 1959 Bad Godesberg conference that the German SPD decided to get rid of its most antiquated ideology. Across the channel, the British Labour Party was unable to do away with its much-contested 1918 Clause IV (nationalisation) until Tony Blair managed to do so in the mid-1990s. The Scandinavian parties, on the other hand, largely adopted the rules of liberal democracy and rid themselves of communist remnants during the interwar years.

Although the Socialist International's organisational structure was designed to bring about its stated objectives, decisions should, according to its principles, be carried out by strengthened relations between the member parties and by "coordinating their political attitudes by consent".[27] Facilitated by a tiny permanent staff located in London, member party politicians met both on a regular and ad hoc basis in different configurations. As such, the SI was an organised network and a forum for discussions, exchange of ideas and shared information. It did not have the power to carry out binding decisions based on majority voting.

In practical terms, it involved that congresses, the organisation's supreme body, were convened every two or three years to which member parties with voting rights could send six representatives.[28] It stated its principles, determined its statutes and admitted new members. During a congress, a wide range of topics were discussed and at the end resolutions were issued. To keep tabs on current political affairs and developments, the SI Council met on a regular basis, at least once a year. It consisted of two delegates from each member party with voting rights. It discussed present-day affairs and issued resolutions.

The organisational set-up also included the Bureau which was put together by 13 members. It was tasked with convening conferences, committees and Working groups, and setting their agenda. It was also responsible for more down-to-earth practical and organisational tasks. Its secretary general who possessed organisational responsibility also was responsible for organising the exchange and distribution of information between member parties. Subject to the agreement of the Bureau, regional conferences with a limited membership could also be arranged. This organisational structure also involved the means for appointing ad hoc committees and working groups, and for convening conferences if and when required. It did not exclude any group of member parties to arrange meetings outside the remits of the Socialist International.

The Socialist International also produced and disseminated information to its member parties. On a regular basis, it circulated the *Socialist International Information*, which from 1970 was renamed *Socialist Affairs*. It also circulated the *Bulletin of the International Council of Social Democratic Women*. The *Socialist International Information* provided the member parties with a substantial amount of information regarding social democratic activities, elections and current affairs among member parties. It comprised speeches by prominent politicians; reports from national parliaments, national parties, and general elections; information about political developments in the member countries; often reports from conferences and working groups; and sometimes also feature articles written by prominent social democratic politicians. Thus, one of the important roles for the SI was to facilitate and disseminate communication among its constituent parties.

The main topics on the Socialist International's agenda during the 1950s and 1960s included peace and disarmament, the German problem, decolonisation and the political situation in Africa and Asia, the current challenges and achievements of democratic socialism and not least cooperation and integration in (Western) Europe. The latter is well placed to illustrate how and in which ways the Socialist International operated as a political actor seen in the light of institutionalism, socialisation and interest formation.

The Socialist International, social democrats and the making of post-war Europe

In the early phase, European socialist and socialist democratic parties found themselves hopelessly divided on international questions and foreign policy – notably on issues pertaining to the process of European integration which clearly involved a North–South dimension.[29] Divisions also went deep on the German problem – which also included the position of the German labour movement within the Socialist International, the role of a divided Germany in Europe, and towards the mid-1950s also the question of German membership of NATO. A thorny issue was how the parties of the left too close to the communist position should be dealt with – such as the Italian socialists who were excluded until they changed their mind.[30]

In 1948, the French socialists suggested that the thrust for closer cooperation provided by the Marshall Aid should be a groundwork upon which a European federation could be built. This had been countered by the British who strongly opposed any move towards some form of, or even the use of the word, federation. When the Council of Europe was set up in 1949, the socialist parties again were divided over whether to participate and how. The disagreement between the parties widened even further on a North–South divide when Schuman proposed the creation of a European Coal and Steel Community (ECSC) in May 1950. In Britain, Denis Healy pointed out that it was "no accident that in their approach to European unity since 1945 the socialist parties of Britain and Scandinavia have been most conservative – for they have most to conserve".[31] An important reason, he argued, was that economic planning, which was a key feature and a buzzword in socialist policies, reinforced the trend towards nationalism in a governing socialist party.

In preparation for the negotiations in the wake of Schuman's proposal, the Socialist International, or rather its forerunner the COMICO, created a *Study Group on European Unity* in an effort to heal the breach which had been caused by the non-participation of the UK and Scandinavia in the Schuman Plan.[32] This illustrates one vital aspect of the Socialist International's modus operandi. Not only did it discuss the implications of difficult issues at congresses or in the Council, but it also often put together working groups, study groups or committees to sort out disagreements or investigate an issue. Although continental socialists eventually realised the importance of the ECSC and declared their support, the British and Scandinavian parties were reluctant. Consequently, at the first conference of the SI in 1951, Van der Goes van Naters of the Dutch Labour Party (PvdA) castigated the socialist movement for its failure to come up with a unifying vision of European integration as a way of avoiding the evils of nationalism.[33]

When the proposal for a European Army under supranational control, and the remilitarisation of Germany, was presented by the 1950 Pleven proposal for a European Defence Community (EDC), the Socialist International was yet again divided.[34] The EDC split the ranks of the French and was dismissed outright by the German socialists, which was concerned with German unification. The Scandinavians and British sided with the Germans. Disagreement also divided the parties internally. In the British Labour Party, people like Morrison and Attlee were at odds over the move to incorporate Germany into the EDC. Morrison would have welcomed British links with the EDC, while Attlee was deeply sceptical of such an association.

In order to remedy the unfortunate developments, and because the *Study Group on European Unity* neither had been able to bridge the internal divisions, nor possessed the necessary political authority to do so, a new *European committee* was set up. When it presented its report at a conference early in 1954, it yet again displayed the disagreement between the French and German social democrats over the EDC. However, in spite of German opposition – and in spite of Finnish, Swedish and Swiss abstentions – a call for European parties to re-examine their position on the EDC was passed.[35] When the EDC was rejected by the French National Assembly in August 1954, other issues surfaced and moved up the transnational socialist agenda.

At its 1955 Congress in London, at which the Messina initiative was discussed – which eventually would culminate in the Rome Treaty and the setting up of the European Economic Community – the tone in the SI appeared to be less sharp but the North–South division still lingered. The Dutch, Belgians and to a large extent the French were still in favour of more integration, while the British and Scandinavians, and to some extent also the Germans were reluctant. This time there was no resolution issued. Yet the socialist group of the ECSC Assembly called for strengthened links with the Socialist International, suggesting that a representative of each body be present at each other's meetings. At its 1957 congress, the SI decided to convene a joint conference on the Rome Treaty with the socialist groups of the Council of Europe and the Assembly of the ECSC.

Growing out of the socialist group of the ECSC Assembly, social democrats in the Community eventually also formalised their cooperation by the setting up of the *Liaison Bureau of the Socialist Parties of the European Community* in 1957. Its declared purpose was to strengthen interparty relations and, "in particular, to define joint, freely agreed positions on problems raised by the existence of the European Community".[36] Socialist politicians in the Community often were leading politicians in their respective national parties, and in that role often participated in the context of the Socialist International. From the early 1960s, observer representatives from the SI and from the Socialist Group in the Consultative Assembly of the Council of Europe were invited to the Liaison Bureau's congresses. This illustrates how social democrats and socialists met and cooperated across borders and networks.

In the late 1950s, the socialist parties of the EEC largely supported the European integration process, while their northern siblings – the labour parties in Britain and Scandinavia – remained reluctant. The French socialist party had largely been among the protagonists of European integration in the post-war years. Although the German Social Democratic Party voted against concrete integration projects in the early 1950s, it supported the setting up of the 1957 Rome Treaties and West German membership of the EEC. In much the same way, the Italian, Dutch and Belgian socialist parties, although approaching the issue in different ways during the early fifties, supported the Rome Treaties and the creation of the Common Market.[37] Hence, on the eve of the 1960s, continental Western European socialist parties supported the European integration process, although initially mainly brought about by conservative and Christian social parties.

The Socialist International, the European issue and converging perceptions

From 1960 onwards, the European issue took a new twist when the Tory government redefined British European policies, eventually leading to the mid-1961 application to join the EEC. The foundering of the European Free Trade Area negotiations and the following formation of EFTA had created a new and urgent situation which encouraged the Socialist International to strengthen talks on European developments. In turn, this led to reconfigured and also new transnational socialist cooperation patterns.[38] Induced by the new and urgent situation, the Socialist International intensified talks between leading socialists by setting up a *Conference of Party Leaders*, a *Contact Committee* and a *Working Party* to study issues of European integration. The latter was put together by socialist parties across the EEC-EFTA divide in order to examine a range of proposals that had been discussed in the Contact Committee.[39]

The SI conference of party leaders formed an arena in which the leaders of the socialist parties discussed present-day issues in a privatised arena. During the long 1960s, when Britain and the other applicants opted for EEC membership, they met 13 times at important junctures in the process of European integration.[40] A core question in social democratic circles was if and to what extent it would be possible to carry out socialist policies as full members of the EEC. At a mid-1961 meeting of the SI *Contact Committee on European Cooperation and Economic Integration*, the British expressed doubt as to whether it would be possible to carry out socialist planning as set out by the Labour Party if Britain joined the EEC.[41] Spokesman for the German Social Democratic Party, Willy Birkelbach, reassured that even as a full member of the EEC national economic planning would still be possible.[42] The British concerns, widely shared by the Scandinavians, were repeatedly reassured by European Community socialist leaders who stressed that membership would not frustrate socialist policy objectives.[43] On the basis of ten years' experience, they emphasised the development of the Community had been "no obstacle to the achievement of socialist aims: quite the contrary".[44]

Another key issue was if and to what extent social democratic parties would be able to coordinate and formalise common policy objectives. At their May 1960 Congress, the EEC socialist parties agreed that at the present stage of European integration, it was necessary to "work out a common European programme" in order to bring about socialist objectives. The idea evolved inside socialist networks throughout the decade. In the mid-1960s, the EEC socialist parties reiterated their call for the establishment of regular contacts between the national parties' research bodies to see whether a revision of its structure could enable it to "give a positive lead to socialist policy at a community level".[45]

By the end of the decade, well-connected and networked social democratic leadership outside the EC believed membership was in accordance with their programmatic objectives and initiated work on a European-level social democratic programme.[46] At the eve of the 1970s, therefore, concerted efforts existed to pick up and develop the 1960 Liaison Bureau's initial plans for a social democratic programme for Europe. In the early 1970s, the North–South divide had faded, and policy preferences in the northern European periphery had largely fallen into line with those of the socialist parties of the EC.

Efforts to draw up a common socialist programme were followed by attempts to set up a European socialist party, notably by PvdA representatives who from the mid-1960s put forward proposals to this end. At the 1966 Berlin Congress of the EEC socialist parties, the Dutch proposed a list to be presented on how to increase socialist influence in the Community. Inspired by these proposals, a number of initiatives were taken among social democrats towards the end of the decade with a view to creating a European party.[47] In May 1969, a broader group of EC social democrats, including British Labour Party representatives, meeting under the chairmanship of PvdA's Henk Vredeling, insisted on the formation of a European socialist party.[48] Following these efforts, Vredeling and his associates formed a European Political Action Group to work for the creation of a European socialist or progressive party.[49]

In the same vein, the president of the Liaison Bureau, Lucien Radoux, and the chairman of the socialist group of the European Parliament (EP), Francis Vals, had proposed to reform the EC Liaison Bureau to give it a more appropriate structure.[50] At the time, also social democratic commissioners Sicco Mansholt (PvdA) and the Italian Socialist Party's (PSI) Lionello Levi-Sandri were deeply concerned with the issue of strengthening organised socialist influence at EC level and put forward proposals to set up a European party.[51] However, although pressure was building up, some members of the Liaison Bureau had reservations about creating a European party.[52]

Such initiatives of which many emanated from the SI also influenced the Scandinavians. The regional transnational network of parties and trade union confederations, the *Scandinavian Cooperation Committee of the Nordic Labour movement* (SAMAK), initially demonstrated little enthusiasm for European integration.[53] Much like the SI, SAMAK had been re-established after the war and turned into a vibrant network with a broad agenda involving the European issue.[54] Yet a closer examination of its activities and cooperation patterns demonstrates significantly decreased interest, intensity and frequency of these meetings during the 1960s as compared with the 1950s.[55]

As cooperation brought about by the SI intensified, the attention of Scandinavian socialist party leaders was redirected to a wider European framework in the early 1960s. The explanation appears to reside in new challenges combined with the SIs activities by creating new and strengthened cooperation patterns. By actively contributing to these developments, the Scandinavians implicitly redirected their attention towards a European arena at the expense of their established regional network.

At the end of the 1970s, the tone inside the Socialist International had changed. By then a common purpose underpinned social democrats to pick up and develop the 1960 Liaison Bureau's initial plans for a social democratic programme for Europe supported by a European-level socialist party. Policy preference on the European issue in the northern European periphery evidently had converged and was more in line with those of the socialist parties of the EC.[56] At the Socialist International's June 1969 Congress in Eastbourne, an important topic was how to bring into being a socialist programme for the European Community.[57] By then, the undertaking was supported also by former reluctant SI members. During the latter part of the 1960s, and in the context of the SI, even the Norwegian Labour Party put substantial efforts into developing a social democratic programme for Europe.[58]

A key point in this context is that participation in transnational socialist networks brought individuals in the parties directly, as well as indirectly, into contact with processes of deliberation in other countries' parties and labour movements. Thus, they offered an opportunity for socialist leaders and politicians to engage in discussions of sensitive issues as, for instance, the process of European integration. It also involved travelling and experiencing how other national political parties operated. Both implicitly and explicitly, the networked party elites were exposed to perceptions and positions held by other individuals and parties, and information and impressions from these encounters were channelled into intraparty policy-making processes.

The common denominator for structural and organisational changes taking place during the 1950s and 1960s was that the Socialist International contributed by bringing party elites across national and institutional borders closer together. As indicated by Featherstone and others, a consensus on a more positive perception of joining the EC emerged which eventually became embedded also in former reluctant British and Scandinavian networked party leaderships.[59] An important reason for modified perceptions appears to be transnational contacts facilitated by the Socialist International.

During the early 1950s, the Socialist International largely appeared to be involved in co-ordinating national policies rather than making one of its own. On the eve of the 1970s, this had changed, and a new dimension had been added. In the case of European Integration, the Socialist International was involved in efforts to introduce a common socialist policy and the setting up of a European-level political party. These developments are examples that hardly can be detached from activities instigated and brought forward by the Socialist International. On the contrary, they appear to be significant determinants when analysing the SI as a political actor.

Yet it is also evident that political leaders could change their opinion, tactics and policies. Moreover, political leaders could lose their positions and be substituted by less networked individuals or politicians. In the British case, the rise of the Left in the Labour Party during the 1970s, and its antagonism to the Tory government – and the perceptions of the EEC as a capitalist club – resulted in the Labour Party adopting a policy of leaving the European Community, splitting and almost destroying the party in the early 1980s.

The Socialist International as political actor

It may be argued that activities in the Socialist International had little effect, as suggested by Sassoon, since international relations was in the hands of the superpowers and could not be affected by a powerless talking club of socialists, and that domestic politics was determined by national structures and socioeconomic conditions. This line of reasoning apparently is supported by the fact that the Socialist International produced compromise resolutions based on unanimity and with limited impact.

Although compromise resolutions may inspire policymaking and put a mark on politicians, evidence is pointing towards the significance of cooperation and socialisation in transnational networks. By convening congresses and council meetings, organising conferences, committees and working groups, and by bringing leading politicians across institutional and national borders together, the Socialist International, in accordance with propositions put forward by Axelrod and Checkel, produced conditions for strengthening pro-norm behaviour and offered structures conducive to the formation of intersubjective understandings. Consequently, in line with interpretative and constructivist propositions, contacts, discussions and discourses in transnational contexts potentially had a number of functions with repercussions for the Socialist International's role as a political actor.

First, participation in a network in the context of the Socialist International, party leaderships and party individuals were brought in closer contact with processes of deliberation in other parties and networks, providing them with information on developments and policies on relevant issues. As demonstrated by this study, and corroborated by relevant literature, close relationships existed between the Socialist International and socialist individuals and networks in the ECSC/EEC, the Council of Europe and the well-established Cooperation Committee of the Nordic Labour Movement.[60] It indicates that activities organised by the SI facilitated cooperation and information sharing in and between individuals and social democratic networks.

Second, being embedded in similar ideological traditions, networking over time also allowed socialist party elites to define and elaborate common policy objectives. Many developments outside national control had consequences for national policies, and the networks were adequate structures in which participants could discuss and promote policies based on party preferences and ideology. To some extent transnational networks developed a shared social system of perceiving the world which led politicians to work out solutions for societal challenges. Studies have demonstrated how cross-border networks influenced interstate bargaining.[61] The present study has indicated that perceptions of the process of European integration converged, eventually leading to the Socialist International's joint efforts to prepare a socialist programme for Europe and set up a transnational social democratic party within the context of the EC on the eve of the 1970s.

Third, the web of contacts facilitated by the Socialist International also was valuable for identifying suitable partners for discussing ideas and developing and implementing policy objectives. By bringing together social democrats and socialists across national and institutional structures, the SI enabled social democratic and socialist politicians and parties to expand and enrich their network. As demonstrated above, social democrats were divided over integrative steps taken in the late 1940s and early 1950s. Yet interparty discussions requiring cooperation across national borders carried an inherent potential for adjusted perceptions. In this context, the SI and its forerunner COMISCO were appropriate arenas in which individuals and working groups were put together in order to identify and put together individuals and working groups to investigate possible ways ahead. Identifying suitable partners were appropriate when engaging in trans- and international negotiations on specific issues.

Fourth, according to theoretical propositions offered by constructivist and interpretative approaches, participation in these networks had the capacity to influence both individuals and ultimately policy formation, party policies and politics.[62] Deepened transnational networking over time not only created a framework conducive to socialisation but also had the capacity to build lasting cross-border social trust.[63] Despite early disagreements over the European integration process, networks facilitated by the SI enabled socialist leaders to build trust in the form of normative and emotional bonds. Regular meetings over time allowed participants to share their political beliefs and policy preferences, ultimately having the capacity to enable convergence of perceptions.[64]

Finally, contacts instigated by the SI largely were independent of being in power. Regular connections between governments and ministers easily were weakened or cut off if a party was voted out of power. Interactions in the context of the Socialist International's networks existed and were maintained largely independent of a party's position within the polity.

Conclusion: What was the role of the Socialist International as a political actor?

In this chapter, I have analysed the role of the Socialist International as a political actor by highlighting its potential, ability and capacity to influence individuals and policymaking and thus bring about policy change. By focussing on transnational networks and socialisation, underpinned by insights from interpretative and constructivist approaches, it demonstrates that the Socialist International was an organised transnational network in which party elites were likely to be influenced by values, world views and policy preferences held by other individuals and parties.

The 1951 (re)construction of the SI implied that social democratic and socialist parties decided to devote time and resources to trans- and inter-national cooperation, and it involved the formation of a well-structured and long-lasting transnational network. It brought together socialist groups across national and institutional borders, and when appropriate or necessary, it put together conferences, committees and working groups. Such arrangements and activities enabled social democrats to discuss, investigate and advise on particular issues. Committees and study groups could be set up on an ad hoc basis alongside long-term contacts and arrangement. An important generic characteristic was that the organisation brought individuals and political parties together in different configurations, often for protracted periods of time.

Conditions in these transnational arenas to a large extent met the specific criteria set out by scholars under which socialisation is likely to take place. Inside and across transnational social democratic and socialist networks, in which the Socialist International was a core actor and facilitator, members identified with prevalent ideas, values and norms and regarded them as legitimate. They participated on a voluntary basis and harboured few prior ingrained beliefs that were inconsistent with basic values. They also acknowledged the authority of in-group members and interacted with individuals based on principles of serious deliberative argument. In a context absent of instructions or demands, members usually are susceptible to arguments and deliberations. These processes involved that intersubjective understandings were likely to become internalised and take on "taken-for-grantedness". As such, the theoretical argument put forward in this study indicates that ideas were being transferred and internalised, and that members of the networks adjusted perceptions and policies accordingly.

Although far from all observed policy changes can be attributed to the SI, it is an underestimated aspect of activities undertaken by the Socialist International. By bringing together leading socialists and social democrats across Europe in transnational configurations, it facilitated and developed long-time relations and trust. Moreover, the creation of networks was instrumental and rational in order to facilitate and develop policies and bridge divisions. Because complicated choices are expected to rely on calculations of the probability of outcomes, the intellectual and institutional climate in which decisions are made is vital.

Yet the theoretical argument put forward in this study does not specify the conditions under which contacts, cooperation and networking were likely to influence participants. Nor does it indicate who influenced whom. Nevertheless, theoretical propositions brought to notice by transnational and constructivist approaches and the concept of socialisation offer plausible explanations to the process of converging perceptions of post-war European integration among European networked socialists and social democrats. It also demonstrates that the role of the SI went far beyond being a "Cold War organization which did little else besides formulate compromise resolutions which never had the slightest importance", as suggested by Donald Sassoon.

Notes

1 Donald Sassoon, *One Hundred Years of Socialism* (London: I. B. Tauris Publishers, 1996), 210.
2 An obvious exception is Julius Braunthal, *History of the International 3. World Socialism 1943–1968* (London: Nelson, 1980). Otherwise see Pascal Delwit, *Social Democracy in Europe* (Bruxelles: Editions de l'Université de Bruxelles, 2005); Hans Keman, *Social Democracy. A Comparative Account of the Left-Wing Party Family* (London: Routledge, 2017); Hans Keman, "Theoretical Approaches to Social Democracy", *Journal of Theoretical Politics* 5, no. 3 (July 1993), 291–316; Donald Sassoon, *One Hundred Years of Socialism* (London: I. B. Tauris Publishers, 1996); Kevin Featherstone, *Socialist Parties and European Integration. A Comparative History* (Manchester: Manchester University Press, 1988); Michael Newman, *Socialism and European Unity. The Dilemma of the Left in Britain and*

France (London: Junction Books, 1983); Byron Criddle, *Socialists and European Integration. A Study of the French Socialist Party* (London: Routledge, 1969); Richard T. Griffiths, ed., *Socialist Parties and the Question of Europe in the 1950's* (Leiden: E. J. Brill, 1993); Klaus Misgeld, "Den svenska socialdemokratin och Europa från slutet av 1920-talet till början av 1970-talet", in *Socialdemokratin och svensk utrikespolitik. Från Branting till Palme*, edited by Bo Huldt and Klaus Misgeld (Stockholm: Utrikespolitiska institutet, MH Publishing, 1990), 195–210; Klaus Misgeld, "As the Iron Curtain Descended. The Co-ordinating Committee of the Nordic Labour Movement and the Socialist International between Potsdam and Geneva (1945–1955)", *Scandinavian Journal of History* 13, no. 1 (1988), 49–63; Kristian Steinnes, "A Socialist Europe? Democratic Socialist Party Ideas and the Process of European Integration 1960–1973", in *European Parties and the European Integration Process, 1945–1992*, edited by Lucia Bonfreschi, Giovanni Orsina, and Antonio Varsori (Bruxelles: P.I.E. Lang, 2015); Arne Lyngstad, *Europa – debatt i Den Sosialistiske Internasjonale 1955–1963* (Trondheim: unpublished MA thesis, University of Trondheim, 1992).

3 By this definition, political parties are transnational actors. Despite their national basis and close relations to state institutions, their functional role and political behaviour is largely independent of the state. As of late, transnational network approaches have increased their focus on functions at the cost of structural frameworks. While overlapping the areas between intergovernmental and transnational activities, transnationalism in this conception does not refer exclusively to a level, but rather to social phenomena that link different functions. See Wolfram Kaiser and Peter Starie, eds., *Transnational European Union. Towards a Common Political Space* (London: Routledge, 2005), 5.

4 See for example D. C. Phillips, "The Good, the Bad, and the Ugly: The Many Faces of Constructivism", *Educational Researcher* 24, no. 7 (1995), 5–12.

5 Institutionalism is often subdivided into rational choice, historical and sociological approaches. Historical and sociological institutionalism tends to define institutionalism more broadly than rational choice variants. See for instance Paul Pierson, "The Path to European Integration: A Historical Institutional Analysis", *Comparative Political Studies* 20, no. 2 (1996), 123–63; Paul Pierson, *Politics in Time. History, Institutions, and Social Analysis* (Princeton: Princeton University Press, 2004).

6 See, for example, the definition of institutionalism put forward by Armstrong and Bulmer as "formal institutions; informal institutions and conventions; the norms and symbols embedded in them; and policy instruments and procedures" in Kenneth A. Armstrong and Simon J. Bulmer, *The Governance of the Single European Market* (Manchester: Manchester University Press, 1998), 52.

7 Thomas Risse, "Social Constructivism and European Integration", in *European Integration Theory*, edited by Antje Wiener and Thomas Diez (Oxford: Oxford University Press, 2004), 1.

8 These debates are heavily inspired by, and even amalgamated in the works of, Anthony Giddens and his development and elaboration of the structuration theory. The structuration theory attempts to show how social structures are both constituted by human agency and at the same time the very medium of this constitution. See for instance: Anthony Giddens, *New Rules of Sociological Method. A Positive Critique of Interpretative Sociologies* (New York: Basic Books, 1976) and Anthony Giddens, *The Constitution of Society. Outline of the Theory of Structuration* (Cambridge: Polity Press, 1984).

9 See, for example, Alastair Iain Johnston, "Treating International Institutions as Social Environments", *International Studies Quarterly* 45, no. 4 (2001), 487–515 (especially 494–96); Frank Schimmelfennig, "International Socialization in the New Europe: Rational Action in an Institutional Environment", *European Journal of International Relations* 6, no. 1 (2000), 109–139; Robert Axelrod, "Promoting Norms: An Evolutionary Approach to Norms", in *The Complexity of Cooperation*,

edited by Robert Axelrod (Princeton: Princeton University Press, 1997), 58–59; Jeffrey T. Checkel, "Why Comply? Social Learning and European Identity Change", *International Organization* 55, no. 3 (2001), 553–588.
10 Frank Schimmelfennig, "Transnational Socialization: Community-Building in an Integrated Europe", in *Transnational European Union. Towards a Common Political Space*, edited by Wolfram Kaiser and Peter Starie (London: Routledge, 2005), 63.
11 Alastair Iain Johnston, "Treating International Institutions as Social Environments", *International Studies Quarterly* 45, no. 4 (2001), 495. This is a point elaborated by Hall who argues that "orders" of learning are an adequate way of dealing with the degree of internalisation. He argues that first-order learning takes place when actors adjust policy techniques and settings while holding policies constant, that second-order learning occurs if policy goals and instruments are altered, and that third-order learning is present if an organisation's or a group's paradigm of world view and overarching goals are changed. Peter Hall, "Policy Paradigms, Social Learning, and the State: The Case of Economic Policymaking in Britain", *Comparative Politics* 25 (1993), 275–296.
12 See Leann M. Brown, "Learning and Food Security in the European Union", in *Organizational Learning in the Global Context*, edited by Leann Brown et al. (Hampshire: Ashgate, 2006), 25.
13 Robert Axelrod, "Promoting Norms: An Evolutionary Approach to Norms", in *The Complexity of Cooperation*, edited by Robert Axelrod (Princeton: Princeton University Press, 1997), 58. See also Alastair Iain Johnston, "Treating International Institutions as Social Environments", *International Studies Quarterly* 45, no. 4 (2001), 495.
14 Jeffrey T. Checkel, "Why Comply? Social Learning and European Identity Change", *International Organization* 55, no. 3 (2001), 562–63.
15 Anthony Crosland, *The Future of Socialism* (London: J. Cape, 1956).
16 See Iring Fetscher, "The Changing Goals of Socialism in the Twentieth Century", *Social Research* 47, no. 1 (1980), 36–62.
17 Although we analytically can distinguish between reformism and revisionism, the dividing lines between the two are unclear in much of the literature. Revisionist arguments relate to interpreting in a new way the original ideas and goals of social democracy, while reformist strategies deal with the piecemeal management of democratic socialism within capitalist democracies.
18 Talbot C. Imlay, *The Practice of Socialist Internationalism: European Socialists and International Politics, 1914–1960* (Oxford: Oxford University Press, 2017).
19 At first an information bureau was established, the Socialist Information and Liaison Office (SILO) 1946–1947, later the Committee of the International Socialist Conferences (COMISCO) 1947–1951. The COMISCO changed into the Council, and the subcommittee into the Bureau of the SI.
20 To a fair extent it was the work of the British Labour Party and Scandinavian social democrats. Donald Sassoon, *One Hundred Years of Socialism* (London: I. B. Tauris Publishers, 1996), 210.
21 *Aims and Tasks of Democratic Socialism*, part 1, paragraph 2. Declaration of the SI adopted at its First Congress held in Frankfurt-am-Main on 30 June–3 July 1951.
22 Donald Sassoon, *One Hundred Years of Socialism* (London: I. B. Tauris Publishers, 1996), 210.
23 Julius Braunthal, *History of the International 3. World Socialism 1943–1968* (London: Nelson, 1980), 513.
24 In later years, the SI has been criticised because it included too many non-democratic parties, and in 2013, the German SPD formed a new organisation, the Progressive Alliance, of former and current members of the SI. In 2020, the Progressive Alliance claimed 140 participants from around the world.
25 See Richard Lowenthal, "Democratic Socialism as an International Force", *Social Research* 47, no. 1 (1980), 63–92.

26 Hans Keman, *Social Democracy. A Comparative Account of the Left-Wing Party Family* (London: Routledge, 2017), notably 37–47.
27 Statute of the Socialist International. International Institute of Social History (IISH), SI, 249, 6th Congress, Hamburg, 14–17 July 1959.
28 Congresses were convened every second year from 1953 and every third year from 1963.
29 See for instance: Klaus Misgeld, "As the Iron Curtain Descended. The Co-ordinating Committee of the Nordic Labour Movement and the Socialist International between Potsdam and Geneva (1945–1955)", *Scandinavian Journal of History* 13, no. 1 (1988), 49–63; Richard T. Griffiths, ed., *Socialist Parties and the Question of Europe in the 1950's* (Leiden: E. J. Brill, 1993).
30 Richard T. Griffiths, ed., *Socialist Parties and the Question of Europe in the 1950's* (Leiden: E. J. Brill, 1993), 14–24.
31 Quoted from Edmund Dell, *The Schuman Plan and the British Abdication of Leadership in Europe* (Oxford: Oxford University Press, 1995), 190.
32 Richard T. Griffiths, ed., *Socialist Parties and the Question of Europe in the 1950's* (Leiden: E. J. Brill, 1993), 16.
33 Richard T. Griffiths, ed., *Socialist Parties and the Question of Europe in the 1950's* (Leiden: E. J. Brill, 1993), 17.
34 Divisions were clearly demonstrated at the SIs December 1951 Council meeting. Donald Sassoon, *One Hundred Years of Socialism* (London: I. B. Tauris Publishers, 1996), 214.
35 Richard T. Griffiths, ed., *Socialist Parties and the Question of Europe in the 1950's* (Leiden: E. J. Brill, 1993), 19–20.
36 Declaration of the first Congress of the EEC socialist parties in Luxembourg, January 1957, IISH, SI 45, Socialist International Information (SII), 1977, 111.
37 Wilfried Loth, "The French Socialist Party, 1947–1954", in *Socialist Parties and the Question of Europe in the 1950's*, edited by Richard T. Griffiths (Leiden: E. J. Brill, 1993), 25; Denis Lefebvre, "The French Socialist Party, 1954–1957", in *Socialist Parties and the Question of Europe in the 1950's*, edited by Richard T. Griffiths (Leiden: E. J. Brill, 1993), 56; Rudolf Hrbek, "The German Social Democratic Party, I", in *Socialist Parties and the Question of Europe in the 1950's*, edited by Richard T. Griffiths (Leiden: E. J. Brill, 1993), 63, 74; Jürgen Bellers, "The German Social Democratic Party, II", in *Socialist Parties and the Question of Europe in the 1950's*, edited by Richard T. Griffiths (Leiden: E. J. Brill, 1993), 78–89; Ennio di Nolfo, "The Italian Socialists", in *Socialist Parties and the Question of Europe in the 1950's*, edited by Richard T. Griffiths (Leiden: E. J. Brill, 1993), 90–98, 106–134; Thierry E. Mommens and Luc Minten, "The Belgian Socialist Party", in *Socialist Parties and the Question of Europe in the 1950's*, edited by Richard T. Griffiths (Leiden: E. J. Brill, 1993), 140–61.
38 See Kristian Steinnes, "Socialist Party Network in Northern Europe. Moving towards the EEC Application of 1967", in *The History of the European Union. Origins of a Trans- and Supranational Polity 1950–72*, edited by Morten Rasmussen et al. (London: Routledge, 2009), 93–109.
39 It had been set up at a July 1960 meeting of the SI Contact Committee. IISH, SI, SII vol. X, 1960, 472 and SI, 590, European Cooperation and Economic Integration Contact Committee 1960–61, 27 February 1961.
40 The first conference took place in Salzburg in January 1961. The subsequent conferences were held in July 1961 (Elsinore, Denmark), October 1963 (Marseilles), 12 April 1964 (Chequers, London), 9–10 January 1965 (Salzburg), April 1965 (London), 24–25 October 1965 (Paris), 4–5 January 1967 (Rome), 9 December 1967 (Chequers, London), 30 March 1969 (Vienna), 6–7 July 1969 (Harpsund, Sweden), 21–22 March 1970 (Brussels) and 2–4 September 1971 (Salzburg). An extraordinary conference of party leaders was convened in February 1963 (Brussels), in the wake of the breakdown of the British membership negotiations during the previous month.

The most intense cooperation at the conference of party leaders corresponds with the period in which Britain and the other applicants sought to join the EEC during the 1960s.
41 IISH, SI, 590, 2 July 1961, and report from SI, Labour Archives Manchester (LAM), International Dept., box EEC memoranda etc., Finance and Economic Policy Sub-Committee, 27 July 1961.
42 SPD spokesman Willy Birkelbach. Report from SI, Meeting of the Contact Committee on European Cooperation and Economic Integration, 2 July 1961, Circular No. 49, 1961, 27 July 1961. See also LAM, International Dept., box EEC memoranda etc., Finance and Economic Policy Sub-Committee, 2 and 27 July 1961.
43 IISH, SI, 590, 2 July 1961, Summary report of meeting of the Contact Committee of the Socialist International, which referred to fears of the Scandinavian Cooperation Committee of the Nordic Labour Movement (SAMAK).
44 IISH, SI, SII Vol XII, Documents of the Fifth Congress of the Socialist Parties of the European Community, 5–6 November 1962, 713.
45 Statement by the Berlin Liaison Bureau Congress on 17–18 November 1966. Simon Hix and Urs Lesse, *Shaping a Vision. A History of the Party of European Socialists 1957–2002*, Party of European Socialists (PES) (Brussels: http://urs-lesse.de/History_PES_EN.pdf, 2002), 17.
46 The Swedish Labour Movement's Archives and Library, Stockholm (ARAB), SAMAK, Report, Social Democratic Nordic Congress on European Integration, Helsinki, 18–19 December 1970, 5.
47 European Union Archives, Florence (EUA), Group Socialiste Parlement européen (GSEP) 51, Vers un Parti Européen Progressiste, PE/GS/21/1970.
48 IISH, SI 595, Socialist Co-operation, April 1970, 19. See also Harold Wilson at the 1969 SI Eastbourne Congress, Harold Wilson, 17 June, 16–20 June 1969, IISH, SI, SII 1969.
49 Socialist Co-operation, April 1970, 19–21, IISH, SI 595.
50 EUA, GSEP 50, PE/GS/125/69.
51 IISH, SI 595, Socialist Co-operation, April 1970, 19.
52 EUA, PS/CE/68/69, Procès-verbal de la réunion du Bureau de liaison, 14 November 1969.
53 Mikael af Malmborg, *Den ståndaktiga nationalstaten. Sverige och den västeuropeiska integrationen 1945–1959* (Lund: Lund University Press, 1994); Richard T. Griffiths, ed., *Socialist Parties and the Question of Europe in the 1950's* (Leiden: E. J. Brill, 1993), 178–200, 201–20, 221–38.
54 Although having been set up in 1912, the SAMAK lay prone most of the interwar years. After a couple of wartime talks, it was re-established in 1945 after which the leadership of the parties and trade unions met regularly, normally twice a year.
55 The Norwegian Labour Movement's Archives and Library, Oslo (AAB), The Norwegian Labour Party (DNA), Da 1945, box 5, Da 1946, box 11, Da 1947, box 17, Da 1948, box 21, Da 1949, box 28, Da 1950, box 37, Da 1951, box 47; The Danish Labour Movement's Library and Archives, Copenhagen (ABA), Socialdemokratiet (SD), SAMAK, Ks, 326, Ks 327–28 (1952–54), Ks 329–30 (1955–58), Ks 331 (1959–62); ABA, Per Hækkerup papers (PHA), Ks 653; ARAB, Tage Erlander papers (TEA) and Olof Palme papers (OPA).
56 Kristian Steinnes, "Northern European Social Democracy and European Integration, 1960–1972. Moving towards a New Consensus?", in *Consensus and European Integration. An Historical, Perspective*, edited by Daniela Preda and Daniele Pasquinucci (Brussels: P.I.E. Peter Lang, 2012), 107–122.
57 Kristian Steinnes, "A Socialist Europe? Democratic Socialist Party Ideas and the Process of European Integration 1960–1973", in *European Parties and the European Integration Process, 1945–1992*, edited by Lucia Bonfreschi, Giovanni Orsina, and Antonio Varsori (Bruxelles: P.I.E. Lang, 2015), 67–80.

58 The party's 1970–1973 manifesto explicitly stated that the objective was to "initiate cooperation between Western European Social Democratic parties to prepare a European programme" on which a "Europe characterised by democratic socialist principles" could be built. Statement DNA, European Cooperation, January 1967, AAB, Finn Moe papers (FMA), box 0009; and International Committee, European Cooperation, 18 January 1967, FMA, box 0008. See also EEC questions to DNAs leadership, by Helge Hveem at the Norwegian International Peace Research Institute (PRIO), 26 November 1970, AAB, Per Kleppe papers (PKA), box 45.

59 Kevin Featherstone, *Socialist Parties and European Integration. A Comparative History* (Manchester: Manchester University Press, 1988); Kristian Steinnes, *The British Labour Party, Transnational Influences and European Community Membership, 1960–1973* (Stuttgart: Franz Steiner Verlag, 2014), 144–153.

60 See for instance Simon Hix and Urs Lesse, *Shaping a Vision. A History of the Party of European Socialists 1957–2002*, PES (Brussels: http://urs-lesse.de/History_PES_EN.pdf, 2002); Donald Sassoon, *One Hundred Years of Socialism* (London: I. B. Tauris Publishers, 1996); Richard T. Griffiths, ed., *Socialist Parties and the Question of Europe in the 1950's* (Leiden: E. J. Brill, 1993); Klaus Misgeld, "As the Iron Curtain Descended. The Co-ordinating Committee of the Nordic Labour Movement and the Socialist International between Potsdam and Geneva (1945–1955)", *Scandinavian Journal of History* 13, no. 1 (1988), 49–63; Kevin Featherstone, *Socialist Parties and European Integration. A Comparative History* (Manchester: Manchester University Press, 1988).

61 See for example: Katja Seidel, *The Process of Politics in Europe: The Rise of European Elites and Supranational Institutions* (London: I.B. Tauris, 2010); Brigitte Leucht, *Transatlantic Policy Networks and the Formation of Core Europe*, PhD Thesis (Portsmouth: University of Portsmouth, 2008); S. Bugdahn, "Travelling to Brussels via Aarhus: Can Transnational NGO Networks Impact on EU Policy?", *Journal of European Public Policy* 15, no. 4 (2008), 588–606.

62 Frank Schimmelfennig, "International Socialization in the New Europe: Rational Action in an Institutional Environment", *European Journal of International Relations* 6, no. 1 (2000), 109–139 and Frank Schimmelfennig, "Transnational Socialization: Community-Building in an Integrated Europe", in *Transnational European Union. Towards a Common Political Space*, edited by Wolfram Kaiser and Peter Starie (London: Routledge, 2005), 61–82.

63 For a discussion on social and instrumental trust, see: Roderick M. Kramer and Tom R. Tyler, *Trust in Organizations: Frontiers of Theory and Research* (London: Sage, 1996).

64 Some of the social democratic leaders possessed leading roles in parties and government for long periods during the 1950s and 1960s. Tage Erlander was party leader and prime minister of Sweden for 23 years, and the Norwegian Halvard Lange was foreign minister for almost 20 years. Danish Jens Otto Krag and British Harold Wilson were influential politicians in their respective countries and active participants in European socialist networks.

2 From democratic socialism to neoliberalisation

Political and ideological evolution of Nordic Social Democrats and Portuguese Socialists after the economic crisis of the 1970s

Sami Outinen, Ilkka Kärrylä and Alan Granadino

In the wake of the economic crises of the 1970s, Socialists and Social Democrats in Southern and Northern Europe modified their discourses and policies in order to adapt to new economic and political circumstances. Keynesian post-war full employment policies faced recurrent crises in the Nordic countries, while in the Iberian Peninsula, the transitions to democracy opened the possibility of redefining the economic policies of the main political actors. This chapter examines the policies and concepts of democracy and economy of Nordic Social Democratic parties and the Portuguese Socialist Party (PS), including topic-relevant transnational reflexive comparisons during the 1970s and the early 1980s, years of political transformations in Southern Europe and global economic transition.[1] This chapter contributes to a transnational and comparative history of peripheral European Social Democratic parties. It crosses the conventional East–West division while analysing political history in the cold war context as well as urges to avoid archetypal Western–Eastern division in European intellectual history.[2] The chapter leans methodically on conceptual history and transnational comparative reflexivity,[3] in addition to researching direct transnational connections. This enables us to historise how Nordic Social Democrats and Portuguese Socialists sketched their own scopes of action in positive and negative relation to major ideologies[4] and redefined their conventional meanings.[5]

Academic literature on Social democracy is vast.[6] Political scientists usually contextualise their analysis, writing a brief historical account of post-war Social Democracy. These accounts often follow the subsequent explanatory line: in post-war Europe, a class compromise between the organised working class and large businesses emerged, facilitated by sustained growth and the Keynesian employment commitment. Capitalist profits were redistributed, and, thanks to progressive taxation, welfare states could be expanded. This political and socio-economic deal started to crumble in the 1970s because of slowing economic growth in the developed countries due to Asian competition and saturation of consumer goods markets, high wages, the end of the Bretton Woods system and an abrupt increase in the price of oil. From this decade on, globalisation and the collapse of Communism in the East, coupled with the reduction of the working class in

DOI: 10.4324/9781003181439-3

Western Europe, broadly explain the overall crisis of Social Democracy. The roots of the Social Democratic ideological retreat are found in the 1970s and the 1980s, but the real breaking-point with the Social Democratic tradition is considered to have occurred with Labour's Third Way and the reforms of Schröder in Germany.

Although this narrative is overall convincing, it is in some respects problematic because, as it has been pointed out in the introduction to this volume, the determinism implicit in the emphasis on structural international, economic and social factors obscures many aspects of the evolution of European Social Democracy. For example, it overlooks the predictable relevance of human agency and the alternative ideas that might have been relevant despite not prospering.

Historians have added complexity to this narrative in monumental works[7] and through more narrowly focused case studies. They have provided evidence that different timelines can be found for explaining the retreat of so-called traditional Social Democratic ideas. Moreover, they have demonstrated that Social Democrat transnational relations were intense and relevant in the 1970s, notably during the transitions to democracy in Southern Europe[8] and as a response to the developments taking place at the EC level.[9] These works show that the history of this ideological family is entangled and that the transnational relations of Social Democrats must be considered to understand the political, organisational, identity and ideological evolutions of these parties.

Adopting a transnational approach is especially helpful for studying the Portuguese case. Literature on the Carnation Revolution shows that European Social Democracy's involvement in Portugal was intense and relevant. In this chapter we connect this instance of Social Democrat transnational cooperation to the transformation of the PS's political economy and concepts of democracy. This approach is also useful, although perhaps less relevant, for analysing the Finnish and Swedish cases. The domestic contexts in the Nordic countries were different, more stable, than the Portuguese one. Hence, transnational cooperation was not as relevant for explaining the transformations observed in the Social Democratic Party of Finland (SDP) and the Social Democratic Party of Sweden (SAP) as it was in the case of the PS. Notwithstanding this fact, contacts between Finnish and Swedish Social Democrats were frequent and relevant, sometimes leading to conceptual transfers among themselves and with other big European Social Democratic parties. Seen in a European context, the three cases are examples of a general trend among Social Democratic parties. They offer different explanations to the questions of how and why Social Democrats started to change their previous ideological convictions.

Our argument is that in this period, we can observe in both Northern and Southern Europe early signs of what we could conceptualise as the neoliberalisation of the economic policies of the Social Democrat/Socialist parties. Moreover, we contend that, besides the international and national structural factors affecting these parties, the transnational relations between European Social Democrat leaders and the asymmetrical relationships among their parties are factors to take into account in order to better explain these early signs pointing towards neoliberalisation – this concept being considered as a variegated, partial and hybridised process.

One should be careful not to treat neoliberalism as too unified and coherent a doctrine. Political economist Jamie Peck has pointed out how neoliberalism's outspoken ideals have not been fully realised anywhere, but it has rather produced new forms of regulation and state interventionism to support generally shared tendencies towards freer markets and commodification of new spheres of life. Peck argues that it is more appropriate to talk about "neoliberalisation" than "neoliberalism".[10] In this chapter, we stick to this consideration.

Early signs of change: the case of the Portuguese Socialist Party

The PS was created in 1973 in the Federal Republic of Germany, in a Congress organised with the support of the Friedrich Ebert Foundation. At the congress, Mário Soares was elected Secretary General. The party was basically composed of a group of friends – middle-class intellectuals that were renowned opponents to Salazar's regime – who did not have connections with the working class nor grassroots support in Portugal.[11]

The fact that the party was created abroad gives a glimpse of how dependent on international support the PS was from its inception.[12] It also shows that the Portuguese Socialists were connected to the network of European Social Democrats before the beginning of the Carnation Revolution, as Ana Monica Fonseca shows in greater detail in her chapter in this volume. However, although the party was created in the FRG, one of its ideological points of reference was the French Socialist Party (PSF).[13] Soares and other members of the executive committee lived exiled in Paris, and they had been especially influenced by PSF's renovation in the late 1960s and early 1970s. The ideological renewal of the French Socialist Party was characterised by the rejection of capitalism, the aim to build socialism in freedom through the implementation of *autogestión* (self-management) and the union of the French left (in 1972, Socialists, Communists and Left Radicals signed the common programme of the left). The latter seemed to be profitable for the French socialists at the expense of the more powerful Communist Party. As the PS coexisted with a strong Communist party in the clandestine opposition to Salazar's regime, the French example was an important source of inspiration for Portuguese socialists.[14]

When it comes to economic policy, at the moment of its creation, the PS divided it into long-term and short- to medium-term objectives. The long-term objective was

> to build in Portugal a classless society [...]. The PS understands that this aim [...] can only be achieved through [giving] the power to workers within the frame of the collectivisation of the means of production and distribution, and [through] economic planning respecting plural initiatives.

Regarding the short- and medium-term objectives, PS considered that for achieving the final aim, first it was necessary to promote a process of quick economic development based on democratic economic planning. The party advocated agrarian reform and the nationalisation of the main Portuguese companies. It also aimed at transforming the working relations within companies, recognising the workers right to manage them democratically. Finally, the PS considered that the private sector should be respected, but only in the domain of the activities that were not crucial for the process of economic development. Therefore, it should be subordinated to the general planning of the economy.[15]

PS's economic policy was connected to the overall objective of the party of building socialism in freedom, what they called democratic socialism. PS understood this concept as a combination of grassroots democracy (*autogestão*) and representative parliamentarian democracy. Soares explained how he conceived this combination of democracies two months before the beginning of the revolution.

> I am in favour of assemblies permanently controlling the ones elected, and [in favour] of the wide participation of the people in the [political] decision-making process [...]. However, I consider a danger for the democratic movement to choose *basismo* [grassroots self-management] as a system, decapitating the movement from a responsible and coordinated direction at a national level. [...] Since the events of May 1968, [...] direct democracy has progressed everywhere. [...] For me it is a phenomenon to congratulate ourselves that still should be developed. This is, in essence, the problem of *autogestão*, of which I am a convinced supporter.

Soares was in favour of grassroots democracy only if it went together with, and was subordinated to, a system of representative democracy. According to him, the combination of these two kinds of democracy could lead to a new kind of democratic socialism. He considered that *autogestão* was incompatible with both capitalism and State centralism, but also that, if it was unrestrained, it could lead to anarchy. By imposing democratic parliamentary control over grassroots self-management, the diversion of this movement into anarchy could be prevented. This would lead to a more perfect kind of democracy.[16]

At the moment of the outbreak of the Portuguese Revolution on the 25th of April 1974, the international context was characterised by several factors that, in combination, made the revolution an international, especially European, affair.[17] The international economic crisis initiated in 1973, the peak of the process of Cold War deténte, the geo-political instability in the Mediterranean, the Portuguese Colonial wars, the rise Euro-communism in Southern Europe and the relative decline of the US hegemony, were all factors that interacted with the change of regime in Portugal. Since the Iberian country was a NATO member in the suddenly unstable Southern Europe, with a strong Communist party and colonies that claimed independence, the Carnation Revolution became a relevant international issue.

Only one week after the military coup, the new Portuguese President, Antonio de Spínola, requested Soares to travel to the main capitals of the EC countries in order to explain Portugal's new situation and to convince them that Portugal would respect its international alliances. Soares started his European tour with an additional objective, which was to obtain advice and support for the PS from its European sister-parties.[18]

In London, Soares got the promise of support from the British government and Labour Party.[19] In Bonn, he had a meeting with the American ambassador in Germany, and while discussing the economic situation of Portugal, Soares declared that the challenges ahead "must be solved without resort to extreme right or Leftist solutions". In facing the future economic challenges, Soares said: "liberty in Portugal – to which the Socialists are very attached – would be maintained".[20] As the British put it in a confidential report of the South European department of the Foreign Office, after Soares' European tour: "two themes that emerge clearly are the socialist attachment to liberty and the need for middle-of-the-road policies".[21]

In this European tour, Soares disregarded the programme of his own party. These statements show the pragmatism and opportunism of the leader of the PS. In order to get Western support and approval, he was willing to clarify before Portugal's allies any doubt about his party's commitment to the rules of the game existing in the West – Atlanticism, liberal democracy and capitalism. The fact that Soares' statements were at odds with the PS programme can be further explained by two recent experiences. Firstly, the Chilean coup d'état in September 1973 against the Socialist President Salvador Allende which had shown the limits of Socialist experiences in certain places that were geo-strategically important for the equilibrium of the Cold War. Secondly, the situation in Portugal had changed since the PS wrote its programme in 1973, when it was still an illegal party. In addition, the programme of the PS left some room for changes and flexible interpretations. At the beginning of the text it said: "[the programme represents] a point of reference [...] it is a starting point for further ideological discussion, reflexion and development".[22] However, the feeling that Soares' statements provoke is that he was not as committed to his party's programme – which he himself had written to a great extent[23] – as he was to taking advantage of the state of affairs that offered him the possibility of obtaining the support of the Western powers for his party, as well as for the political evolution of Portugal along Western lines.

The overthrowing of the Portuguese dictatorship unleashed long-repressed social tensions, demands and needs, which contributed to the radicalisation of the revolution from the very beginning.[24] With the Portuguese right in disarray and with the Communists trying to benefit from the situation and to become the avant-garde party of the revolution, the focus of the political struggle in Portugal shifted from the Left versus Right confrontation to one that took place within the Left. The main contenders were the PS and the PCP, although their disputes radiated to the Armed Forces Movement (MFA). This confrontation reached its peak in the summer of 1975, after the MFA, supported by the PCP, strengthened its control over the state apparatus, nationalised the banks and insurance companies and initiated the agrarian reform.

In this context, the PS held a Congress in December 1974, where the party developed and approved a new programme. The section on economic policy was very similar to the previous one, and the whole programme was stuffed with radical, revolutionary rhetoric. Before the Congress, Soares made public statements that were at odds with what he said in private to his European counterparts: "Portugal [needs] a complete modification of its economic structures, because it [is] not a question of adjusting the most inequitable aspects of capitalism, but of destroying capitalism".[25] Immediately after the Congress he stated that if the Socialists were to win the elections that would be held in the spring of 1975, "the PS will not save capitalism".

While the Socialists radicalised their proposals in a revolutionary context, the European Social Democratic parties and governments started to coordinate their activities in 1975 for promoting a democratic solution to the revolution. For doing so, they increased their support (financial, material, moral and public) to the PS, and they tried to persuade the Portuguese Socialists to change their radical discourse for a more moderate social democratic one. The Portuguese did not change their discourse, as they needed to satisfy the abovementioned social demands at least rhetorically, but they combined their radical rhetoric with a moderate stance in private. To control the development of the revolution, the Socialists needed external support, and to get it, they accepted the core ideas that the European Social Democrats wanted to promote in Portugal, namely the establishment of a Western kind of democracy, the development of regulated capitalism and the anchorage of the country to the West.

In May 1975, after the elections to the constituent assembly were won by the PS but disregarded by the Communists and the Military, the leaders of the Southern European Socialist parties (French, Spanish, Greek, Italian, Portuguese and Belgian) met in the summerhouse of François Mitterrand, leader of the PSF, to analyse the Portuguese situation and to study the possibility of establishing a common strategy on how to deal with the Communist parties.

In the meeting, Soares was clear about the fact that Portugal could not hold on for a long time in the economic crisis created by the confluence of decolonisation, revolution and international crisis. Therefore, he thought that to boost the economy, the Socialists would "encourage the private initiative, facilitate investments and [would] get credits from Western Europe".[26] He thought that European support was very important at both the political and economic levels.[27]

In fact, an economic plan was already taking shape at the European Economic Community (EEC) level. The idea was to offer financial aid to Portugal under the condition that the country would evolve towards a Western kind of democracy.[28] This was an initiative born in the Council of Ministers of the EEC, where Social Democrats were the majority. Soares also considered that such measures would be effective for reorienting the direction of the revolution. In July 1975, he met with the British and the ambassador in Lisbon on several occasions. In these meetings, he emphasised the Portuguese need for economic assistance, and he suggested that the Europeans should offer a programme of economic aid "conditioned to the development of a democratic regime".[29] Also in July 1975, Victor Rego, Soares' chief of Cabinet, stated in a SI Bureau meeting that the EEC should link its economic assistance to "the problem of democracy in Portugal" and "the position of the Portuguese Socialist Party",[30] meaning the leading position of the PS in the government.

In spite of maintaining this stance in private, in July 1975, the PS published a document entitled *Vencer a crise. Salvar a Revolução* [Beat the crisis. Save the revolution], in which they presented a new economic plan. The Socialist solution for saving the revolution was the creation of a government of National Salvation, with a composition that "should respect the popular will", which in practice meant the results of the Constitutive Assembly elections of April won by the PS. One of the immediate tasks of this government should be to tackle the economic problems of Portugal. For doing so, the PS proposed an economic programme, the *Plano Económico de Reconstrução Nacional*. Its aim was "the development of the productive forces, in the frame of the progressive substitution of the capitalist relations of production by socialist relations of production". However, the PS argued that in order to reach this goal, "it would be necessary to insert Portugal in a wide and diverse frame of international co-operation" – which meant consolidating their links with Europe and the Portuguese-speaking countries. The economy of transition to socialism implied the planning of the economy, fomenting "self-management experiences where possible", but also "reaffirming a coherent policy of public and private investments, national as well as international". In order to successfully carry out this policy of investments, it was "indispensable to re-establish a climate of confidence internally and externally". This implied that the private sector of the economy had to be guaranteed in order to attract international investors.[31]

Around the same days, on 22 July, the Prime Minister of Sweden Olof Palme, in a joint initiative with Willy Brandt, invited all the leaders of the northern European Social Democracy (Harold Wilson, Bruno Kreisky, Willy Brandt, Helmut Schmidt, Joop den Uyl, Trygve Bratteli, Anker Jörgensen and Kalevi Sorsa) plus Mário Soares and François Mitterrand, to an informal meeting in Stockholm to be held on 2 August.[32] The aim of the meeting was "to discuss ways in which democratic processes in Portugal could be supported".[33] Also, as British Labour put it, this was "an opportunity for us to give Dr Soares any advice that might help him to play his hand steadily and sensibly over the difficult times ahead of him".[34]

Once in Stockholm, the Social Democrat leaders created the Committee of Friendship and Solidarity for Democracy and Socialism in Portugal, whose most immediate objectives were to help to establish a Western kind of democratic regime in Portugal with a government that would reflect the results of the April elections and to fight against Portuguese international isolation. Financial support for the PS and international pressure against the Communist takeover remained crucial.[35]

The revolution is considered to have come to an end between September and November 1975. Shortly after the creation of the new provisional government (Sixth Provisional Government), formed in correspondence with the electoral results of April, which means with a majority of Socialist ministers, the Western powers coordinated their responses to the Portuguese events and the EEC[36] and the United States[37] conceded economic aid to Portugal. They made it very clear that this gesture was a sign of support for the new government and that economic aid was conditional to the development of a liberal democracy in Portugal. They also publicly supported a Portuguese request to the International Monetary Fund (IMF) for balance of payments aid. Thus, Portugal entered a dynamic of international economic dependence that would anchor the country to the West. As the Western support was linked to the promotion of the PS as the main bulwark against Communism, this dynamic would ultimately be a crucial international factor in the process of moderation of the PS in ideological terms in the late 1970s and early 1980s.

Some months later, after winning the elections in April 1976, the Socialists had another Congress, in which Soares defended the following economic policy:

> We should not be reluctant to carry out the necessary measures and to apply a realist [economic] policy, because [...] to be leftist is to defend the interests of the working classes avoiding, with a policy of good common sense and prudency, the return of Fascism. [...] The economic situation of Portugal is extremely unique, and it could constitute a very important [laboratory] for the progressive parties and movements of Europe. The enlarged public sector, the experiences in workers-self management, and the agrarian reform, despite its totalitarian perversions, can be applied without destroying the functioning of the companies. [...] However, in Portugal – we should not harbour any illusions – given our geo-strategic situation and the balance of forces within our society, Socialism is not for today, and we cannot go further in the current historical context.

This meant that the PS

> [will] not destroy the market economic mechanism that are fundamental for the development of any country that wants to preserve democracy. [...] It is inevitable to offer stimulus to the public and private sectors in order to increase production. It is a policy of national survival that if it is not implemented by a socialist government, it will be inevitably imposed by a new dictatorship. [...] Our economic policy will be based on the dynamization of the public sector, the encouragement of the private sector and for an attractive policy for national and foreign investors.

In the international conjuncture described above, the economic consequences of both the colonial policy of the dictatorship and of the revolution became another key factor influencing the evolution of PS's economic policy in the following years. Only in 1975 Portugal had negative economic growth, −4.3% of the GDP and a huge trade deficit. The PS inherited this situation, and in 1977, a government led by Soares resorted to a conditional programme of the IMF, which forced the PS government to adopt unpopular economic restructuring and stabilisation policies. In 1979, the PS went to the opposition and when it reached power again in 1983, it was in a coalition with the centre-right party PSD (the Central Bloc) again in a difficult economic context and when the negotiations for EEC membership were coming to an end. The government, again led by Soares, resorted once more to IMF support in 1983 and implemented another austerity programme.[38]

Nordic programmatic Democratic Socialism, economic democracy and practical orientation towards neoliberalism

The Social Democratic Party of Finland (SDP) stressed at the party congress in 1975 that democratic socialism was their ideological glue. It aimed at "socialist society" and "equality between people", which would be achieved by seeking the support of the majority of citizens. Social Democrats declared, for example, that the central means of democratic economic planning were "the effective regulation of capital movements, strong expansion of state companies and co-operatives and the regulation of foreign trade". They also favoured industrial democracy, endorsed the societal control of commercial banks and insurance companies and wanted to increase public services.[39]

There seemed to be three main motives to stress democratic socialism by different Social Democrats in Finland at that time. Firstly, this was meant to win the support of the post-war baby boom generation, which had partly radicalised in the late 1960s.[40] This tactical manoeuvre to tame the attraction of the Communist Party was complemented by the will to stabilise the position of the adherents of the party leader Rafael Paasio who had unified the divided party in the 1960s but resigned from his post in 1975.[41] Accordingly, some of the most radical Social Democrats would have set abovementioned programmatic goals as a precondition to co-operate with bourgeois parties in future coalition governments.[42]

The Social Democratic Party of Sweden (SAP) positioned itself in a manner similar to the SDP as the representative of democratic socialism between communist planned economy and capitalism in its party conference in 1975. Olof Palme defined himself as a reformist who believed in the idea that the reality always changed in a series of steps instead of in a big, violent and immediate bang.[43]

The SAP committed to a long-term planning of the economy (*planmässig hushållning*), co-determination of wage-earners and strong consumer influence (konsumentinflytande). Planning the economy represented for the SAP the counterweight to multinational companies, concentrated private power and giant international consortia. It aimed at increasing the influence of strong and free trade union movement and active popular movements.[44]

The SDP decided to transform its *practical* short-term policy in the meeting of SDP's Directorate at Siuntio Spa in January 1977. Party leader Kalevi Sorsa argued that the SDP had gathered "at Bad Sillanpää" (a spa of the Miina Sillanpää Foundation) to transform its policy towards favouring export sector profitability and distance itself from its socialist image. "Bad Sillanpää" refers to the German sister-party SPD's Bad Godesberg programme in 1959. This is because SDP's meeting was arranged at a spa in a manner of SPD's Bad Godesberg meeting where Germany's Social Democrats disconnected themselves from Marxism.[45]

SDP's "Bad Sillanpää strategy" meant decreasing company taxation, increasing productivity, improving the export sector's cost-competitiveness and practising strict financial and monetary policy. This was meant to stabilise Finland's economic recession together with an anti-inflation policy (moderate wages policy) and income tax reliefs. The strategy was applied by a new left-centre coalition government headed by SDP leader Kalevi Sorsa from the summer of 1977 onwards.[46] Only a minority of SDP's decision-makers would have practised counter-cyclical economic policy to fight increasing unemployment. The party had more freedom for manoeuvre vis-à-vis the Communists compared to the PS because also Communists participated in Sorsa's government and thus were committed to the premises of Bad Sillanpää strategy.[47] SDP's economists partly motivated this by perceived weaker export sector competitiveness compared, for example, to Sweden and disappearing custom tariffs in the shipbuilding, textile and clothing industries based on Finland's concluding agreement with European Community (EC) in the early 1970s.[48]

In 1978, Palme announced his readiness for austerity measures, "tight and hard" economic policy and lower living standards for workers.[49] New economic ideas were making a breakthrough also within the Swedish Social Democrats, a few years later than in other European countries. After their defeat in the parliamentary election of 1979, SAP formed an expert working group to formulate a new economic policy for the party. The traditional Social Democratic policy did not seem to function in the internationalised and more volatile economy with high inflation and growing unemployment. The economists in the working group were greatly influenced by transnational trends of neoclassical and monetarist economics. They wanted to take these new ideas seriously and investigate which parts of the right-wing or "neoliberal" agenda could be appropriated to serve Social Democratic goals. For the economists, it was clear that the welfare state and the public sector had to be reformed in order to preserve them.[50]

In 1980, Palme drew the SAP Executive Board's attention to the Japanese state's investment in research and technological development. For Palme, this meant the ideological acceptance of a "mixed economy" in the manner of the SPD in Germany, diverging from the "more dogmatic" Labour in Britain.[51]

SAP's party government stressed in 1981 that there were no possibilities to decrease Sweden's dependence on free trade while small country's employment, living standard and economic growth were based on the export sector's "international competitiveness".[52] This was followed by SAP's "Crisis Program" in 1981, which was strongly based on the economist group's ideas. The programme opposed the idea that state budget and current balance of payment deficits, as well as high inflation, should be used to generate production and increase employment. Ingvar Carlsson presented the programme at SAP's party conference. He stressed that the labour movement's traditional way to understand the fight against inflation and high employment as opposite phenomena didn't hold up anymore. SAP won parliamentary elections and returned to the government party in Sweden in 1982. New Finance Minister Kjell-Olof Feldt stressed that the government's economic policy would be based on the Crisis Program.[53]

SAP's employment policy reached a central feature of SDP's Bad Sillanpää policy by preferring low inflation and industrial sector competitiveness over full employment during the first years of the 1980s. The reverse reasoning of the relationship between inflation and employment was strengthened due to the simultaneous existence of increased unemployment and inflation, i.e. stagflation. However, this indicates that neoliberal ideas had touched Nordic Social Democrats. This happened even though Sweden's and Finland's Social Democrats still criticised neoliberalism, capitalism and radical right-wing thoughts as a rhetorical tool in the public battle over voter acceptance in the late 1970s and in the early 1980s.[54]

Olof Palme tried to combine stable economic growth and full employment with United Nations' New International Economic Order (NIEO) initiative.[55] UN's General Assembly had accepted an NIEO-resolution, 1 May 1974. This meant, for example, the aim to guarantee every state a sovereign economic and social system, including effective control over their economic activities. The SAP combined the NIEO process with the will "to promote an international economic policy which prioritizes full employment and at the same time fights against inflation" in 1978.[56] However, the NIEO initiative was finally buried by the proponents of the "magic of the market", mainly Reagan, Thatcher and Kohl, at the Northern and Southern Country Summit in Mexico in October 1981.[57]

The NIEO initiative was meant to be an alternative to IMF's austerity-driven stabilisation programmes, which were preconditions to its loans.[58] IMF was the institution through which the impact of neoliberalism was felt in Finland in June 1975, in Britain in 1976 and in Portugal in 1977–1978. Prime Minister Kalevi Sorsa committed to IMF's stand-by loan to Finland. This meant engaging to stabilise the currency exchange rate, practise strict economic policy as well as balance public expenditure and current balance of payments deficit.[59] In Sweden, by contrast, Olof Palme reminded in 1977 that Sweden has to avoid the fate of the British Labour-government which had received loans from IMF against only "draconian propositions on social disarmament and hard restrictive measures".[60]

Furthermore, Finland's Prime Minister Sorsa suggested European coordination of Neo-Keynesian economic policy to European Social Democratic leaders in the spring of 1983. SAP's representatives had actively promoted similar goals in the OECD at that time. Sorsa's idea was nullified in Paris as a consequence of French socialists political U-turn.[61] The latter refers to the French socialist government's failure to implement successfully a reflationary and counter-cyclical economic policy, which involved also increasing company taxation and nationalising private banks and companies due to the pressure of capital flight.[62]

After these failures, also the SAP and the SDP committed to capital market liberalisation in the mid-1980s.[63] Despite inner-party critics on the increasing power of market forces and weakening productive investments, Sorsa labelled this as a necessary measure and SAP's Minister of Finance Kjell-Olof Feldt believed that this would decrease interest rates.[64] Embracing capitalism as a consequence of capital market liberation represented a strong commitment to the central principle of neoliberalism by the SAP and the SDP.

As Finnish and Swedish Social Democrats modified their economic policies, their views on the relations of democracy and the economy changed as well. Concepts like "economic democracy" and "industrial democracy" had for long been key elements in Social Democratic rhetoric and visions of the future. They referred to democratic, state-led steering and planning of economic activity, as well as employee and trade union influence, in workplaces and labour market relations.[65] In the early 1970s, Swedish Trade Union Confederation, LO (*Landsorganisationen*), had also introduced the idea of "wage-earner funds" as means to extend democracy in the economic sphere and distribute wealth and income more equally. The initial plan meant establishing collective trade union-governed funds, which would have collected shares of corporate profits in the form of stock. In a few decades, the funds could have become the majority owners of the largest Swedish enterprises.[66] Due to strong support among the trade union movement, SAP agreed to promote the idea while trying to manoeuvre it into a more moderate form.[67] Employer and business representatives condemned the idea and launched a public campaign against it, which aggravated the political atmosphere in Sweden.[68]

The new Social Democratic policy orientation meant that centralised steering and planning of production and investments became less legitimate as components of economic policy. Economic crises and internationalisation were perceived to narrow the leeway of national economic policy and "economic democracy". Social Democratic rhetoric turned to emphasise supporting private business and its profits as main sources of investment and employment.[69] The market mechanism became a more desirable principle of resource allocation than economic planning, partly as a necessity for international competition and national interest but partly as it was considered to promote individual autonomy and responsibility, which had become stronger legitimation concepts.

Proposals for economic democracy began to concentrate on the "micro level" of workplaces and the "meso level" of collective capital formation through wage-earner funds or a more market-based and individualised system. Democratisation of working life was strongly advocated by SAP leader and Prime Minister Olof Palme and promoted through several reforms during the 1970s in both Sweden and Finland. These included legislation on employee representation in corporate governance, work environment, protection against dismissal and co-determination.[70] They strengthened employees' position against the employer, gave them power on issues concerning work environment and organisation, and improved the flow of information in workplaces. However, they did not redistribute strategic power over investments, plant closures, relocations and other major decisions affecting employment. In most decisions, the employer side retained the final authority.[71]

Even though Social Democrats and trade unions continued to demand more employee influence,[72] radical ideas of democratic control and even concepts like industrial and enterprise democracy were mostly left aside. The concept of self-management (*autogestion*) was appropriated from French socialists in the late 1970s and remained a buzzword for some years. Especially in Finland, the Social Democrats used self-management as a way of acknowledging the strong critique of bureaucracy and representative democracy and presenting a vision of grassroots democratic activity that would engage regular people.[73] However, self-management remained a rhetorical device and did not lead to concrete reform proposals. The concept may even have contributed to the ongoing delegitimisation of collectivism. During the 1980s, the emphasis in general turned from collective interest representation and conflicts between capital and labour to individual participation in working life. Instead of democracy, new organisation and management methods were legitimised with efficiency, flexibility and competence that would contribute to the common goods of competitiveness and economic growth.[74]

The issue of wage-earner funds, in turn, was geared into a moderate form in the course of several years of debate and preparation. In both Sweden and Finland, Social Democrats argued that some forms of collective ownership would be desirable, for example, worker cooperatives, but large-scale transfer of ownership to trade unions or other collectives was not advocated. When established, Swedish wage-earner funds' possibilities to increase employee power in the economy remained very limited. They were instead legitimised as means of capital formation for the benefit of the national economy. In effect, they became market-based investment funds, whose share of ownership in individual companies was limited and investment decisions mostly based on the objective of profit.[75] In Finland, SDP's stance on wage-earner funds became even more careful, as they wanted to avoid a similar conflict that had broken out in Sweden. Eventually SDP advocated company-specific but collectively owned "cooperation funds", which in negotiations with employers and bourgeois parties were turned into individualised and voluntary "personnel funds". This resembled earlier centre-right and employer ideas of dispersing ownership to individual employees and citizens.[76]

Reforms of the 1980s were adapted to the demands of the market economy and global competition, which at the time were significantly shaping economic practices and labour markets. Increasing employee influence at workplaces or their collective ownership had become difficult in other than consultative and voluntary forms. Democracy was becoming a less relevant concept in the context of the economy and working life. Actors across the political spectrum were adopting an ideational constellation, where enterprises would be governed by competent managers, while employees could be given operational power in their own work and possibly a share of its profits without accompanying influence. The new mode of thought was based on the belief of converging interests of capital, labour and the nation in the context of globalising economy and structural renewal, where only the most efficient and profitable industries, employees and nations would prevail.

Conclusion

Both Nordic Social Democrats and Portuguese Socialists combined programmatic democratic socialism and practical capitalist economic policy while running the affairs in the stabilised Nordic welfare states and Portugal, which was in the middle of transition towards democracy after the mid-1970s. Common denominators were also a strong impact of Social Democrats of big European countries and international organisations to both Southern and Northern Social Democrats as well as presenting the ideas of industrial democracy and self-management as alternatives to both capitalism and socialism.

In the turn of the 1970s and 1980s, Nordic Social Democrats took policy elements from the neoliberal toolbox and made a rightward shift in their economic policy. This could justify calling Nordic policies at least contributions to "neoliberalisation" at that time. Furthermore, Nordic Social Democrats would have favoured European or global decisions to practise Keynesian full employment policy and tamed global capital. After this failed to materialise, not least because of neoliberal's strong role in international organisations, the Bad Sillanpää and Crisis Policy strategies remained compatible with global capitalism. Maintaining export sector competitiveness-based employment strategy required in this situation committing to market-friendly economic policy. In Portugal, in its turn, the cold war constellation, and the PS's dependence on international support, is a major explanation behind a substantial influence of European Social Democrats to tame "socialism" in the politics of Portuguese Socialists into a more market-friendly direction.

In the period analysed, both Nordic and Portuguese Social Democrats/Socialists steered away from radically deepening democratic socialism or industrial democracy. In the case of the Nordic parties, the demands of market economy and global competition distorted the debates on different kinds of democracy and made them less relevant. In the case of the PS, achieving a Western kind of representative democracy became the objective of the Socialists for gaining control over the revolution in the last months. Thus, external support coupled with the domestic political evolution led the energies of the party to work for a Liberal democracy, marginalising other conceptions of democracy considered before. On the other hand, capitalist counter-reaction to democratic economic regulation in the 1980s was too strong to avoid a neoliberal orientation in order to maintain short-term economic fortunes in both the Northern and Southern peripheries.

Notes

1 Hellema, D., *The Global 1970s. Radicalism, Reform and Crisis* (Abingdon and New York: Routledge, 2018).
2 Nygård, S., J. Strang, and M. Jalava, "Facing Asymmetry: Nordic Intellectuals and Center-Periphery Dynamics", in *Decentering European Intellectual Space*, edited by Jalava, M., et al. (Leiden and Boston: Brill, 2018), 1–15.
3 Kettunen, Pauli, and Klaus Petersen, "Introduction: Rethinking Welfare State Models", in *Beyond Welfare State Models. Transnational Historical Perspectives on Social Policy*, edited by Pauli Kettunen and Klaus Petersen (Cheltenham and Northampton: Edward Elgar Publishing, 2011), 1–15.
4 Freeden, Michael, "Conceptual History, Ideology and Language", in *Conceptual History in the European Space*, edited by Willibald Steinmetz, Michael Freeden, and Javier Fernández-Sebastián (New York and Oxford: Berghahn, 2017), 122–130.
5 Koselleck, Reinhart, "Introduction and Prefaces to the Geschichtliche Grundbegriffe", *Contributions to the History of Concepts* 6, no. 1 (2011): 31.

6 Przeworski, Adam, *Capitalism and Social Democracy* (Cambridge: Cambridge University Press, 1985); Scharpf, Fritz, *Crisis and Choice in European Social Democracy* (Ithaca, NY and London: Cornell University Press, 1991); Paterson, William E. and Alaistair H. Thomas (eds.), *Social Democratic Parties in Western Europe* (London: Croom Helm, 1977); Brenner, Robert, *The Economics of Global Turbulence: The Advanced Capitalist Economies from Long Boom to Long Downturn, 1945–2005* (London: Verso, 2016); Callaghan, John, *The Retreat of Social Democracy* (Manchester: Manchester University Press, 2000); Giddens, A., *The Third Way: The Renewal of Social Democracy* (Malden: Polity, 1999); Kitschelt, Herbert, *The Transformation of European Social Democracy* (Cambridge, New York, and Melbourne: Cambridge University Press, 1994). Lavelle, Ashley, *The Death of Social Democracy: Political Consequences in the 21st Century* (Aldershot: Ashgate, 2008); Moschonas, Gerassimos, *In the Name of Social Democracy. The Great Transformation, 1945 to the Present* (London and New York: Verso, 2002).
7 Droz, Jacques, *Histoire Général du Socialisme. Tome IV: De 1945 à nous jours* (Paris: Presses Universitaires de France, 1978); Sassoon, Donald, *One Hundred Years of Socialism. The West European Left in the Twentieth Century* (London: Fontana Press, 1997).
8 Muñoz Sánchez, Antonio, *El amigo alemán. El SPD y el PSOE de la dictadura a la democracia* (Barcelona: RBA Libros, 2012); Granadino, Alan, "Possibilities and Limits of Southern European Socialism in the Iberian Peninsula: French, Portuguese and Spanish Socialists in the Mid-1970s", *Contemporary European History* 28, no. 3 (August 2019): 390–408; Ortuño Anaya, Pilar, *Los socialistas europeos y la transición española (1959–1977)* (Madrid: Marcial Pons, 2005); Sablosky, Juliet Antunes, *O PS e a transição para a democracia. Relações com os partidos socialistas europeus* (Lisboa: Editorial Notícias, 2000); Salm, Christian, *Transnational Socialist Networks in the 1970s. European Community Development Aid and Southern Enlargement* (Basingstoke and New York: Palgrave Macmillan, 2016).
9 Steinnes, Kristian, "Between Independence and Integration: European Social Democratic Parties and Direct Election to the European Parliament in the 1970s", in *Les partis politiques européens face aux premières élections directes du Parlement Européen*, edited by Raflik and Thiemeyer (Baden-Baden: Nomos, 2015).
10 Peck, Jamie, *Constructions of Neoliberal Reason* (Oxford: Oxford University Press, 2010).
11 Martins, Susana, *Socialistas na Oposição ao Estado Novo* (Lisboa: Editorial Notícias, 2005), 98.
12 Muñoz Sánchez, Antonio, "Entre solidaridad y realpolitik. La socialdemocracia alemana y el socialismo portugués de la dictadura a la democracia", *Hispania Nova* 15 (2017): 243–273.
13 Granadino 2019.
14 Granadino, Alan, "Between Radical Rhetoric and Political Moderation: The Portuguese PS and its International Networks in the Carnation Revolution", in The End of Social Democracy? The Moderate Left since 1945, its Transformation and Outlook in Europe, special issue of *ÖZG Österreichische Zeitschrift für Geschichtswissenschaften – Austrian Journal of Historical Studies*, 1 (2018): 85–110.
15 Declaração de principios e programa do Partido Socialista, 1973, p. 5.
16 Soares, Mário, "Resposta ao inquerito do Expresso", Mário Soares Foundation, Arquivo Mário Soares, (s.d.), "Diversos de OUT.66 a FEV.74", CasaComum.org, Disponível: http://hdl.handle.net/11002/fms_dc_93356 (2015-10-10).
17 Del Pero, Mário, "A European Solution for a European Crisis. The International Implications of Portugal's Revolution", *Journal of European Integration History* 15, no. 1 (2009): 15–34; Del Pero, Mário. "'Which Chile, Allende?' Henry Kissinger and the Portuguese Revolution", *Cold War History* 11, no. 4 (2011): 625–657.

18 Confidential report from R. H. Baker (FO, South European Department) to Lord Bridges, 10 May 1974, UKNA, FCO 9/2072, Dr. Soares' visit to UK and other European capitals May 1974. This document has been partially used in do Paço, António Simões, "Friends in High Places – o Partido Socialista e a 'Europa Connosco", in *Revolução ou Transição? História e Memória da Revolução dos Cravos*, edited by Varela, Raquel (Lisboa: Bertrand, 2012), 117–138.
19 Telegram from James Callaghan to Henry Kissinger, 2 May 1974, UKNA, FCO 9/2072, Dr. Soares visit to UK and other European capitals May 1974.; document quoted in Del Pero, Mario, Víctor Gavín, Fernando Guirao, and Antonio Varsori, *Democrazie. L'Europa meridionale e la fine delle dittature* (Florence: Le Monnier, 2010), 126. Also in Del Pero 2009.
20 Confidential report from R. H. Baker (FO, South European Department) to Lord Bridges, 10 May 1974, UKNA, FCO 9/2072, Dr. Soares visit to UK and other European capitals May 1974.
21 Confidential report from R. H. Baker (FO, South European Department) to Lord Bridges, 10 May 1974, UKNA, FCO 9/2072.
22 Programa do Partido Socialista, 22.AGO.1973 (Arquivo Mário Soares – Pasta 2249,001, im. 156).
23 Reis, António, "O Partido Socialista na revolução. Da via portuguesa para o socialismo à defesa da democracia pluralista", in *O Partido Socialista e a democracia*, edited by Vitalino Canas (Oeiras: Celta Editora, 2005), 53.
24 Accornero, Guya, *The Revolution before the Revolution. Late Authoritarianism and Student Protest in Portugal* (New York: Berghahn Books, 2016); Ramos Pinto, Pedro, *Lisbon Rising. Urban Social Movements in the Portuguese Revolution, 1974–75* (Manchester and New York: Manchester University Press, 2013).
25 *La Croix*, 25 September 1975, Robert Pontillon's Collection, Centre Jean-Jaurès, Paris. Quoted in Kassem, Fadi, "Choosing a Foreign Policy for French Socialists. The Case of the Democratic Revolution in Portugal (1974–1981)", *Zeitgeschichte* 2, vol. 40 (2013): 94.
26 450RI1, Blanca, Antoine, Etat de situation au 10 Juin 1975. Centre d'Archives Socialistes (CAS), Fondation Jean-Jaurès.
27 41RI1, "Latche (Landes) 23/24.5.75", Conférence des PS de Europe du Sud (Latche) mai 1975, CAS, Fondation Jean-Jaurès.
28 Conversações com o Ministro Britanico dos Negocios Estrangeiros, 27/06/1975, Arquivo Histórico Diplomàtico de Negocios Estrangeiros, Fundo PEA 43/1975/ Processo 330 GBR. Conversa entre sexa o ministro Melo Antunes e o senhor Callaghan.
29 Meeting between Mário Soares and Nigel Trench, 12/07/1975, UKNA, FCO 9/2270, Internal political situation in Portugal, 1975. Document already used in Del Pero et al. 2010, 149.
30 Portugal-summary of discussion at Bureau meeting, Dun Laoghaire, Ireland, July 12–13, 1975, IISH, SI Archives, 780 (Portugal 1975–1976).
31 "Vencer a Crise, Salvar a Revolução, 1975 – Provas finais do livro organizado pelo Secretariado Nacional PS", Fundação Mário Soares/DAR – Documentos António Reis, 1977, http://hdl.handle.net/11002/fms_dc_79970 (2021-9-23). Around the same time, the proposals of other parties, such as the PPD, were influencial in the design of the economic policy that would be applied in Portugal at the end of the revolution. See: Noronha, Ricardo, *"A Banca ao Serviço do Povo". Política e economia durante o PREC (1974–75)* (Lisbon: Impresa de História Contemporânea, 2018). Especially chapter 9.
32 Letter from Ole Jödahl to Harold Wilson, 22/07/1975, UKNA, PREM 16/1053, The PM's visit to Stockholm for a meeting of Socialist leaders to discuss Portugal Policy. PM's meeting in London Sept. 1975.
33 Letter from P. J. Weston to Harold Wilson, "Meeting of Socialist Leaders on Portugal", 22/07/2013, UKNA, PREM 16/1053, The PM's visit to Stockholm for a meeting of Socialist leaders to discuss Portugal Policy. PM's meeting in London Sept. 1975.

34 Telegram from Callaghan to the No. 10 Downing Street and to the Cabinet Office, 25/07/1975, UKNA, PREM 16/1053, The PM's visit to Stockholm for a meeting of Socialist leaders to discuss Portugal Policy. PM's meeting in London Sept. 1975.
35 Castaño, David. "'A Practical Test in Détente': International Support for the Socialist Party in the Portuguese Revolution (1974–1975)", *Cold War History* 15, no. 1 (2015): 15–22.
36 The European aid was provided by the European Investment Bank, which gave 150 million ecus to Portugal.
37 Moreira de Sá, Tiago, *Os Americanos na Revolução Portuguesa (1974–1976)* (Lisboa: Editorial Notícias, 2004); Moreira de Sá, Tiago, *Carlucci versus Kissinger. The USA and the Portuguese Revolution* (Washington, DC, and Londres: Lexington Books, 2011).
38 Gallagher, Tom, "The Portuguese Socialist Party: The Pitfalls of Being First", in *Southern European Socialism. Parties, Elections, and the Challenge of Government*, edited by Gallagher, Tom and Williams, Allan M. (Manchester: Manchester University Press, 1989); Costa Lobo, Marina, and Magalhães, Pedro C., "Room for Manoeuvre: Euroscepticism in the Portuguese Parties and Electorate 1976–2005", *South European Society and Politics* 16, no. 1 (2011): 81–104.
39 Outinen, Sami, "From Steering Capitalism to Seeking Market Acceptance. Social Democrats and Employment in Finland 1975–1998", *Scandinavian Journal of History* 42, no. 4 (2017): 389–413.
40 Lehtinen, Lasse, *Aatosta jaloa ja alhaista mieltä. Urho Kekkosen ja SDP:n suhteet 1944–1981* (Helsinki: WSOY, 2002), 590.
41 Lipponen, Paavo, *Muistelmat I* (Helsinki: WSOY, 2009), 414–416.
42 Outinen, 2017.
43 Outinen, Sami, "Nordic Social Democrats, Employment and Globalization 1975–1998", Manuscript.
44 Outinen, Manuscript.
45 Sassoon 1997, 249–251; Outinen 2017, 394–395.
46 Puoskari, Pentti, *Talouspolitiikan funktiot ja instituutiot. Teorian rekonstruktio ja elvytyksen talouspoliittinen anatomia* (Helsinki: Helsingin yliopisto, 1992), 9.
47 Outinen 2017, 394–395; Outinen, Sami, *Sosiaalidemokraattien tie kansantalouden ohjailusta markkinareaktioiden ennakointiin. Työllisyys sosiaalidemokraattien politiikassa Suomessa 1975–1998* (Helsinki: Into Kustannus, 2015), 81–112.
48 Outinen 2015, 76.
49 Outinen, Sami, "From Democratic to Market-Driven Regulation of Employment: The Swedish and Finnish Social Democrats, the Third Way and Emerging Economic Globalization, 1975–86", in *Nationalism and Democracy in the Welfare State*, edited by Pauli Kettunen, Saara Pellander, and Miika Tervonen (Cheltenham: Edward Elgar, 2022), Chapter 6.
50 Andersson, Jenny, *Between Growth and Security. Swedish Social Democracy from a Strong Society to a Third-Way* (Manchester and New York: Manchester University Press, 2006), 107–109; Mudge, Stephanie L., *Leftism Reinvented. Western Parties from Socialism to Neoliberalism* (Cambridge, MA: Harvard University Press, 2018), 317–321.
51 Outinen 2022.
52 Outinen manuscript.
53 Outinen 2022.
54 Outinen 2022.
55 Vivekanadan, B., *Global Visions of Olof Palme, Bruno Kreisky and Willy Brandt. International Peace and Security, Co-operation and Development* (Basingstoke: Palgrave Macmillan, 2016), 15–32.
56 Outinen 2022.
57 Doyle, Michael, "Stalemate in the North-South Debate: Strategies and the New International Economic Order", *World Politics* 35, no. 3 (1983): 426–464; Toye, John,

and Richard Toye, *The U. N. and Global Political Economy: Trade, Finance, and Development* (Indiana: Indiana University Press, 2004); Bair, Jennifer, "Taking Aim at the New International Economic Order", in *The Road from Mont Pèlerin. The Making of the Neoliberal Thought Collective*, edited by Philip Mirowski and Dieter Plehwe (Harvard: Harvard University Press, 2009), 347–385, 355.
58 Agarwala, P. N., *The New International Economic Order. An Overview* (New York: Pergamon Press, 1983), 4–5.
59 Outinen 2022; Heikkinen, Sakari, and Seppo Tiihonen, *Hyvinvoinnin turvaaja. Valtiovarainministeriön historia III* (Helsinki: Valtiovarainministeriö., 2010), 141–2; Keränen, Seppo, *Ehdollinen demokratia. Urho Kekkonen ja työmarkkinapolitiikka* (Turku: Turun yliopisto, 2010), 254–9; Kuusterä, Antti, and Juha Tarkka, *Suomen Pankki 200 vuotta II. Parlamentin pankki* (Helsinki: Otava, 2012), 412–4.
60 Outinen manuscript.
61 Outinen 2022; Outinen 2015, 147–8; Outinen 2017, 401; Blåfield, Antti, and Pekka Vuoristo, *Kalevi Sorsan suuri rooli* (Helsinki: Kirjayhtymä, 1985), 183.
62 Lordon, Frédérik, "The Logic and Limits of Désinflation Compétitive", in *Social Democracy in Neo-Liberal Times. The Left and Economic Policy since 1980*, edited by Andrew Glyn (Oxford: Oxford University Press, 2001), 111–120; Browne, Matthew, and Yusaf Akbar, "Globalization and the Renewal of Social Democracy. A Critical Reconsideration", in *Social Democracy. Global and National Perspectives*, edited by Luke Martell (Basingstoke: Palgrave, 2001), 63–4.
63 Bieler, Andreas, *Globalisation and Enlargement of the European Union. Austrian and Swedish Social Forces in the Struggle over Membership* (London: Routledge, 2002), 41–2; Ryner, J. Magnus, *Capitalist Restructuring, Globalization and the Third Way. Lessons from the Swedish Model* (London and New York: Routledge, 2002), 149–150; Outinen 2017, 399.
64 Outinen 2022; Outinen 2017, 399.
65 Friberg, Anna, *Demokrati bortom politiken. En begreppshistorisk analys av demokratibegreppet inom Sveriges socialdemokratiska arbetareparti 1919–1939* (Stockholm: Atlas, 2012); Pontusson, Jonas, *The Limits of Social Democracy. Investment Politics in Sweden* (Ithaca: Cornell University Press, 1992).
66 Viktorov, Ilja, *Fordismens kris och löntagarfonder i Sverige*. Stockholm Studies in Economic History 51 (Stockholm: Acta Universitatis Stockholmiensis, 2006); Ekdahl, Lars, *Mot en tredje väg. En biografi över Rudolf Meidner 2. Facklig expert och demokratisk socialist* (Lund: Arkiv, 2005); Sjöberg, Stefan, *Löntagarfondsfrågan – en hegemonisk vändpunkt. En marxistisk analys* (Uppsala: Uppsala universitet Stockholm, 2003); Ryner 2002; Blyth, Mark, *Great Transformations. Economic Ideas and Institutional Change in the Twentieth Century* (Cambridge: Cambridge University Press, 2002); Nycander, Svante, *Makten över arbetsmarknaden. Ett perspektiv på Sveriges 1900-tal. Tredje upplagan* (Lund: Studentlitteratur, 2017); Stråth, Bo, *Mellan två fonder. LO och den svenska modellen* (Stockholm: Altas, 1998); Pontusson 1992; Åsard, Erik, *Kampen om löntagarfonden. Fondutredningen från samtal till sammanbrott* (Stockholm: P A Norstedt & söners förlag, 1985).
67 Viktorov 2006; Ekdahl 2005; Sjöberg 2003.
68 Viktorov 2006, 220–224; Blyth 2002, 213–219; Ryner 2002, 169–170; Stråth 1998, 173, 233–235.
69 Outinen 2017; Outinen 2015; Lindberg, Henrik Malm, and Stig-Björn Ljunggren, *Från jämlikhet till effektivitet. Om lärande socialdemokratin under 1980-talet* (Stockholm: Hjalmarson & Högberg, 2014); Andersson 2006; Lindvall, Johannes, *The Politics of Purpose. Swedish Macroeconomic Policy after the Golden Age* (Göteborg: Göteborg University, 2004); Ryner 2002.
70 Bergholm, Tapio, *Kohti tasa-arvoa. Tulopolitiikan aika I. Suomen Ammattiliittojen Keskusjärjestö 1969–1977* (Helsinki: Otava, 2012); Bergholm, Tapio, *Tulopolitiikan aika II. Laatua ja vapaa-aikaa. Suomen Ammattiliittojen Keskusjärjestö vuodesta 1977*

(Helsinki: Suomalaisen Kirjallisuuden Seura, 2018); Nycander 2002; Stråth 1998; Pontusson 1992; Mansner, Markku, *Suomalaista yhteiskuntaa rakentamassa. Suomen Työnantajain Keskusliitto 1956–1982* (Helsinki, Teollisuuden kustannus Oy, 1990); Schiller, Bernt, *"Det förödande 70-talet", SAF och medbestämmandet 1965–1982* (Stockholm: Arbetsmiljöfonden, 1988); Simonson, Birger, *Arbetarmakt och näringspolitik. LO och inflytandefrågorna* (Stockholm: Arbetsmiljöfonden, 1988).

71 Johansson, Anders L., and Lars Magnusson, *LO. 1900-talet och ett nytt millennium* (Stockholm: Atlas, 2012), 170–179; Pontusson 1992, 183–185; Simonson 1988, 132–137, 151–157, 187–189; Schiller 1988, 128–133.

72 E.g. Bryt upp från MBL-tröttheten, Tiden 8 (1979), 418–420. *Solidarisk personalpolitik* (Stockholm: Landsorganisationen i Sverige (LO), 1981), 110–122; Written question on the implementation of the Cooperation Act, KK 155/1980, Finnish parliamentary documents 1980; Surakka et al. 1980; Louekoski, Matti, "Halutaanko päätösvaltaa todella, kokemuksia ja näkemyksiä yt-lain soveltamisesta", *Sosialistinen aikakauslehti* 2 (1982), 34–37.

73 E.g. Tikka, Seppo, *Pehmeään politiikkaan* (Helsinki: Kirjayhtymä, 1979), 73–74; von Sydow, Björn, "Jämlikheten och närdemokratin", *Tiden* 3 (1984): 162; *Economic Democracy and Wage-Earner Funds* (Helsinki: Suomen ammattiliittojen keskusjärjestö (SAK), 1985), 3, 33–40; Platform of the Social Democratic Party of Finland 1987. On *autogestion* see also Sassoon 1996, 561–564.

74 Cf. Boltanski, Luc, and Éve Chiapello, *The New Spirit of Capitalism* (London: Verso, 2005); Kärrylä, Ilkka, *Democracy and the Economy in Finland and Sweden since 1960: A Nordic Perspective on Neoliberalism* (Cham: Palgrave Macmillan, 2021).

75 Viktorov 2006, 108–109; Ekdahl 2005, 304–306, 313–314; Sjöberg 2003, 125–127; Pontusson, Jonas, and Sarosh Kuruvilla, "Swedish Wage-Earner Funds. An Experiment in Economic Democracy", *Industrial and Labour Relations Review* 45, no. 4 (1992): 779–791, 283–285.

76 Committee report 1987: 40. *Productive participation in renewing working life.* (Helsinki: Government of Finland, 1987); Yliaska, Ville, *Tehokkuuden toiveuni. Uuden julkisjohtamisen historia Suomessa 1970-luvulta 1990-luvulle* (Helsinki: Into Kustannus, 2014, 222–228; Mansner, 2005, 327–334).

3 Put (Southern) Europe to work
The Nordic Turn of European Socialists in the early 1990s

Mathieu Fulla

During the 1980s, social democracy in Western Europe experienced significant electoral and ideological defeats. The purported "Thatcher-Reagan revolution" disrupted the compromise between democratic socialism and capitalism that had persisted in the wake of the Second World War. As Geoff Eley concludes, "Keynesian economics, comprehensive Welfare states and [the] expanding public sector, corporatism, and strong trade unions crumbled".[1] Rather than signifying a reversal, these fundamental shifts – which have informed the thinking of European socialist elites regarding economic and social issues – had originated in the second half of the 1970s, only a few years before Margaret Thatcher and Ronald Reagan seized power. In the United Kingdom and West Germany, the Callaghan and Schmidt governments had gradually adopted austerity and supply-side policies, which they presented as the only viable means of competing with the powerful American and Japanese economies, as well as with emerging challengers in Southeast Asia.

At the turn of the 1990s, this mentality prevailed among key socialist leaders and experts in Northern and Southern Europe, most of whom accepted the pro-market Single European Act (SEA) and the Economic and Monetary Union (EMU). In France, Pierre Bérégovoy, the Minister of the Economy and Finance, relentlessly professed his faith in hard currency, the so-called *politique du franc fort*, which prioritised economic policies focusing on a balanced budget and curtailing inflation rather than a commitment to full employment. In 1990, the *Financial Times* "rewarded" the French socialist government by naming it the best disciple of Friedman's monetarism.[2] In Sweden, the administration of Olof Palme initiated a major shift in its economic policy in 1985. Palme's objective was to curb inflation, but the tools he applied signalled "the beginning of a set of austerity budgets" that transformed employment "from a social citizenship entitlement to a market variable".[3]

Beginning in the early 1990s, however, "a huge public debt, inflation, unemployment, and currency problems resulted in a serious crisis".[4] The Soares and Gonzalez administrations in Portugal and Spain endorsed similar policies as an efficient means of averting economic crisis, typified by the rampant protectionism supported by Salazarism and Francoism for years. The political scientist Cornel Ban describes the economic philosophy of Gonzalez and his aides

DOI: 10.4324/9781003181439-4

as "embedded neoliberalism": "When Spain was hit by the European recession triggered by Germany's unification and the Danish vote against the Maastricht Treaty, the government essentially reran the 1982 macro-stabilization package, with its attendant austerity and labour market liberalization reforms".[5] It is important to note, however, that most European socialist elites did not willingly embrace this ideological turn. When the French Socialist government officialised its conversion to austerity in 1983, a shift that it had discreetly initiated in late 1981,[6] resignation prevailed over enthusiasm. Confidential records of several French Socialist Party meetings reveal members' growing doubts about the possibility of building an alternative socialist economic and social policy. The concerns expressed by the French Prime Minister Pierre Mauroy and his Swedish and Greek counterparts Olof Palme and Andreas Papandreou firmly echoed the cool, straightforward analysis offered by Portuguese president Mario Soares, who claimed:

> In southern Europe, we arrived in power not through expansion (as in the North), but in crisis and because of the crisis. The problem was then how not to disappoint and to retain power. [...] In Portugal, we had a revolution, but it veered in the direction of a popular democratic type of regime. The Socialist Party opposed it. [We] reintroduced market-based elements into a quasi-collectivised economy. As a result, we were unable to either conduct a social policy or satisfy the capitalists. We retook power because the conservatives failed! We are going to defend the mechanisms that we denounce (such as the IMF). How can this contradiction be untied?[7]

In other words, the profound transformation of global capitalism during the 1970s and 1980s, marked by the increasing assimilation of Western European countries into the world economy and the advent of an "Age of Finance",[8] propelled Europe's socialist leaders towards the progressive adoption of supply-side policies at the cost of their traditional commitment to full employment.

Disregarding current debates over the role of "neoliberalism" in shaping the radical growth of capitalism over the past 40 years,[9] the acceptance of this dominant economic paradigm within the socialist parties had a significant impact on the architecture of the EMU. Their tacit support of the Maastricht Treaty facilitated the triumph of free-market ideology, while initiatives in favour of a "Social Europe" remained secondary and were a source of intense debate among member states.[10] Although they relentlessly called for the rebalancing of economic efficiency and social justice, before the creation of the Party of European Socialists (PES) in November 1992, European socialists remained vague on this topic. The creation of this more structured organisation indicated improved relations between elite party members and created an "intimate atmosphere" that was propitious to more ambitious initiatives.[11] Like the president of the European Commission, French socialist Jacques Delors, the PES advocated for "the shaping of capital-labour relations at a supranational level", one of the goals promoted by supporters of a more socially oriented European framework.[12]

The achievement of the "Road to Maastricht" coincided with the revival of socialist influence on European policymaking. In June 1993, Jacques Delors urged the Copenhagen European Council to "look far and wide" regarding the structural problem of unemployment in the European Union (EU).[13] Contending that member-state policies since the early 1980s had failed to overcome mass unemployment and induce a competitive framework that was able to compete with the United States and Japan, Delors called for significant changes in employment policy. He considered labour to be a key feature of social integration and therefore insisted that European growth be oriented towards adding jobs in accordance with the GDP, as well as increased flexibility in member-state labour markets and accommodation of low-skill workers.[14] Convinced by Delors' arguments about structural unemployment and issues of growth and competitiveness in the EU, the Copenhagen European Council granted the Commission a mandate to write a White Paper for its session in Brussels in December.[15] While the Confederation of the Socialist Parties of the European Community (CSPEC) had failed to address European policymaking in the 1980s, the PES approach to employment policy strongly influenced the Commission White Paper. This success was primarily due to the design of the European Employment Initiative (EEI), which was written by a team of European Socialist politicians and experts in conjunction with the European Commission on the White Paper. Routinely amended and refined by the PES experts and Members of the European Parliament (MEPs) of the Socialist Group in European Parliament (SGEP), the EEI can be understood as a key source of inspiration for the employment title that was inserted into the 1997 Amsterdam Treaty.

This chapter considers the genesis of this "success story", which is not without ambiguity. Although the EEI found its way into the complex channels of European policymaking, its impact on the general economic framework of Europe remained inadequate. Neither the European Socialists nor Jacques Delors fully succeeded in subverting the ordoliberal framework constructed in the 1980s by member states. Although they have continued to influence European social and industrial policies, the principles supported by the German ordoliberals, namely free enterprise "anchored in framework treaties, with a primary focus on guaranteeing respect for property and contract, protecting free competition, and honouring monetary prudence", has generally prevailed.[16] The EEI nevertheless signalled an important ideological renewal within European social democracy. The initiative attracted the attention of Jacques Delors – who envisioned a more socialist orientation to post-Cold War and post-Maastricht Europe – primarily due to the "Nordicisation" of employment policy implemented by the PES in 1992 and 1993. Leading politicians and economic experts of the Nordic social democratic parties, particularly the Swedish Social Democratic Party (SAP), and trade unionists seized this opportunity for ideological leadership on employment policy within Western European socialist circles. In the early 1990s, the political influence of the German SPD, the leading force of socialist internationalism since the late 1950s, was waning because of major organisational, ideological and strategic divisions. As James Sloam observed, the failure of the SPD to develop an original vision for Europe rallied "a joint CDU/CSU, FDP, and SPD motion in support of a 'unified Europe'".[17] The French Socialist Party and British Labour Party, both facing dire internal leadership crises, lacked the resources to fill this ideological and political void. This chapter illustrates how a small group of Nordic politicians and experts used the PES to Europeanise a Nordic approach to the social policy forged in the 1980s by the SAP.

Several political scientists highlighted the prominent role of the PES in the Delors White Paper, officially entitled *Growth, Competitiveness, Employment*. Shortly after the document was published, Simon Hix noted that it was not by chance "that the final version [...], which was adopted by the European Council on 11 December 1993, contained many of the proposals from the Larsson report [the unofficial title of the EEI]".[18] A few years later, Karl Magnus Johansson expanded upon this point, notably tracing the emergence of a transnational coalition of socialists, trade unionists and experts who promoted a socialist agenda within the European Council and the Commission. Johansson also called attention to the Nordic origins of the employment policy designed by the PES through the EEI.[19] A considerable amount of the political science literature on this subject has emphasised the ideological and political factors that allowed the PES to influence European policymaking at the time.[20] This body of research, although insightful, has left three questions unanswered. First, it tends to overlook rivalries among PES experts. The appointment of a group chaired by Allan Larsson, a Swedish socialist MP, and former Finance Minister in the Carlsson government (1988–1991), coincided with the marginalisation of the official partisan working group on social issues, which was developing a more Keynesian and voluntarist approach to employment policy. Further, the chronology of the drafting process and the identity and roles of the members of the Larsson group remain largely undocumented – although Johansson made important comments on these points. Last, although this body of work has highlighted the influence of the Larsson group on the Delors cabinet despite a lack of details about the effective channels of cooperation, the reciprocal impact of the Delors cabinet on the broader Socialist movement remains unknown. "One can assume a cross-flow ideas and information", wrote Robert Ladrech, although without further developing this hypothesis.[21] This chapter illustrates that the Larsson group seriously considered the numerous amendments suggested by Jacques Delors and his aides, thereby facilitating the Europeanisation of this Nordic socialist approach to employment policy.

An examination of multilevel archival fonds opened the "black box" of the Larsson report: The archives of the presidency of Jacques Delors at the European University Institute in Florence (the Centre for History at Sciences Po Paris also holds a digital copy); the unclassified archives of the Forward Studies Unit (*Cellule de Prospective*) at the Historical Archives of the European Commission in Brussels; the archives of the PES held by the *Fondation Jean-Jaurès*, a French Socialist think-tank based in Paris; and the archives of SAMAK at the Swedish Labour Movement's Archives and Library in Stockholm. The first section of this chapter traces the developments that advanced the Nordicisation of the approach to employment policy within the PES. The second section highlights the gradual Europeanisation of the Larsson report by way of the Delors cabinet. The conclusion demonstrates that the EEI can be understood as an ideological offensive whose goal was the promotion of a "Third Way" on the scale of European social democracy a few years before the advent of Blair and Schröder's ideological agenda.

PES expertise rejuvenated by the Nordic labour movement

In early September 1993, the PES leaders held a conference in Arrabida, Portugal. Two years later, Peter Brown-Pappamikail, then a senior official in the PES, delivered an interesting testimony about the atmosphere of the conference:

> In the late summer of 1992, the national leaders of the Party of European Socialists agreed to meet for two days in Portugal for an informal "think-in". That the meeting took place at all was remarkable enough; that it took place away from the media and public attention, and without advisors or assistants, even more so. But most remarkable was the way, in the relaxed atmosphere of a mountainside monastery, the leaders sat down as equals in this European arena of party leaders, whatever their status in other national and European fora. For one of the first times that I have witnessed, party leaders did not defer or pull rank according to national (or) governmental protocol.[22]

During the two-day conference, the issue of persistent unemployment was the principal topic of debate. The Spanish Prime Minister Felipe Gonzalez suggested that the PES establish a high-level working group for the purpose of developing a socialist employment initiative, a proposal that was widely welcomed by peers.[23] Socialist leaders officially requested that the SAP draft a working paper addressing the following topics: halving unemployment, creating new jobs, preserving European competitiveness and modernising worker social protections. The SAP leader, former Prime Minister Ingvar Carlsson, delegated this task to his former Minister of Finance, Allan Larsson. Larsson, the son of a foundry worker, was employed as a journalist for several publications with close links to the Social Democrats. In the early 1980s, he served as the editor-in-chief of a current affairs magazine, *Vi*. He was subsequently a public servant under several Social Democratic administrations and developed extensive knowledge of employment policy during his tenure as the head of Sweden's Labour Market Board between 1984 and 1989.[24]

From an outsider perspective, it may seem surprising that Socialist leaders deferred to the SAP on this crucial issue. The SAP was not an official member of the PES, although Sweden had formally applied to join the European Union in 1991. Moreover, during his appointment as Minister of Finance, Allan Larsson implemented similar austerity measures to those of his Socialist and Conservative counterparts then in office in EEC member states.[25] These considerations did not deter the Socialist leadership from appointing him because of their conviction that

PES expertise on social issues had long suffered from a lack of pragmatism and expert involvement. From their perspective, Allan Larsson embodied the modern social democratic conception of employment policy in an increasingly globalised and Europeanised economic framework. Shortly before his work for the PES, the Swedish politician had gained the confidence of leading Nordic trade unionists with his accomplishments within SAMAK, "the cooperation committee between the social democratic parties and trade union confederations in the Nordic countries".[26] Since 1990, SAMAK's members were attempting to "respond to the devaluation of political means on the national and Nordic levels by upgrading to the European level".[27] Even before his involvement with SAMAK, Larsson was strongly convinced that the future of the "Nordic model of Welfare" was closely linked to Europeanisation. As Minister of Finance, he stressed that Sweden's economic future was irrevocably tied to that of the EC and, like Bengt Dennis, the governor of the Central Bank, he hoped to see the *krona* enter the European Monetary System (EMS) exchange rate mechanism as soon as Brussels would permit it.[28]

SAMAK and Larsson's plan to Europeanise their approach to social issues encountered the deep dissatisfaction of Socialist leaders with previous solutions proposed by several PES working groups regarding "Social Europe". From the second half of the 1980s onwards, the CSPEC and the SGEP expressed their wish to counterbalance the pro-market economic and financial goals inserted into the SEA and the EMU with a set of measures that would guarantee "a social coverage, and acceptable activity and living conditions" for every European citizen.[29] In 1989, despite persistent conflicts between member parties, the electoral manifesto presented by the CSPEC highlighted the social deficits of Europe's economic framework. The document called for "an active communitarian social policy", contending that economic growth was insufficient to resorb unemployment.[30] Several working groups were consequently nominated to address the issue, but none succeeded in producing a document that Socialist leaders were willing to endorse. The "Social group" appointed by the CSPEC in March 1990 is a telling example of the prevailing distrust of PES experts.[31] Chaired by Elena Flores, the vice-president of the Spanish Socialist Party (PSOE) and a former MEP, the group failed to draft a single paper and was fiercely criticised by the leaders of the CSPEC and their counterparts in the SGEP. The deputy of the group, Eisso Woltjer from the Dutch Labour Party (PvdA), expressed his disappointment in the party's inadequacies with respect to social affairs, which had been designated as a top priority two years earlier.[32] A few months later, the Bureau of the CSPEC also chastised the social group. The former MEP Mario Didò of the Italian Socialist Party (PSI) characterised its work as "lamentable" and Ralf Pittelkow, a close aide of the Danish Social Democratic Party's rising star Poul Nyrup Rasmussen, urged his comrades to find an alternate solution to revitalise the socialist perspective on these matters.[33]

Socialist MEPs and their colleagues at the CSPEC felt the need to rejuvenate their approach to social Europe, which had reached a stalemate according to the SGEP president, the French Socialist Jean-Pierre Cot in a meeting between the group and the CSPEC in May 1992.[34] Having previously supported rapid ratification of the Maastricht Treaty – which was unpopular among member-states' citizens, as illustrated by its defeat in the Danish referendum – MEPs called for "a political response to social injustice, unemployment, and growing regional imbalances" at a European level to address inequalities perpetuated by the single market.[35] In this climate of uncertainty, a speech delivered to the SGEP in Stockholm by Allan Larsson in July 1992 sparked strong interest among members and played a decisive role in his appointment one year later as leader of the PES's social experts.[36] Provocatively entitled "Can Europe afford to work?" – a symbolic allusion to Ernst Wigforss's famous 1932 pamphlet, *Can we afford to Work?* (although radically different in content)[37] – Larsson's presentation was primarily based on his research for SAMAK, which had concurrently created a working group on employment policy titled "Europagruppe".[38]

Larsson's speech played a crucial role in reviving the credibility of the social expertise of the PES. It could be interpreted as heralding the Europeanisation of the "Social Policy in the Third Way", which was designed and refined by numerous politicians and SAP experts throughout the 1980s.[39] In his presentation, Larsson denounced the OECD's passive employment policies during this decade: "Practically all European countries prefer to pay people to stay away from working life…It is not (a) lack of financial resources that forces 16 to 17 million people into unemployment".[40] He proposed that the employment policies designed by the Nordic social democratic parties could restore Europe to full employment, challenging the conventional "Eurokeynesian" approach to unemployment that had been promoted in the transnational socialist circles since the 1970s.[41] Recalling the stark contrast between high EU member-state unemployment rates and low unemployment rates in Japan and the United States, Larsson underscored the social and economic ramifications of the situation:

> A major part of Europe's population has been excluded from the normal labour market; many are long term unemployed, totally dependent on allowances, and rejected by society. Unemployment is also a heavy burden for public finances. In Western Europe, […] the costs for unemployment benefits and early retirement can be calculated to no less than 125 billion US dollars.[42]

From Larsson's perspective, Europe would be well-advised to emulate the precedent set by Japan, which had succeeded in combining strong economic growth with low unemployment and low inflation in the 1980s. Although Larsson understood that Japanese employment policy was not replicable within a European context, he nevertheless called attention to the European labour market's contrasting inability to create numerous jobs despite economic expansion. Given the critical connection between employment and socialisation, the Swedish MP lamented that "the way the labour market policies have been applied in [the] Europe of the 1980s looks more like a demolition process than anything else. It gives the impression that the underlying theory is that Europe cannot afford to work!"[43]

Larsson thus introduced his three main points: the European labour market is too rigid; the skilled labour shortage perpetuates a "mismatch" between supply and demand; the EMU is insufficient to provide jobs and welfare for all Europeans. Larsson encouraged European leaders to closely examine the Japanese model of youth education and training, "but most of all of adult training in the [industrial] job".[44] He called for an active employment policy, for which Nordic – from his perspective, Swedish – and Japanese models could provide a strong source of inspiration. He argued for increased labour market flexibility – a taboo term in Southern European socialist milieux – coupled with improvements in the welfare of workers:

> The real lever for increased productivity and employment is to improve training, education, and skill levels and to reform work organisation. We need more flexibility—not through a general lowering of workers' terms and conditions—but through higher skills and productivity among those who are, or run the risk of becoming, unemployed. [...] It is necessary to create a clear vision for the employment policy, which is just as clear and distinct as the one that applies to the monetary policy today if we are to turn Europe away from mass unemployment towards full employment.[45]

Allan Larsson proposed ambitious goals for European Socialists that included halving unemployment in the following five years and "moving eight million unemployed Europeans from the dole towards active measures as a step to productive jobs in the ordinary labour market".[46] He also insisted that achieving these goals would not require considerable public expenses, thus rendering his project fully compatible with the Maastricht economic and monetary framework. According to Larsson, an active employment policy, combined with ambitious investments in industry and infrastructure in accordance with requests made by the European Trade Union Confederation (ETUC), would restore full employment in the EU. The Larsson project offered a translation of the "Third Way for Social Policy" designed by the SAP which "subordinated 'security' to growth and the need to create economic efficiency by reducing social expenditure".[47]

The MEPs were persuaded by Larsson's presentation. In September, Derek Reed of the British Labour Party expressed to his colleagues working on employment and growth issues that "it is clearly sensible to maintain close contact between the Nordic working group and our own conference preparations".[48] He proposed that they invite SAMAK to send an observer to all preparatory meetings for the group's conference and maintain close informal contacts with the committee. Two months later, Frode Forfang, the general secretary of SAMAK, invited the leaders and experts of the PES to attend SAMAK's annual general meeting. In the same month, the Bureau of the Socialist group in EP decided that the speech delivered by Allan Larsson in July 1992 should be the political backdrop of a conference on growth and employment the following February in Brussels.[49] A meeting between a SAMAK delegation led by Larsson and several MEPs further cemented his growing influence.[50]

The new approach to economic and social issues developed by SAMAK instigated the "Nordicisation" of the social expertise of the PES. In the early 1990s, numerous Nordic Social Democrats and leading trade unionists, in addition to economic experts committed to the Nordic labour movement, endorsed a "supply stimulating policy", temporarily renouncing the goal of full employment in the name of bolstering the international competitiveness of private firms.[51] This philosophy corresponded with the principles of the European Socialist leaders. Accordingly, "Put Europe to Work", the official title of the Larsson report which provided the theoretical framework of the upcoming European Employment Initiative, "was a translation from a report in Swedish—'Sätt Europa I arbete'— drafted by SAMAK's Larsson working group".[52]

Despite the warm reception of Larsson's active employment policy, the Nordic approach to the labour market did not immediately become dominant in European Socialist arenas. In December 1992, the PES had created a working group on economic and social issues co-chaired by the French Socialist Gérard Fuchs (a close aide of former Prime Minister Michel Rocard and one of the vice-presidents of the PES) and the Italian Socialist Mario Didò, who had just regained his seat as an MEP.[53] The Southern European Socialists were considerably more influential within the group than its Nordic members. According to its list of affiliates, only 2 of its 30 members belonged to a Nordic social democratic party (one Finnish and one Swede). In August 1993, the group issued a paper entitled "Eight recommendations for growth and employment". The document characterised its analytical framework as a derivative of "communitarian Keynesianism" largely inspired by the European Growth Initiative adopted by member states at the Edinburgh European Council meeting in December 1992. The Fuchs-Didò group supported a voluntarist industrial policy, echoing the "neo-mercantilist" initiatives developed by the European Commission in the early 1980s.[54] In light of the protectionist Japanese and American industries, the report's authors called for a significant increase in the EU budget in support of large-scale research and development investment. This return to neo-mercantilist principles was paired with a call for adopting the principle of *préférence communautaire* in EU commercial policy i.e. giving priority to member states when a non-EU country failed to provide minimal social protection for its workforce.[55] Last, the working group raised the controversial issue of working time reduction, which was strongly opposed by the British Labour Party and the Greek PASOK. Symbolically, Allan Larsson, who was supposed to join the group, never attended a single meeting.[56] In September, the document was submitted to the socialist leadership in Arrabida, but it failed to spark their interest: Larsson's ideas prevailed. The Fuchs-Didò group was abruptly side-lined in favour of the Larsson group, which promoted an approach to employment policy that the leaders considered to be more practical within the EMU framework and closer to their own economic policy vision. The defeated Southern Socialist experts were bitter about these developments. In a letter to Michel Rocard, then (ephemeral) general secretary of the French Socialist Party, Gérard Fuchs fiercely criticised the philosophy of the Larsson report. He considered the document questionable on numerous points, particularly its lack of interest in using Keynesian public borrowing to curtail mass unemployment.[57]

In summary, although PES socialist leaders and directors never objected to the Fuchs-Didò group, they regarded Larsson's approach as more pragmatic. Larsson's subsequent appointment to the PES was anticipated and effectively facilitated connections between the PES and the Delors cabinet.

The Europeanisation of the Larsson report

The decision made in Arrabida signified an important moment in the early history of the PES. As Brown-Pappamikail put it:

> Unlike the different working groups set up by the PES and the Confederation before it, (which tended to ramble without conclusions or clear objectives and suffered from a lack of political authority due to low participation from national parties), this group was to be made up (of) personal representatives of the Party Leaders, with the authority and mandate to speak and act on behalf of their respective leader.[58]

The Larsson group report was intended to strengthen and influence the imperatives of the European Commission – primarily voiced by Jacques Delors and his aides – regarding employment and the growth and competitiveness of the European economy. As chairperson of the group, Allan Larsson was able to rely on the influential socialist network that he had cultivated since serving as Minister of Finance. Prior to the official formation of the working group, he "made some important visits in the summer of 1993", establishing "contact with the Commission and the European Trade Union Congress (ETUC), and in London he met with leading spokesmen for (the Labour Party) on employment and finance, namely Andrew Smith and Gordon Brown".[59] Brown, then shadow Chancellor of the Exchequer for the British Labour Party, was one of the 23 members who attended the first meeting of the Larsson group in early September.[60] The list of members found in the archives of the European Commission affirms Brown-Pappamikail's testimony: most of the parties' members delegated top-level politicians and experts to the group. For instance, the PSOE appointed Joaquin Almunia, a former Minister of Labour, then its spokesperson in the Budget Commission in Parliament. The Italian Socialist Party (PSI) sent its own president Gino Giugni, the labour minister in the Ciampi government. The French Socialist Party was a notable exception, however, as illustrated by its decision to appoint secondary experts such as André Gauron, a former adviser of the Minister of Finance Pierre Bérégovoy, and the economist Dominique Taddeï, a former French deputy.[61] This choice can be construed as a reprisal against the marginalisation of the Fuchs-Didò group, and more fundamentally as a reflection of the historically marginal interest of PS elites in international and European socialist organisations.[62] It is also worth noting the conspicuous lack of gender diversity in the Larsson group. The sole female representative of the team was Marianne Andreassen, a political adviser in the Norwegian Ministry of Foreign Affairs and a former member of the Larsson Employment group within SAMAK. Last, several experts involved in the Fuchs-Didò group joined the Larsson team. The Belgian Socialist Party and the Luxemburg Socialist Workers' Party delegated the same individuals to both groups.[63]

The involvement of individual group members in the drafting process varied widely. It is almost certain, for instance, that Gordon Brown and the successive British representatives played no role in shaping the Larsson report. Other members were more engaged in the process and submitted substantial amendments. The majority of these individuals went on to become high-level politicians: Siegmar Mosdorf from the German SPD, then the Party spokesperson on economic and financial affairs; Luc Hujoel from the Belgian Socialist Party, a close adviser of its president Philippe Busquin; Jens Stoltenberg, the Minister of Industry and Energy, from the Norwegian Labour Party; and Joaquin Almunia, who also made significant contributions to the final report.[64] Their additions to Larsson's draft primarily concerned the modalities of the relaunch in European public investments (i.e. social and public infrastructures and environmental goals). By contrast, none questioned the merits of the active employment policy outlined by the Swedish MP in his speech to the SGEP in July 1992.

Unlike the Fuchs-Didò group, which had no formal relations with the European Commission, Allan Larsson maintained a personal relationship with Jacques Delors, whom he had met during his tenure as Minister of Finance.[65] Both men participated in the conference on "Growth and Employment" organised by the SGEP in early February 1993, during which Larsson presented the "Nordic model".[66] The head of the European Commission attentively read successive drafts of the report – Larsson wanted to keep him informed of each stage of the process[67] – and personally met with Larsson a few days prior to the publication of the final version.

Broadly speaking, the Delors cabinet warmly welcomed the Larsson initiative. "Larsson is taking very seriously his task of writing the paper on employment for the Socialist leaders. All are pleased that he was asked to do it and wish it to complement the Commission's White Paper", Chris Boyd wrote in a note to Delors after a trip to Sweden, during which he met with Larsson and Ingvar Carlsson.[68] The head of the Commission was amenable to supporting Larsson's efforts because his own diagnosis of the structural crisis of the EU and approach to employment policy were compatible with those promoted by the Swedish MP. Several members of his cabinet were closely involved with the Larsson group. In early November, Jérôme Vignon, the chair of the Forward Studies Unit and one of Delors' closest advisers, addressed a series of comments that were inserted into the final draft of Larsson's text. Vignon's analysis reflected the feelings of the Delors cabinet towards the work initiated by the PES. After praising Larsson for "rendering great service to the European Social Democratic movement" by calling for an active employment policy, which Vignon considered especially pertinent, he expressed concerns about the macroeconomic framework within which the Larsson group would implement this employment policy. He regretted that the text did not emphasise the economic potential of the second phase of the EMU, which would allow the Commission to increase public borrowing at the community level. Vignon also noted that the document neglected to address the sensitive issue of working time – likely a deliberate choice made by Larsson to avoid the fate of the Fuchs-Didò group – which could have been a strong vehicle for improving the flexibility of the work organisation.[69] Most of these comments were addressed in the final version of the EEI, which included a large section entitled "Investing in a new work organisation and new models of working time". Like the Delors cabinet, the Larsson report authors remained tentative on the topic, declining to commit to a concrete goal such as the 35-hour-work week.[70] Moreover, the archives of the Forward Unit Studies contain numerous records of correspondence between Delors' aides and the members of the Larsson group. Shortly after the Arrabida conference, Pascal Lamy informed Jacques Delors of a long conversation he had shared with the MEP Luigi Colajanni, who was preparing a document addressing the central issues raised in the White Paper. Lamy wrote, "We spoke about it together and he wrote the joint proposal that seems to me to go in the right direction to the extent that the social and technological aspects […] are included".[71]

Conversely, although it was not officially cited, the EEI exerted a tangible influence on the social chapters of the Commission White Paper. Delors wished to avoid potential criticism about a supposed partiality in favour of European social democracy.[72] Nevertheless, although the final version of the text echoed numerous elements of the EEI, the White Paper should not be interpreted as a direct translation of the document. The Commission adhered to the macroeconomic criteria established by the Maastricht Treaty and staunchly opposed any substantial changes to the strict regulation of the budgetary policies of the member states in the interest of adopting a single currency by the late 1990s:

> The gradual reduction in public deficits is necessary during the initial phase to bring indebtedness under control and to continue to increase public saving during the second phase. This will call for increased efforts to restructure spending—and particularly to curb operating expenditure—in favour of public resources allocated to tangible and intangible investment and to an active employment policy. Stable monetary policies consistent with the aim of low inflation will be a constant benchmark throughout the period.[73]

These goals were a distinct departure from the "European New Deal" presented in the EEI, although the differences should not be overestimated. The Larsson report authors also emphasised a commitment to sound budgeting, which they deemed essential to the reduction of unemployment in Europe.[74]

The contents of the Commission White Paper nevertheless demonstrate that Delors partly fulfilled his expressed goal of using "his office to implement at least parts of a Social Democratic agenda".[75] The arguments concerning employment policy contained in the White Paper affirm the proximity of Larsson and Delors' viewpoints: "Both the White Paper and the Larsson report can be seen as efforts towards a coherent Social democratic strategy against recession and unemployment which would not question the only recently ratified Maastricht Treaty".[76] Taking care to avoid explicit references to Keynes, both documents called for a supply-side relaunch through private and public investment rather than consumption, which would induce inflation due to an increase in wages. Both claimed that to halve unemployment, member states had to implement coordinated employment policies. Both underscored the necessity of increased flexibility in the labour market of member states. On this point, the Nordic influence is particularly evident. While the EEI was intentionally vague on the subject out of consideration for the Southern Socialist parties, the White Paper was more explicit: "In several southern countries, the laws on the conditions under which workers on unlimited contracts may be laid off need to be made more flexible, with greater assistance being given to the unemployed and with less recourse to precarious forms of employment".[77] As the political scientist Hélène Caune has observed, the Commission White Paper connected the need for increased flexibility in the labour market with a re-evaluation of the training and mobility of European workers throughout their professional lives.[78] Put another way, Delors inserted a Nordic conception of active labour employment policy into the White Paper, while rejecting the model implemented in the Netherlands at the time. In a private meeting with Emilio Gabaglio and Jean Lapeyre, the leaders of the ETUC, Delors fiercely criticised the PvdA's Minister of Finance Wim Kok, one of the primary architects of the Dutch active employment policy, whom he accused of being inflexible on economic issues and voluntarily deaf to the proposals made by the White Paper.[79] Conversely, Delors publicly praised the Swedish model during the campaign organised by the Commission to promote the White Paper in early 1994:

> The improvement of unemployment policies is a question that should be familiar to the social-democratic family because if there is a country that has succeeded in this area, it is Sweden, even today. Why has it succeeded? Because in Sweden, employment policy consists of an obsession with providing each person who presents themselves to the agency offices say "I do not have a job and I am looking for one" with a job, an activity, or a training program, and in the end, almost as a last resort, to pay them unemployment benefits.[80]

The body of research regarding the 1993 Commission White Paper highlights the reasons why, in the short term, it failed to launch a new course in the economic and social agendas of member states.[81] By contrast, the EEI exerted a more tangible impact on European social democracy. Systematically updated, the document remained the official European socialist position on employment policy until 1997.

This resurgence of social democratic influence on European policymaking induced two significant ideological turns. First, the primacy of pro-market policies within the EU was no longer contested, nor was the project to instate a common currency by the end of the 1990s. The Larsson report argued that European socialists were willing to unify an economic relaunch through investment (i.e. a supply-side economic policy), an active employment policy furthering social and environmental goals, and "good housekeeping with public resources" (which was tirelessly championed by most European governments regardless of their political affiliations). In other words, the PES followed the example of its national member parties in the 1980s and parted with Keynesian principles, which were unpopular with the heads of state and government of the EU, socialists included. The "New Deal" concept introduced in the EEI functioned primarily as an appeasement to Michel Rocard, the leader of the French PS,[82] rather than a meaningful attempt to reintroduce Keynes through the channel of "Eurokeynesianism". As Delors remarked in a conference dedicated to the legacy of Pierre Mendès France, "I can occasionally quote Keynes in European meetings without causing heart attacks, but barely".[83]

Second, a consensus emerged among the European socialist leaders and the experts of the Larsson group that GDP growth must precipitate the creation of new jobs, as in the United States and Japan. Like the SGEP, SAMAK had expressed scepticism towards growth as a universal remedy for the unemployment crisis. The delegation emphasised the plight of the long-term unemployed who were in particular need of assistance and encouraged worker mobility throughout their professional lives.[84] Many of the ideas suggested by the members of SAMAK found their way into the PES and the Delors cabinet, including halving unemployment in Europe within five years as a step towards regaining full employment, significant material and immaterial investment in the private sector, thereby prioritising the decrease of interest rates, breaking with the "passive employment policy" implemented by Western European governments in the 1980s, and promoting an "active employment policy" with the goal of reintroducing unemployed labourers into the workforce.

Conclusion: a different Third Way prior to "Blair-Schröder's Third Way"

The "Nordicisation" of PES social policy was swift and far-reaching. It played a substantial role in the political and ideological turn of European social democracy during the 1990s. In May 1994, socialist leaders urged Allan Larsson to update his report with the European general election in mind. An ad hoc group designated the "European Employment Initiative" was appointed.[85] The developments that took place between this election and the 1997 Amsterdam Treaty are beyond the scope of this chapter, but it is important to note that Larsson played a prominent role in these developments, first in the PES and later in the DGV, the Commission's directorate for employment of which he was appointed as director-general in 1995.[86] Larsson's departure from the working group did not undermine the Nordic ethos of European socialists' approach to employment policy. The MEP Elisabeth Guigou, a former economic adviser of Delors and Mitterrand in the 1980s and early 1990s, continued to invoke Nordic expertise after taking charge of the EEI with her adviser, Richard Corbett. In an interview, Corbett called attention to the "convergence between the EP and the Swedish government regarding employment issues and the alliance between Guigou and Lund, the Swedish representative in the reflection group".[87]

Because it aligned with the monetary and macroeconomic framework established in the Maastricht Treaty, SAMAK's approach to employment policy entered the *doxa* of European socialists. In this regard, the success of the Larsson initiative arguably signified a preference towards a third way prior to Blair and Schröder's "Third Way/*Neue Mitte*". Both projects reflect the "market turn" of socialist leaders and their advisers, who favoured supply-side economic policy at the time. The two projects also promoted "social democratic workfare" at a European scale. The EEI's commitment to flexibility (coupled with additional reforms) in the labour market echoed the ideas later developed in the 1999 Blair-Schröder manifesto, which contended that "adaptability and flexibility are at an increasing premium in the knowledge-based service economy of the future".[88] Broadly speaking, both ideologies prioritised labour as a core social value, underlining the significance of a return to full employment. Nevertheless, the social imperative of employment security was more central to the Larsson project. The EEI was a loyal translation of the formal "Nordic active employment policy", a key concept in the European debate over labour policy in the 1990s, which re-emerged in the 2000s with Danish attributes.[89]

Ultimately, the "Nordicisation" of PES employment policy epitomised the way in which European socialists planned the somewhat elusive aspiration of a "Social Europe" in the 1990s. The ambitious project to radically reform capitalism in the early 1970s led by charismatic figures such as Willy Brandt, Olof Palme and Bruno Kreisky had become outdated.[90] The PES had conceded by subordinating its perspective on social issues to the ordoliberal framework established by the Maastricht Treaty. The transformation of this framework was no longer European socialists' central objective and was replaced by the goal of improving it from within, as Allan Larsson explained to Ingvar Carlsson (who had just been re-elected as prime minister) a few days before the 1996 IGC Council:

> Improved employment is the essential mechanism through which the union's economic, social, and environmental goals can be reconciled with the necessary commitment to sound public finances. The aim is also to achieve such a high rate of productivity that common social standards can be fulfilled, and inflationary pressures counteracted.[91]

The EEI can thus be understood as a third way before the "Third Way". The Blair-Schröder manifesto resembles a radicalisation of the updated EEI by bolstering the call for flexibility and minimising the aspects that concerned the security of workers rather than calling for a radical break with the dominant paradigm among European social-democratic elites.

Acknowledgement

I would like to thank Michele Di Donato and Marc Lazar for their comments on earlier versions of this chapter.

Notes

1 Geoff Eley, *Forging Democracy. The History of the Left in Europe, 1850–2000* (Oxford and New York: Oxford University Press, 2002), p. 7.
2 "Mitterrand, the Monetarist", *Financial Times* editorial, 20 April 1990.
3 J. Magnus Ryner, "Neo-Liberalization of Social Democracy: The Swedish Case", *Comparative European Politics* 2 (2004), pp. 97–119, p. 101. Jenny Andersson and Kjell Östberg, "The Swedish Social Democrats, Reform Socialism and the State after the Golden Era", in *European Socialists and the State in the Twentieth and Twenty-First Centuries*, edited by Mathieu Fulla and Marc Lazar (Cham: Palgrave Macmillan, 2020), pp. 323–343, pp. 336–339.
4 Niels Finn Christiansen and Pirjo Markkola, "Introduction", in *The Nordic Model of Welfare*, edited by Niels Finn Christiansen and *alii* (Copenhagen: Museum Tusculanum Press, University of Copenhagen, 2006), pp. 9–29, p. 26.
5 Cornel Ban, *Ruling Ideas: How Global Neoliberalism Goes Local* (New York: Oxford University Press, 2016), p. 34.
6 Mathieu Fulla, "Quand Pierre Mauroy résistait avec rigueur au 'néolibéralisme'", *Vingtième siècle. Revue d'histoire* 138, no. 2 (2018), pp. 49–63.
7 Mario Soares, Meeting of the Socialist Heads of State and Government, "*Les acteurs du changement*", Handwritten Report, 18 May 1983, p. 3, Center of Socialist Archives of the Foundation Jean-Jaurès (below CAS-FJJ), Archives of Lionel Jospin, First Secretary of the French Socialist Party, 2 PS 455.
8 Pierre François and Claire Lemercier, *Sociologie historique du capitalisme* (Paris: La Découverte, 2021), pp. 213–265.
9 Daniel Rodgers, "The Uses and Abuses of 'Neoliberalism'", *Dissent* (Winter 2018), https://www.dissentmagazine.org/article/uses-and-abuses-neoliberalism-debate [Accessed June 17, 2021].
10 Laurent Warlouzet, *Europe contre Europe: entre liberté, solidarité et puissance depuis 1945* (Paris: CNRS Editions, in press, Winter 2022).
11 Gerassimos Moschonas, "The Party of European Socialists", in *Encylopoedia of European Elections*, edited by Yves Deloye and Michael Bruter (Basingstoke and New York: Palgrave MacMillan, 2007).
12 Helen Drake, *Jacques Delors: Perspectives on a European Leader* (New York: Routledge, 2000), p. 115.
13 Jacques Delors, "*Entrer dans le XXIe siècle. Les perspectives de l'économie européenne*", SEC (93) 993, 21 June 1993, Centre for History at Sciences Po (below CHSP), Jacques Delors Papers, JD-1134.
14 *Ibid.*
15 Jérôme Vignon, one of the closest Delors' advisers, recalled: "In European Commission administrative jargon, a white paper is a communication with a comprehensive impact generally covering several policy spheres and taking a longer-term view. Unlike green papers, white papers contain proposals for legislative decisions". See Jérôme Vignon, "The Rich Legacy of the White Paper on Growth, Competitiveness and Employment", Notre Europe Jacques Delors Institute, note 2, p. 6.
16 Rutger Claasen and *alii*, "Rethinking the European Social Market Economy: Introduction to the Special Issue", *Journal of Common Market Studies* 57, no. 1 (2019), pp. 3–12, p. 6.
17 James Sloam, *The European Policy of the German Social Democrats: Interpreting a Changing World* (Basingstoke: Palgrave Macmillan, 2005), p. 135.
18 Simon Hix, "Parties at the European Level and the Legitimacy of EU Socio-Economic Policy", *Journal of Common Market Studies* 33, no. 4 (December 1995), pp. 527–554, p. 547.
19 Karl Magnus Johansson, "Tracing the Employment Title in the Amsterdam Treaty: Uncovering Transnational Coalitions", *Journal of European Public Policy* 6, no. 1

(1999), pp. 85–101, p. 85. This employment title pointed out that employment was "a matter of common concern" and called for member states and the EU to "work towards developing a co-ordinating strategy for employment".

20 See, for example, Robert Ladrech, "Political Parties and the Problem of Legitimacy in the European Union", in *Legitimacy and the European Union: The Contested Polity*, edited by Thomas Banchoff and Mitchell Smith (London: Routledge, 1999), pp. 94–114; Andreas Aust, "From 'Eurokeynesianism' to the 'Third Way': The Party of European Socialists (PES) and European Employment Policies", in *Social Democratic Party Policies in Contemporary Europe*, edited by Giuliano Bonoli and Martin Powell (London and New York: Routledge, 2005), pp. 180–196.

21 Robert Ladrech, "Political Parties…", *op. cit.*, p. 106.

22 Peter Brown-Pappamikail, "Europe's Modern Prince? An Insider's View of the Party of European Socialists", Paper prepared for presentation in the panel on "Party Politics in the European Union", at the European Community Studies Association Conference, 11–14 May 1995, Charleston, South Carolina (USA), p. 4 (12 p.).

23 Axel Hanisch, "*Note à l'attention des membres du Bureau et des membres du groupe de travail 'Larsson'*", 3 December 1993, 1 p., Centre of Socialist Archives at the Foundation Jean-Jaurès in Paris (below CAS-FJJ), PES Archives, PS 50 RI PSE 1993.

24 "New Swedish Minister Promises Tighter Economy", *Reuters News*, 27 February 1990.

25 "*Présenté comme 'austère et responsable', le projet de budget suédois est plus libéral que social-démocrate*", *Le Monde*, 15 January 1991. J. Magnus Ryner, "Neo-Liberalization of Social Democracy", art. cit., p. 103 and note 4, p. 115.

26 Frode Forfang, "Annual Meeting of SAMAK, 21–22 January 1993", Oslo, 30 November 1992, 1 p., CAS-FJJ, PS 50 RI PSE. Formally founded in 1932, SAMAK is a joint committee including the autonomous islands of Greenland, Faroe Islands, and Aland.

27 Urban Lundberg, "A Leap in the Dark. From a Large Actor to a Large Approach: The Joint Committee of the Nordic Social Democratic Labour Movement and the Crisis of the Nordic Model", in *The Nordic Model of Welfare, op. cit.*, edited by Niels Finn Christiansen and *alii*, pp. 269–297, p. 289.

28 Robert Taylor, "Sweden and the EC: Sweden Comes in from the Cold – After Decades of Isolation, the Country has Finally Decided to Embrace the EC", *Financial Times*, 14 June 1991.

29 "*Manifeste électoral 1989*", revised version after the 9 February 1989 meeting in Brussels, p. 2, CAS-FJJ, 50 RI UPSCE élections (1988–1989).

30 "*Manifeste électoral 1989*", revised version after the meeting held in Brussels on 9 February 1989, 25 p., p. 2, CAS-FJJ, 50 RI UPSCE élections (1988–1989).

31 CSPEC, "*Note à l'attention des membres du bureau*", Brussels, 29 March 1990, "*Projet de procès-verbal du Bureau, Vienne, 24 mars 1990*", 5 p., p. 4, CAS-FJJ, 50 RI UPSCE 1990–November 1992.

32 CSPEC, "*Projet de procès-verbal de la réunion du bureau du 14.02.91 à Bruxelles*", Brussels, 18 February 1991, 10 p., p. 4, CAS-FJJ, 50 RI UPSCE 1990-November 1992.

33 PES, "*Projet de procès-verbal de la réunion du Bureau Corfou, 08.05.91*", Brussels, 12 June 1991, p. 6 (10 p.).

34 Jean-Pierre Cot, "*Projet de procès-verbal du bureau de l'union 14 et 15 mai à Strasbourg*", Brussels, 2 June 1992, p. 5 (11 p.), CAS-FJJ, 50 RI UPSCE 1990-November 1992.

35 SGEP, "Provisional Conclusions of the Socialist Group on the Architecture of the New Europe adopted in Vilamoura on 4 June 1992", p. 1 (2 p.), Swedish Labour Movement Archives and Library (below SLMAL) in Stockholm, Archives of the *Arbetarrörelsens nordiska samarbetskommité* (SAMAK), 1213/F/1/2.

36 Allan Larsson, speech at the meeting of the Socialist Group of the European Parliament, 2–3 July 1992, 9 p. Allan Larsson, "*En havstang till arbete*", 21 April 1992, 8 p., SLMAL, Archives of SAMAK, 1213/F/1/5.

37 Jenny Andersson, *Between Growth and Security: Swedish Social Democracy from a Strong Society to a Third Way*, Manchester University Press, 2006, p. 114.

38 SAMAKS Europagruppe, list of members, August 1992, SLMAL, Archives of SAMAK, 1213/F/1/5, 2 p.
39 Jenny Andersson, *Between Growth*, op. cit., pp. 105–127.
40 Speech by Allan Larsson, MP, former Minister of Finance at the meeting of Socialist Group of the European Parliament, 2–3 July 1992 in Stockholm, p. 1 (9 p.), SLMAL, Archives of SAMAK, 1213/F/1/5.
41 Andreas Aust, "From 'Eurokeynesianism'", op. cit., p. 181.
42 Speech by Allan Larsson, 2–3 July 1992, doc. cit., p. 3.
43 *Ibid.*, pp. 4–5.
44 *Ibid.*, p. 6.
45 *Ibid.*, pp. 7–8.
46 *Ibid.*, p. 8.
47 Jenny Andersson, *Between Growth*, op. cit., p. 121.
48 SGEP, Derek Reed, "Note to 'Employment and Growth' Circulation List. Re: Employment and Growth: Nordic Working Group", 7 September 1992, 1 p., SLMAL, Archives of SAMAK, 1213/F/1/5.
49 Bureau of the Socialist Group in the European Parliament, report of the decisions, November 1992, 2 p., CAS-FJJ, PS 50 RI PSE.
50 SGEP, *"Note à l'attention des membres 'A' du secrétariat"*, report by Jean-Marie Triacca about the meeting between the SAMAK delegation and MEPs, 9 December 1992, Brussels, CAS-FJJ, PS 50 RI PSE.
51 Urban Lundberg, "A Leap in the Dark", in *The Nordic Model of Welfare*, op. cit., edited by Niels Finn Christiansen and *alii*, p. 290.
52 Karl Magnus Johansson, "Tracing the Employment Title in the Amsterdam Treaty", art. cit., p. 91.
53 PES, *"Projet de procès-verbal du Bureau. Edimbourg le 9 décembre 1992"*, 9 p., CAS-FJJ, PS 50 RI – PSE.
54 Laurent Warlouzet, *Governing Europe in a Globalising World: Neoliberalism and its Alternatives Following the 1973 Oil Crisis* (Routledge, 2018), pp. 123–125.
55 PES, *"Huit pistes essentielles pour l'emploi. Projet de rapport du groupe économique du PSE présenté par Gérard Fuchs"*, 5 August 1993, 5 p., CAS-FJJ, PS 50 RI – PSE.
56 *"Compte rendu de la réunion du groupe de travail 'Economique et social' du 29 mai 1993 à Strasbourg, 12 juillet 1993"*, p. 2 (7 p.), CAS-FJJ, PES Archives, PS 50 RI – PSE.
57 Gérard Fuchs, Letter to Michel Rocard, 5 December 1993, p. 1 (1 p.), CAS-FJJ, PES Archives, PS 50 RI – PSE.
58 Peter Brown-Pappamikail, "Europe's Modern Prince?", op. cit., p. 4.
59 Karl Magnus Johansson, "Tracing the Employment Title in the Amsterdam Treaty", art. cit., note 6, p. 98.
60 He was then replaced by Alistair Darling, who was himself replaced by Andrew Smith.
61 *"Réunion groupe de travail ad hoc "PES Employment Programme". Première réunion – 20 septembre 1993"*, list of members of the Larsson group, 2 p., Historical Archives of the European Commission (below HAEC), Forward Studies Unit, box 346.
62 Mathieu Fulla, "Partager une culture économique sans le savoir. Les experts socialistes français et britanniques des années Soixante-dix", *Ventunesimo Secolo*, 44 (2019), pp. 64–87.
63 *"Groupe de travail 'économique et social'"*, attendee list, Strasbourg, 12 March 1993, CAS-FJJ, PS 50 RI – PSE.
64 PES, Bernard Tuyttens, "Note for the Attention of the Members of the Ad Hoc Group 'European Employment Programme' Chaired by Allan Larsson", 9 November 1993, CAS-FJJ, PS 50 RI – PSE.
65 Report of a meeting between Jacques Delors and Allan Larsson, 6 March 1991, CHSP, Jacques Delors Papers, JD-552.
66 SGEP, *"Croissance et emploi"*, 6 January 1993, Programme of the conference which will held on 4 February 1993, 2 p., CAS-FJJ, PS 50 RI PSE.

66 *Mathieu Fulla*

67 PES, Axel Hanisch, Letter to Jacques Delors, 12 November 1993, 1 p., and the third version of the Larsson report attached, HAEC, Forward Studies Unit, box 346.
68 Chris Boyd, "Note to the File" about his trip to Stockholm, 14–15 October 1993, p. 1 (2 p.), HAEC, Forward Studies Unit, box 351.
69 Jérôme Vignon, *"Quelques commentaires sur* 'Yes, Europe can Afford to Work'", 4 November 1993, 5 p., CAS-FJJ, PS 50 RI – PSE.
70 Allan Larsson, "Put Europe to Work", Report over the European Employment Initiative to the Leaders of the member parties of the PES", 3 December 1993, 20 p., CAS-FJJ, PS 50 RI – PSE 1993.
71 Pascal Lamy, *"Note pour le président", Objet: croissance-compétitivité-emploi – projet de Luigi Colajanni*, 8 September 1993, p. 1 (1 p.), HAEC, Forward Studies Unit, box 351.
72 *"Documentation Livre Blanc"*, Fall 1993, 7 p., HAEC, Forward Studies Unit, box 346.
73 *Ibid.*, p. 12.
74 Allan Larsson, "Put Europe to Work", doc. cit., p. 10.
75 George Ross, *Jacques Delors and European Integration* (Cambridge: Polity Press, 1995), quoted in Andreas Aust, "From 'Eurokeynesianism'", *op. cit.*, p. 184.
76 Andreas Aust, "From 'Eurokeynesianism'", *op. cit.*, p. 188.
77 European Commission, *Growth, Competitiveness, Employment. The Challenges and Ways Forward the 21st Century. White Paper*, Luxembourg: Office for Official Publications of the European Communities, 1994, p. 17.
78 Hélène Caune, *"Le modèle danois et la flexicurité européenne. Une 'stratégie à deux bandes' de persuasion par l'expertise"*, Gouvernement et action publique, 2014/2, n°2, pp. 55–79, p. 59.
79 Patrick Venturini, *"Note pour le Président"*, 19 January 1994, p. 2 (4 p.), CHSP, Jacques Delors Papers, JD-1871.
80 Jacques Delors, *"Conférence de Jacques Delors. Monnaie-croissance-emploi, ou la pensée de Pierre Mendès France confrontée aux réalités d'hier et d'aujourd'hui. 14 janvier 1994"*, 24 janvier 1994, p. 12 (14 p.), CHSP, Jacques Delors papers, JD-1869.
81 Helen Drake, "Towards a New European Society?", *op. cit.*, pp. 134–136; Ken Endo, *The Presidency of the European Commission under Jacques Delors: The Politics of Shared Leadership* (Basingstoke: Palgrave Macmillan, 1999), pp. 191–206.
82 Jean-Michel Thenard, *"Les socialistes européens programment en commun"*, Libération, 8 November 1993.
83 Jacques Delors, *"Conférence de Jacques Delors. Monnaie-croissance-emploi, ou la pensée de Pierre Mendès France confrontée aux réalités d'hier et d'aujourd'hui. 14 janvier 1994"*, 24 January 1994, p. 2 (14 p.), CHSP, Jacques Delors papers, JD-1869.
84 European Commission, *Growth, Competitiveness*, op. cit., p. 17.
85 Letter from Willy Claes to Gérard Fuchs, *"Follow up du rapport d'Allan Larsson"*, 18 January 1994, 2 p., CAS-FJJ, PS 50 RI PSE.
86 Karl Magnus Johansson, "Tracing the Employment Title in the Amsterdam Treaty", art. cit., pp. 93–94.
87 *Ibid.*, p. 94.
88 Tony Blair and Gerhard Schröder's Manifesto, "Europe: The Third Way/Die Neue Mitte", June 8, 1999, http://miroirs.ironie.org/socialisme/www.psinfo.net/dossiers/gauche/3voie/blairvo.html [Accessed June 30, 2021].
89 Hélène Caune, "Le modèle danois…", art. cit.
90 Aurélie Andry, *"Social Europe" in the Long 1970s. The Story of a Defeat*, PhD dissertation, European University Institute, Florence, 2017.
91 Allan Larsson, "A Vision for IGC 1996: A European Employment Union – To Make EMU Possible", April 25, 1995, p. 1 (14 p.), SLMAL, Archives of SAMAK, 1213/F/1/9. The original version of this paper was written in Swedish.

4 Social democracy, globalisation and the ambiguities of "Europeanisation"

Revisiting the Southern European crises of the 1970s

Michele Di Donato

What is "Southern Europe"? As this definition gained currency on the heels of the post-2008 economic and Eurozone crises, scholars tasked with tracing its origins insisted on the historically and politically constructed nature of our understanding of regional demarcations. "In present day Southern Europe, the Cold War, decolonisation and European integration have been the major forces behind region-building", historian Effie Pedaliu argued in a 2013 paper. "In this respect 'Southern Europe' is a new phenomenon that emerged in the 20th Century roughly at the same time that the categories Western Europe and Eastern Europe acquired increasing political currency, but the term has been used regularly only since the 1970s".[1] Focusing on the 1970s, another historian, Sotiris Rizas, remarked that

> Southern Europe as a region sharing common features emerged as a concept in the thinking of American and British policymakers during the 1970s. The collapse of authoritarian regimes in Portugal and Greece and the end of the dictatorship in Spain, taking place almost simultaneously in the mid-1970s, were the political facts underlying this assumption. It was not however only a problem of transition from authoritarianism to democracy that shaped events. The rise of the Communist Party in Italy and the prospect of communist participation in a NATO member-states parliamentary government posed questions of viability of democracy within the Cold War context.[2]

This chapter will take as a starting point what, with hindsight, appears as a rather exceptional historical peculiarity, namely the geographical and chronological concentration in Southern Europe of a series of discrete but interconnected political developments whose outcomes were perceived by the international community as potentially threatening for European stability, and in which the role of left-wing forces was particularly pronounced – the emergence of a reformed "Eurocommunism" in Italy, France and Spain; the socialist-communist alliance led by François Mitterrand in France and the latter's attempt to organise and lead the other socialist parties of the region on the basis of this model; the role of the Left in the transitions to democracy in Portugal and Spain. While the role formal and informal social democratic networks played in these "Southern European

DOI: 10.4324/9781003181439-5

crises" and in their solution has been closely examined by historiography, this chapter will try to propose a partly different approach, using this as a case study to examine the evolution of the relation between social democratic internationalism and international relations in post-war Western Europe.[3] Differently from Rizas and others, I will frame this evolution not only in the context of the Cold War and détente but also as an aspect of the shift from a Cold War–centred international system to the "shock of the global" of the 1970s, focusing especially on the emergence of "Europeanisation" as a response to new perceived challenges.[4]

The chapter will be divided into four sections. In the first one, I will introduce my framework of analysis and discuss its relevance to the study of post-war social democratic internationalism. I will then move to the 1970s and present the main novelties that characterised that decade.[5] Finally, I will zoom in on two aspects of the "Southern European crises" and propose some tentative conclusions on their significance in the historical trajectory of social democratic internationalism.

*

Internationalism has long been considered as a secondary aspect of the history of European socialist and social democratic parties.[6] Especially in view of the collapse of the Second International in the face of the First World War, the internationalism of the social democrats appeared just as a vague (and rather empty) rhetorical device. The main story, many argued, was that of the "nationalisation" of socialist movements.[7] In recent years, however, this approach has been questioned by several scholars in the context of the growing historiographical interest in transnational networks, relations and circulations. Talbot Imlay, in particular, has remarked that "dismissals of socialist internationalism [...] cannot explain why [social democratic parties] devoted so much time and energy to constructing and maintaining an international community after 1945".[8] In his works, Imlay proposes to focus on the *practice* of socialist internationalism, "defined as the extended effort of socialist parties to cooperate together in international issues".[9] "If socialist parties were clearly embedded in national politics and sometimes governments", he has argued, "this did not prevent them from being active members of an international socialist society [...] not simply a distinct international society but also an oppositional one".[10]

This chapter concurs with this reconsideration of the importance of post-war internationalism, but at the same time proposes a partly different interpretation. It suggests to analyse the history of European social democratic internationalism in the wider framework of the multifarious Western networks of political cooperation, arguing that this is indispensable in order to effectively bridge "the divide between the sub-disciplines of labour and international history".[11] Social democrats were in fact involved in a thick web of contacts and international links, and they partook, in different positions and capacities, in a vast array of international initiatives and developments. Exclusively socialist networks represented only an aspect – albeit a crucial one – of the international socialisation and engagement of party officials and leaders. It often happened that the same person addressed governmental and party gatherings in the space of a few hours. By the mid-1970s, forums such as the "Party Leaders Conferences" of the Socialist International (SI) brought together socialist leaders who also happened to be the heads of government of (among others) West Germany, Britain, the Netherlands, Sweden, Austria and Denmark. Throughout the Cold War period – and beyond – socialist representatives partook in formal and informal organisations that fostered transatlantic cooperation (from the NATO Parliamentary Assembly to private associations such as the Bilderberg Group) as well as in several European institutions. Involved in multiple networks and exposed to different influences, socialist leaders could then transfer their experience to the social democratic movement (in terms of information acquired or development of new outlooks).

It is tempting for the historian of social democratic internationalism to focus exclusively on party networks and on the role they played both in the internal evolution of the socialist movement (in terms of transnational circulation of ideas, models and expertise) and in the international arena. Nevertheless, the analysis of "socialist international relations" should be thoroughly embedded in the international history in which they unfolded, lest one end up cutting off the history of social democracy from the broader course of European and international history. Hence, rather than studying social democratic internationalism simply as part of the history of the Left, the chapter insists on the need to foreground its interactions and overlaps with other instances of international cooperation.

For the decades that followed 1945, a special focus should therefore be kept on the Cold War and transatlantic relations, which decisively shaped the international outlook and initiatives of the European socialist parties. The path that led to the full integration of social democratic parties within the "Atlantic Community" was all but a straightforward one – internal resistances were often significant and conditioned both its timing and its characteristics, which varied in the different European countries. By the late 1950s–early 1960s, however, any residual opposition to "Western" integration among mainstream socialist parties and currents had been marginalised, especially as the German SPD finally abandoned its reservations about European integration and NATO. As Piers Ludlow has argued most cogently, cooperation within the European community should also be understood in its linkage with the Cold War and Euro-American relations.[12] Finally, efforts by European social democrats to reach out to the decolonised and developing countries only gained substance starting from the 1960s, when East-West tensions began to subside.[13]

Adhesion to dichotomous Cold War worldviews became an identity-defining feature of post-war social democracy. Conflictual relationships between social democrats and communists predated the Cold War, but the East-West divide contributed to reshaping and reframing them. To social democrats, opposition to communism also became a vehicle for national and international legitimation, thus showing how the Cold War context, far from representing just an "external constraint" imposed on political and ideological choices, could also be used by "peripheral" actors in order to pursue goals of their own.[14] Partnership in anti-communist action represented just an aspect of a much more profound transatlantic exchange that contributed to refashioning political cultures in postwar Europe. The non-conflictual approach to labour relations entailed by what Charles Maier famously defined as the Marshall Plan's "politics of productivity", as well as the consensual "Cold War liberalism" upheld by the anti-communist intellectuals associated with the Congress for Cultural Freedom (CCF), involved European socialists in a complex process of reception and adaptation, while exchange programmes and sponsored visits to the United States sustained and reinforced their personal networks of contacts.[15] Together with AFL-CIO trade unionists, East coast liberals such as those who would come to be known as John Kennedy's "best and brightest" – one can think of Arthur Schlesinger, Jr., and John Galbraith as quintessential examples – became partners and interlocutors of choice for European social democrats, and played a key role in their international socialisation.[16] It is in this context that the social democratic revisionism thrived since the 1950s, and that political leaders and theorists embraced Keynesian demand-management and redistributive strategies over the traditional focus on nationalisations and control on production.

Encouraged by the Democratic administrations of John Kennedy and Lyndon Johnson as part of their design of liberal modernisation, the "opening to the Left" in Italy and West Germany during the 1960s seemed to seal the Western evolution of European social democracy by completing the integration of what, for different reasons, had been two "deviant" members of this political family, i.e. the Italian PSI and the German SPD.[17] Commenting on a January 1967 Rome meeting of the Socialist International (SI), the local US Embassy did not hide its enthusiasm:

> Recent Rome meeting of International provided striking evidence of increased importance of socialists' role in Europe. Three of parties represented hold or share power in major countries – UK, Germany, Italy. Their delegations were led by ministers whose views carry weight. All parties also represented moderate reformist rather than Bolshevik ideas and attitudes. [...] Impressive fact is that Western European socialists (now including Nenni's socialists[18]) are bringing increasing influence to bear on European and world problems. And in a moderate and restrained fashion.[19]

*

In the space of a few years, several developments blurred this picture of relatively harmonious integration of European social democratic internationalism and transatlantic cooperation. These developments can be linked to three main drivers. The growing global interdependence displayed the limitations of a Cold War–centred reading of international relations. At the same time, Euro-American relations themselves deteriorated and underwent substantial changes. Finally, the political, economic and cultural changes associated with the "crisis of the 1970s" also had a crucial impact. It can be argued that the emergence of cracks in the Cold War order and the crisis of "embedded liberalism" led social democratic internationalism to also grow increasingly "disembedded" from the Western networks of political cooperation with which it had previously interacted.

Historians of US foreign policy and transatlantic relations have thoroughly analysed and discussed the tensions that arose between America and Western Europe since the late 1960s. Even before the major transatlantic rows of 1973 over the Yom Kippur War and the energy crisis, issues such as the US war in Vietnam, international economic and monetary relations and different approaches to East-West détente policies had become crucial catalysts of controversy.[20]

Social democratic parties and leaderships were part and parcel of these developments. The leaders' positions on the Vietnam war ranged from the prudence of Willy Brandt to the radical opposition of Olof Palme (the Swedish Prime Minister since 1969), but the vast majority of the socialist parties' grassroots and delegates were critical of the American intervention.[21] This development was problematic also for staunchly Atlanticist social democrats such as Helmut Schmidt. In a 1968 conversation with a political counsellor of the US embassy in Bonn, the then leader of the SPD *Fraktion* at the Bundestag explained that "he was [...] constantly asked questions during political meetings about the American policy in Southeast Asia. He was in these days increasingly at loss for answers. We should be aware that criticism of our Vietnam policy is growing in Germany. The pressure in the SPD has become very strong to take an outright anti-American stand". As the American officer responded with a classic justification of the Vietnam intervention as part of a global struggle against Communism whose outcomes were crucial for Germany, Schmidt closed the conversation with one of his characteristic matter-of-fact remarks: "Schmidt said that he was familiar with this American theory [...]. He did not seek to argue its validity but gave the impression that few people in his party were willing to accept it under current circumstances".[22]

An "experts' committee" on the reform of the international monetary system was set up by the Socialist International after Nixon's decision of suspending the convertibility of the dollar in August 1971. The proceedings of its first meetings show a certain longing for the "lost world" of transatlantic harmony. The participants agreed that the Bretton Woods system had "worked well", with the British Harold Lever going so far as to define it "by far the best system the world has ever enjoyed". More radical "experts" such as Jean Pierre Chevènement (from the CERES left-wing faction of the French Socialist Party) argued that the crisis of the system should not be considered simply as a "technical" one, and that "as socialists, we must raise the problem of US policy in general and vis-à-vis Vietnam in particular when told about the monetary crisis". Yet even a moderate such as the SI President Bruno Pittermann remarked that "American Labour is more in favour of the present US economic policy than we are", thus signalling that, in the new conjuncture, the "progressive" transatlantic agreement on the benefits of economic liberalism was giving way to protectionist tendencies that were consistent with Nixon's "New economic policy".[23] It was indeed in the United States that post-war liberalism was increasingly contested as a new discourse of limits was emerging which Nixon's *éminence grise*, Henry Kissinger, was translating into a new foreign policy programme.[24] During a SI Party Leaders Conference held in

September 1971, Dutch PvdA's Joop den Uyl had indeed captured the opinion of many by remarking that "Europe had to come to terms with the post-Vietnam world where the United States was unable or unwilling to lead the world in political, monetary or economic matters".[25]

Significantly, all the socialist "experts" endorsed some form of "European initiative" as a response to the monetary crisis. In this as in other cases, social democratic networks participated in a tendency towards "Europeanisation" as a reaction to the transatlantic quarrels of the early decade, epitomised by the active phase of European integration that followed the Hague Summit of December 1969. As highlighted among others by Antonio Varsori, and more recently by Laurent Warlouzet and Aurélie Andry, this process was paralleled by a partial "social democratisation" of Europe and European institutions: as the number of social democratic governments increased (with the 1969 electoral success of the SPD as a watershed), initiatives aimed at reinforcing the "social" aspect of integration gained ground.[26] Social democrats displayed a distinctively "European" approach also in what concerned détente policies. They all endorsed the West German *Ostpolitik*, whose philosophy of promoting gradual change in the East through increased contacts became a keystone of the foreign policy programmes of almost all European SI parties (in spite of the qualms manifested by the two superpowers, which instead sought to stabilise their condominium and feared autonomous initiatives by their junior allies). The personal prestige of Willy Brandt all but reinforced the popularity of this position, which accompanied the definitive confirmation of the status of the SPD as the new leader of the Socialist International.[27] Détente policies effectively came to represent – and to be presented as – a modern and successful expression of the pacifist tradition of social democratic internationalism.[28]

*

It is in this context that the "Southern European crises" of the mid-1970s came about. As stated above, the chapter will not attempt to retell the well-known story of their development or of the role socialist networks played in their denouement. Its goal is rather to highlight the importance these events assumed in the evolution of the relation between social democratic internationalism and international relations during the 1970s. A first aspect that can be stressed, when looking at this interaction, has to do with the perception of the European social democratic movement as a unitary actor in international relations. By definition, this perception can be best identified when looking at the social democratic movement from the outside. Here we shall do so by concentrating on the relations between European socialists and what was then the most important governmental actor in the international arena, i.e. the United States.

From this point of view, the Southern European crises represented a crucial turning point. Focusing especially on the Portuguese democratic transition, the existing historiography has highlighted the contrast between a hawkish, rigidly anti-Communist US approach, represented by Secretary of State Henry Kissinger, and a more nuanced Euro-socialist strategy of support to the Portuguese democratic forces (i.e. to Mário Soares's PS, first and foremost), which was eventually able to win the day.[29] The autonomy of socialist solidarity networks is epitomised by the famous meetings of Stockholm and London (August–September 1975), in which European social democratic leaders manifested their commitment to sustaining the PS as the main rampart against the risk of an anti-democratic drift of the Portuguese situation, after the tensions of the *verão quente*. At the same time, the boundaries between state and party diplomacy were porous, and the role of social democratic solidarity networks was often discussed during intergovernmental meetings.[30] It should also be noted that these discussions took place in the context of an important evolution in transatlantic relations. After the tensions that culminated in the 1973 rows, a practice of close consultation between the United States and the main European powers had re-emerged since 1974.[31] The Southern European crises were discussed in the context of ad hoc quadripartite meetings of the foreign ministers of the United States, the FRG, the UK and France. Dedicated to the crisis of NATO's "Southern Flank", these meetings gave governmental officials the opportunity to exchange freely on the situation of the whole of Southern Europe and the Northern shore of the Mediterranean: Portugal, Spain, France, Italy, Yugoslavia, Greece, Cyprus and Turkey. Briefing material for President Gerald Ford explained that the foreign ministers were in fact "ranging much more broadly over Western interests and policies and as a result a sort of de facto political steering group is emerging". The United States and the main European powers appeared to be building "an organic association in which we seek to cope jointly with common problems".[32] From this point of view, the quadripartite meetings on the "Southern Flank" were closely linked to the emergence of new intergovernmental forums such as the G-6/G-7 summits (the first of these summits took place in November 1975 in Rambouillet, a mere three months after the inauguration of quadripartite consultations).[33]

On the European side, two out of three governments involved in the quadripartite meetings were led by the Socialist International parties. Although he held in high regard some representatives of these governments, such as James Callaghan and (especially) Helmut Schmidt, Kissinger did not conceal his mistrust of the European Left as a whole. He despised what he defined as the latter's "sentimental" approach to foreign policy, which in his view even prevented the European Left from "analyz[ing] its own national interest".[34] The transatlantic rows of the early decade had left him with the image of a left-leaning Western Europe that was on the one hand prone to coalesce around anti-Americanism, and on the other to accede to the Third World's demands for restructuring international economic relations and building an anti-Western New International Economic Order.[35] "The problem for us in Western Europe", Kissinger argued in a May 1975 memorandum for the President,

> is that in many of the countries political life and societies are gradually shifting to the left and that values and orientations will emerge that may over time make the NATO association an anachronism. [...] The trends noted above

would be accelerated by the enduring establishment of a left-radical, neutralist regime in Portugal. Most current European governments are unwilling or unable (because of the political underpinnings on which they rest) to draw these diagnostic conclusions, and even less the policy consequences that would flow from them.[36]

Showing an extremely restricted view of the perimeter of the "Western community", Kissinger frequently voiced his regret of the "opening to the Left" in Italy and West Germany during the 1960s, which he saw as a sort of "original sin" that opened the gates to a leftwards drift of the whole of Western Europe.[37] For its part, the SPD was well aware of this situation, and worked to improve its relationship with American political circles. A working group of the party directorate (*Parteivorstand*) was formed to this end in 1974, whose activities were steadily increased in the following years.[38]

In spite of this deep-seated mistrust, Kissinger had to put up with the fact that Western European socialists had at their disposal unique assets when it came to facing the Southern European crises. As several studies have pointed out, crisis management in Portugal represented a turning point. By December 1975, the US State Department Planning Staff had to acknowledge:

> We already have noted that the European Community can have some influence over political change in Southern Europe […]. The attraction and influence of a reasonably united Western European grouping, with both political respectability and economic benefits to offer, has served our mutual interests in Portugal and may do so again in Spain. The West Europeans […] can do some things that we cannot; certainly they can more openly involve themselves in political developments (including direct support to parties and labor unions) that we could do.[39]

The paper, moreover, recognised a tendency towards "Europeanisation" that "spill[ed] beyond the EC 9" and was giving shape to a new Western European space, less defined by Cold War boundaries. Socialist parties were again playing a key role:

> Socialist party or trade union efforts to influence developments in Southern Europe link some from EC member states with some of Europe's neutrals. Indeed, the recent pattern has been for some non-EC group to broach a new area of "political cooperation" (e.g., Socialist parties on Portugal) before the subject is taken up by the EC as such.[40]

Social democratic leaders were conscious of this development and were much eager to point out its importance to their American interlocutors. In late January 1976, Denmark hosted an SI Party Leaders' Conference – the outcomes of which, as we shall see in the next section of this chapter, were crucial to another "Southern European" debate, on the possibility of socialist-communist alliances in the region. The convenor, Danish socialist prime minister Anker Jørgensen, insisted that Kissinger make a stopover in Copenhagen en route to Moscow, so that he could brief him on the results of the conference. During the meeting, Jørgensen argued for a flexible approach to the Communist issue and tried to impress on his interlocutor the special value of social democratic summits:

> It would be good if the European Community could have good team work within it, but also have cooperation with other parts of democratic Europe – Sweden, Austria. The Social Democratic meetings are a party meeting, but also a mechanism for better collaboration between countries inside and outside the EC, where we can stress how important it is to try to keep democracy and also to develop democracy.[41]

*

This reference to the socialist conference that took place in Helsingør, Denmark, in January 1976, can serve as an introduction to a second crucial aspect of the relation between social democratic internationalism and international relations. So far, we have dealt with the perception of European social democratic parties as a unitary international actor. At the same time, however, analysts and political leaders were well aware of the internal fractures that existed within the social democratic movement.[42] Widely construed as a showdown moment, the Helsingør summit represented the culmination of a political controversy over the direction of the socialist movement in Southern Europe and beyond. The first issue on the agenda was the admissibility of alliances between socialist and communist parties. Originally brought to the fore by François Mitterrand's *Parti socialiste*, which had built a "Union of the Left" with the French Communist Party, the issue had assumed Europe-wide implications as Mitterrand started theorising the existence of a "Southern European socialism" – more radical than "Northern European" social democracy and more open to alliances with communist parties – and organising conferences and other initiatives with, among others, the Portuguese, Spanish and Italian socialists.[43] Emerging against the backdrop of the Portuguese (and later Spanish) transitions, as well as the development of a reformed "Eurocommunist" movement led by the Italian PCI, which was by then advancing its own bid for power in the wake of unprecedented electoral successes, Mitterrand's strategy had immediate Cold War implications. This did not elude the German social democrats, who embarked on a campaign to contain what they saw as the threat of "Mitterrandisme".[44] As further evidence of the unique relevance Southern Europe assumed in this phase, the SPD formed in November 1975 its own working party on "South-Western Europe", which was tasked with monitoring the situation of the Left in the area.[45] A few years later, it was the turn of the British Labour Party's National Executive Committee (hegemonised by the left-wing) to establish a "Western European Sub-Committee" whose activities initially focused on the socialist and communist parties of France, Italy and Spain.[46]

Cold War equilibria represented only part of the issues at stake in the region. Once again, the State Department's Policy Planning Staff proposed extremely perceptive remarks on this point in another paper of December 1975, which is worth quoting at length:

> While détente doubtless has contributed significantly to Italian and French political "permissiveness", the broader causes of disaffection from centrist parties in Latin Europe and elsewhere in the West lie in the widespread lack of direction and disintegration resulting from what has come to be known popularly as "future shock" – the severe pressures of simultaneous unemployment and inflation in the post-Keynesian West; the acceleration of modern technology and communications; the simultaneous fragmentation and globalization of the international system; the fractious encounter of North and South; the widespread decline of authority in executive branches of government; the fading of the idea of progress and lack of genuine energizing ideals; and the buffeting of the individual in the face of political corruption, economic decline and personalized wars.
>
> We therefore face a situation far more complex than the outward manifestation of Western Communist success – a condition which will require far more subtle and comprehensive treatment than simply broad-stroked anti-communist assault.[47]

For the scope of our analysis, we can observe that different positions on the Southern European crises tended to mirror different understandings of these domestic and transnational problems, especially in what concerned the appropriateness of "interventionist", state-centred responses to the economic crisis and globalisation. Left-wing proponents of encroachments on capitalist prerogatives (e.g. not only most currents of the French PS but also the Labour Left and the German Young Socialists) confronted mainstream currents that preferred to uphold and innovate traditional solutions (as in the case of Willy Brandt and Olof Palme), as well as leaders such as Helmut Schmidt and James Callaghan, who argued that the primacy of global markets represented a reality to be reckoned with, which needed social democrats to abandon potentially harmful voluntarist efforts.[48]

The Planning Staff's nuanced understanding of the stakes of the Southern European crises, however, did not lead to a correspondingly subtle policy approach. What Kissinger and his staff retained of the developments of 1974–1975 was the importance of socialist party diplomacy. This, however, did not dissipate their mistrust. In a conversation with the Secretary of State, the US ambassador to Italy, John Volpe, voiced this attitude with a rather eloquent avowal: "Not that I love the Socialists – I hate their guts – but that is all that we have to work with".[49]

On the eve of the Helsingør Conference, the State Department issued an instruction to European embassies to approach socialist parties in the countries to which they were accredited, urging them to use their influence with the parties of Italy, Portugal and Spain to warn them against the danger of cooperating with the communists.[50] The instruction was duly implemented, and US embassy officials met with the social democratic leaders of all of Western Europe, including foreign ministers and heads of government such as Callaghan, Palme and Jørgensen.[51] Henry Kissinger wrote a personal letter to Willy Brandt which was both an acknowledgement of the historical significance of the linkage between social democratic parties and the United States, and a warning to preserve that course by resisting the new "communist threat".[52] Overall, the Helsingør meeting was followed by US diplomats with an attention unheard of for this sort of party gatherings, and exchanges between socialist parties and US embassies officials continued throughout Europe in the aftermath of the conference.[53] On the one hand, this was a sign of the importance attached to socialist internationalism and party diplomacy. On the other hand, the fact that the US government had decided to adopt "such unsubtle and direct tactics", as some British diplomats defined them, as well as the predictably negative reactions of some of its socialist interlocutors, especially in France,[54] witnessed to the fatigue of the more sophisticated and consensual dynamics of American hegemony of the previous decades, as well as to Kissinger's ideological rigidity and resistance to accepting the European socialist movement's tendency to outgrow its 'Cold War internationalism'.

Debates at Helsingør had in fact ranged far beyond the Cold War implications of socialist-communist alliances. Leading the anti-Mitterrand front, Helmut Schmidt did indeed mention the consequences communist participation in Western European countries could have for cooperation within NATO and for military equilibria, but also discussed different aspects, starting from the transnationalisation of political debates – which was such that the French socialists' alliance strategies risked jeopardising the German electorate's confidence in socialists in their own country. Moreover, he discussed what he saw as the consequences of the transformation of the Western economic system in the age of globalisation of capital and stagflation, which in his opinion rendered economic planning in a single country not only impossible but potentially harmful for the overall stability of the system.[55]

These debates invite us to go beyond the acknowledgement of the role socialist networks played in Southern Europe as agents of "Europeanisation". In Southern Europe and beyond, political alternatives did not just relate to "geopolitical" polarities but also to different socio-economic projects. Different socialist representatives discussed the troubling reality of the economic turmoil at different levels, both domestically and internationally, in party forums as well as in intergovernmental meetings. The ambitious projects of the mid-decade would soon give way to new economic priorities, especially after the negotiation of International Monetary Fund (IMF) loans in Italy and Portugal during 1977 (but the problem went beyond Southern Europe: Labour Britain had gone through its own traumatic "IMF crisis" in 1976).[56]

In the space of a few years, the attractiveness of European social democratic models would decline sharply. The prospects of Euro-socialist autonomy appeared less and less rosy as critiques of state intervention in the economy gained ground. Scholarship is currently focusing on the shifts in the European political and cultural panorama that emerged during this phase of uncertainty, and significant attention is being paid to new intergovernmental forums in which these problems were discussed, such as the G7 and European Council Summits.[57] While the crucial role that social democratic leaders such as Helmut Schmidt played in these processes is widely recognised,[58] much is still to be done to analyse how their experiences and outlooks were conveyed to the social democratic movement, as well as the kind of responses and dynamics they activated, especially in relation to the proponents of alternative views who still dominated the networks of party experts.[59]

In this context, the "Europeanisation" of the Southern European crises also ended up setting in motion some ambiguous dynamics. A paper produced in August 1976 by analysts in the Western European Division of the Office of Current Intelligence at the CIA pondered some of them. The main argument of the study was a familiar one: the democratic transitions and the political and economic troubles of Southern Europe had fed a growing sense of "Europeanness" which connected the Northern and Southern parts of the continent. Aid to socialists and democrats in Portugal, spearheaded by the Northern European social democrats, was the most obvious example, but the CIA analysts also mentioned "the loans the other Europeans have made to support the Italian economy" as "concrete evidence of the feeling that 'we're all in it together'". This aid, the paper noted, was however "accompanied by conditions and lectures". And while the tendency towards growing European cooperation and North-South exchange was clear, one also had to take into account resistances on both sides. An example of these was the negative reactions occasioned by some remarks chancellor Schmidt had recently made about the unsettled situation in Southern Europe: "the spate of articles about the re-emergence of the 'ugly German' that followed this episode suggests how easy it remains to overstep the boundaries of acceptable mutual involvement".[60]

It is hard to resist the "presentist" temptation to look at these dynamics from the perspective of the recent Eurozone crisis and of the strained relations between Northern and Southern members of the EU. Comparing the post-2008 crisis to the 1970s, however, entails taking into account both continuities and changes, especially in what concerns the ability of social democrats to set the political agenda and develop a distinctive approach to international affairs and intra-European relations.

*

The Southern European crises represented a watershed moment for social democratic internationalism. In his report about a May 1978 mission to the United States, German social democrat Karsten Voigt commented:

> Contrary to the past, Socialist International politics is the subject of a great attention among US experts. Already after the activities of the SPD in Portugal and Spain, the instrument of international party relations as a component of European politics received more attention as a moment of practical politics. While in recent years I was mainly asked about Eurocommunism, I

have now been asked a lot more questions about the SI, the European Social Democratic parties and also about the impact of the upcoming election campaign on the European direct elections.[61]

In the wake of the crisis of the mid-1970s, socialist international relations and party diplomacy had emerged as crucial features of European politics. Historians have stressed the role relationships with the former Southern European dictatorships played in shaping the "democratic identity" of the European community, as "the central legitimising strategy that had originally moved the project of European integration forward, that of promoting peace, found its complement in the Community's new obligation to promote democratic ideals".[62] Socialist parties and governments played an important role in this process. Insofar as they were able to operate as a unitary actor on the international arena, they displayed a distinctive interpretation of the boundaries and goals of "Europe" and of the "Western community", and could reasonably claim to be operating for putting democratic and social objectives on top of the international agenda. Transnational political exchanges demonstrated their importance both as foreign policy instruments and as avenues for the legitimation of emerging political forces. Moreover, social democratic forums acted as political clearinghouses that made it possible to overcome at least some aspects of the compartmentalisation of intra-European relations between EC and non-EC members, NATO countries and non-NATO countries, thus prefiguring the prospect of a united political space spanning the whole Western portion of the continent.[63] In some cases, their commitment to East-West détente was evidence of an ambitious long-term design of integration of Europe on an even larger scale.[64] With Willy Brandt's election as President of the Socialist International, in November 1976, the SI set out to play a similar role at a global level.

At the same time, however, the internal fractures that emerged over the new political-economic challenges that characterised the 1970s displayed the limits of this "coming of age" of social democratic internationalism. Divided over the responses to the new international economic conditions, the socialist movement would struggle to assert itself as a credible alternative in the age of globalisation.

Notes

1 Effie Pedaliu, "The Making of Southern Europe: An Historical Overview", in *A Strategy for Southern Europe. LSE IDEAS Special Report*, n. 17, October 2013, 9. See also Pedaliu, "Fault Lines in Post War Mediterranean and the "Birth of Southern Europe", 1945–1979: An Overview", in *Détente in Cold War Europe: Politics and Diplomacy in the Mediterranean and the Middle East*, eds. Elena Calandri, Daniele Caviglia, and Antonio Varsori (London: I.B. Tauris, 2013), 15–32.
2 Sotiris Rizas, *The Rise of the Left in Southern Europe: Anglo-American Responses* (London: Pickering & Chatto, 2012), 1.
3 For a comprehensive view see, among others and in addition to Rizas, the special issue of the *Journal of European Integration History*, 15, no. 1 (2009), and Mario Del Pero, Victor Gavín, Fernando Guirao, and Antonio Varsori, *Democrazie. L'Europa meridionale e la fine delle dittature* (Milan: Le Monnier, 2010).

80 *Michele Di Donato*

4 Niall Ferguson, Charles S. Maier, Erez Manela, and Daniel J. Sargent, eds., *The Shock of the Global: The 1970s in Perspective* (Cambridge, MA and London: Belknap Press, 2010); Claudia Hiepel, ed., *Europe in a Globalising World. Global Challenges and European Responses in the "Long" 1970s* (Baden-Baden: Nomos, 2014); Laurent Warlouzet, *Governing Europe in a Globalizing World: Neoliberalism and its Alternatives after the 1973 Oil Crisis* (New York and London: Routledge, 2017).

5 These sections will partly draw on Michele Di Donato, "Internazionalismo socialdemocratico e storia internazionale degli anni Settanta", *Ventunesimo Secolo*, 44 (2019), 11–37 (to which they however add fresh archival material).

6 In the chapter, I will generally use the two terms as synonyms.

7 A typical example of this approach is Donald Sassoon, *One Hundred Years of Socialism. The West European Left in the Twentieth Century* (New York and London: I.B. Tauris, 2010). For a state-of-the-art review of the question see Ettore Costa, *The Labour Party, Denis Healey and the International Socialist Movement. Rebuilding the Socialist International during the Cold War, 1945–1951* (Basingstoke: Palgrave Macmillan, 2018), 1–11.

8 Talbot Imlay, "'The Policy of Social Democracy is Self-Consciously Internationalist': The German Social Democratic Party's Internationalism after 1945", *The Journal of Modern History*, 86, no. 1 (2014), 81–123, here 85. More broadly, see Imlay, *The Practice of Socialist Internationalism: European Socialists and International Politics, 1914–1960* (Oxford: Oxford University Press, 2018).

9 Imlay, "Social Democratic Internationalism after 1914", in *Internationalisms: A Twentieth-Century History*, eds. Glenda Sluga and Patricia Clavin (Cambridge: Cambridge University Press, 2017), 215.

10 Imlay, "Exploring What Might Have Been: Parallel History, International History, and Post-War Socialist Internationalism", *The International History Review*, 31, no. 3 (2009), 521–557, here 549.

11 Daniel Laqua, "Democratic Politics and the League of Nations: The Labour and Socialist International as a Protagonist of Interwar Internationalism", *Contemporary European History*, 24, no. 2 (2015), 175–192, here 177.

12 Piers Ludlow, "European Integration and the Cold War", in *The Cambridge History of the Cold War*, vol. II, *Crises and Détente*, eds. Melvyn P. Leffler and Odd Arne Westad (Cambridge: Cambridge University Press, 2010), 179–198.

13 Peter Van Kemseke, *Towards an Era of Development: The Globalization of Socialism and Christian Democracy, 1945–1965* (Leiven: Leuven University Press, 2006), 9.

14 See Tony Smith, "New Bottles for New Wine: A Pericentric Framework for the Study of the Cold War", *Diplomatic History*, 24, no. 4 (2000), 567–591.

15 Charles S. Maier, *In Search of Stability: Explorations in Historical Political Economy* (Cambridge: Cambridge University Press, 1987), 121–184; Federico Romero, *The United States and the European Trade Union Movement, 1944–1951* (Chapel Hill, NC: University of North Carolina Press, 2000); Lawrence Black, "'The Bitterest Enemies of Communism'. Labour Revisionists, Atlanticism, and the Cold War", *Contemporary British History*, 15, no. 3 (2001), 26–62; Giles Scott-Smith, *The Politics of Apolitical Culture: The Congress for Cultural Freedom, the CIA and Post-War American Hegemony* (New York and London: Routledge, 2002); Julia Angster, "The Westernization of the Political Thought of the West German Labor Movement", in *German Ideologies since 1945: Studies in the Political Thought and Culture of the Bonn Republic*, ed. Jan-Werner Müller (Basingstoke: Palgrave Macmillan, Basingstoke, 2003), 76–98; Holger Nehring, "'Westernization': A New Paradigm for Interpreting West European History in a Cold War Context", *Cold War History*, 4, no. 2 (2004), 175–191.

16 See Leopoldo Nuti, *Gli Stati Uniti e l'apertura a sinistra. Importanza e limiti della presenza americana in Italia* (Roma-Bari: Laterza, 1999), 127 and *passim*. On the international activity of US Labour see two recent surveys: *American Labor's Global Ambassadors: The International History of the AFL-CIO during the Cold War*, eds.

Robert Anthony Waters, Jr., and Geert van Goethem (Basingstoke: PalgraveMacMillan, 2013); Anthony Carew, *American Labour's Cold War Abroad: From Deep Freeze to Détente, 1945–1970* (Edmonton: Athabasca University Press, 2018).
17. See Nuti, *Gli Stati Uniti e l'apertura a sinistra*. For a comparative approach see the special issue of *Ricerche di Storia Politica*, 17, no. 2 (2014), "A cinquanta anni dal primo Centro-sinistra: un bilancio nel contesto internazionale", eds. Giovanni Bernardini and Michele Marchi.
18. Pietro Nenni was the leader of the Italian Socialist Party.
19. US National Archives at College Park, MD (hereafter: NARA), RG 59, Central Foreign Policy Files, Box 2235, POL 12-3 IT, "International Socialist Meeting", 13 January 1967.
20. For a review of the huge literature on European integration and transatlantic relations, see Alessandra Bitumi, "Rethinking the Historiography of Transatlantic Relations in the Cold War Years: The United States, Europe and the Process of European Integration", in *Modern European-American Relations in the Transatlantic Space: Recent Trends in History Writings*, ed. Maurizio Vaudagna (Turin: Otto, 2015), 71–95. On the 1970s as a turning point, see Michele Di Donato, "Landslides, Shocks, and New Global Rules: The US and Western Europe in the New International History of the 1970s", *Journal of Contemporary History*, 55, no. 1 (2020), 182–205.
21. Guillaume Devin, "L'Internationale socialiste face à la Guerre du Vietnam", in *La Guerre du Vietnam et l'Europe, 1963–1973*, eds. Christopher Goscha and Maurice Vaïsse (Bruxelles: Bruylant, 2003), 215–222.
22. NARA, RG 59, Central Foreign Policy Files, Box 2123, POL 12 GER W 67-68, "Helmut Schmidt's Views on Current Issues", 6 February, 1968.
23. International Institute of Social History, Amsterdam, Socialist International Archives (hereafter: IISH, SIA), box 362, "First meeting of monetary experts group, Brussels, 14.10.71. Short Summary"; "Verbatim Transcript of the first meeting of the monetary experts group of the Socialist International, held in Brussels on Thursday, October 14, 1971". On American Labour and US international economic relations, see Judith Stein, *Pivotal Decade: How the United States Traded Factories for Finance in the Seventies* (New Haven, CT and London: Yale University Press, 2010). On the SI, see Kristian Steinnes, "Rearranging the Economic Order. Social Democracy, European Integration and the Economic Crisis during the 1970s", *Ventunesimo Secolo*, 44 (2019), 38–62.
24. Mario Del Pero, *The Eccentric Realist: Henry Kissinger and the Shaping of American Foreign Policy* (Ithaca, NY and London, Cornell University Press, 2010).
25. Labour History Archives and Study Centre, Manchester (hereafter: LHASC), LP, NEC Minutes, 1st October 1971, "Meeting of Socialist Leaders – Salzburg, 3 September 1971".
26. Antonio Varsori, "The European Construction in the 1970s. The Great Divide", in *Europe in the International Arena during the 1970s. Entering a Different World*, eds. Antonio Varsori and Guia Migani (Bruxelles: Peter Lang, 2011), 27–39; Warlouzet, *Governing Europe in a Globalizing World*, 37–56; Aurélie Andry, "*Social Europe*" in *the Long 1970s: The Story of a Defeat*, PhD dissertation, EUI, Florence, 2017.
27. Guillaume Devin, *L'Internationale socialiste. Histoire et sociologie du socialisme international (1945–1990)* (Paris: Presses de la Fondation nationale des Sciences Politiques, 1993), 299–300.
28. See Michele Di Donato, "The Cold War and Socialist Identity. The Socialist International and the Italian "Communist Question" in the 1970s", *Contemporary European History*, 24, no. 2 (2015), 193–211, here 194–197.
29. See Mario Del Pero, "'Which Chile, Allende?' Henry Kissinger and the Portuguese Revolution", *Cold War History*, 11, no. 4 (2011), 1–33.
30. David Castaño, "'A Practical Test in the Détente': International Support for the Socialist Party in the Portuguese Revolution (1974–1975)", *Cold War History*, 15, no. 1 (2015), 1–26. See also Castaño, *Mário Soares e a revoluçao* (Alfragide: Dom Quijote, 2013).

31 N. Piers Ludlow, "The Real Years of Europe?: U.S.–West European Relations during the Ford Administration", *Journal of Cold War Studies*, 15, no. 3 (2013), 136–161.
32 Gerald L. Ford Presidential Library, Ann Arbor, MI (herafter: GFL), Presidential Country Files for Europe and Canada, 1974–77, Box 6. (A different version of the document is cited in Ludlow, "The Real Years of Europe", 148).
33 See Emmanuel Mourlon-Druol and Federico Romero, eds., *International Summitry and Global Governance. The Rise of the G7 and the European Council, 1974–1991* (London and New York: Routledge, 2014).
34 Richard M. Nixon Presidential Library, Yorba Linda, CA, National Security Council Files, Henry A. Kissinger Office Files, Country Files – Europe – General, Box 56, "Memorandum of Conversation, Henry A. Kissinger-Georges Pompidou", 18 May 1973.
35 Giuliano Garavini, *After Empires. European Integration, Decolonization, and the Challenge from the Global South 1957–1986* (Oxford: Oxford University Press, 2012).
36 NARA, RG 59, Helmut Sonnenfeldt Papers, A1 5339, box 4, Memorandum from Henry A. Kissinger to President, "The Impact of Indochina and Future US Policy", May 1975.
37 Ibid., A1 5339-A, Box 3, Memorandum of Conversation, Henry A. Kissinger-Hans-Dietrich Genscher, 16 June, 1975. NARA, RG 59, Records of Henry Kissinger, Box 17, Memorandum of Conversation, Henry A. Kissinger-Joop den Uyl, 11 August 1976.
38 Friedrich Ebert Stiftung, Bonn, Archiv der sozialen Demokratie (hereafter: FES, AdsD), SPD-PV, b. 11337, "Arbeitspapier des Arbeitskreis Nordamerika im Ausschuss für internationale Beziehungen des Parteivorstandes", 21 January 1974.
39 RG 59 Policy Planning Council (S/Pc), Policy Planning Staff (S/P), Director's Files (Winston Lord) 1969–1977, Box 359, "US Policy toward European Unity", 10 December 1975.
40 Ibid.
41 NARA, RG 59, Records of Henry Kissinger, Box 16, Memorandum of Conversation, Henry A. Kissinger-Anker Jørgensen, 20 January 1976.
42 An aspect stressed by Alan Granadino, *Democratic Socialism or Social Democracy? The Influence of the British Labour Party and the Parti Socialiste Français in the Ideological Transformation of the Partido Socialista Português and the Partido Socialista Obrero Español in the Mid-1970s*, PhD Dissertation, EUI, 2016.
43 See Alan Granadino, "Possibilities and Limits of Southern European Socialism in the Iberian Peninsula: French, Portuguese and Spanish Socialists in the Mid-1970s", *Contemporary European History*, 28, no. 3 (2019), 390–408.
44 See Michele Di Donato, *I comunisti italiani e la sinistra europea. Il Pci e i rapporti con le socialdemocrazie* (Rome: Carocci, 2015), 123–155.
45 FES, AdsD, Nachlaß Horst Ehmke, b. 772, "Erste Sitzung der Arbeitsgruppe Südeuropa des Internationalen Ausschusses beim Parteivorstand am 6. November 1975" (V. Isenberg). See also Ehmke's memoir: *Mittendrin. Von der Großen Koalition zur Deutschen Einheit* (Berlin: Rowohlt, 1996), 251–5.
46 For a report on the first meeting see LHASC, LP, NEC Minutes, 26th April 1978.
47 RG 59 Policy Planning Council (S/PC), Policy Planning Staff (S/P), Director's Files (Winston Lord), 1969–1977 Box 359, "Beyond Détente", 10 December 1975.
48 I have discussed this tripartition in Michele Di Donato, *I comunisti italiani e la sinistra europea*, 123–130. It builds on – but differs from – the one proposed by John Callaghan, *The Retreat of Social Democracy* (Manchester: Manchester University Press, 2000). For a recent critical reconsideration, see Aurélie Andry, "Was There an Alternative? European Socialists Facing Capitalism in the Long 1970s", *European Review of History: Revue européenne d'histoire*, 26, no. 4 (2019), 723–746.
49 RG 59, Records of Henry Kissinger, Box 13, Memorandum of Conversation, Henry A. Kissinger – John Volpe, 11 November 1975.

50 National Archives and Records Administration, College Park, Maryland (NARA), General Records of the Department of State, RG 59, Central Foreign Policy Files, created, 7/1/1973 – 12/31/1979, documenting the period 1973-12/31/1979, 1976STATE001386, "Action Memorandum: Meeting of European Socialists in Denmark – January 18–19, 1976", 3 January 1976. See also The National Archives of the UK, Kew, Richmond, Surrey (hereafter: TNA), FCO 33/2871, Lord N. Gordon Lennox to ADS Goodall, Western European Department, "The United States and the French Left", 27 February 1976.
51 See, among others, NARA, RG 59, 1976STOCKH00222, "Discussion with Prime Minister Palme of Socialist Meeting In Denmark – January 18–19", 15 January 1976; 1976LONDON00670, "Callaghan on Communism in Western Europe", 15 January 1976; 1976COPENH00180, "Prime Minister's Reaction to American Views Regarding Communist Participation in Government", 17 January 1976.
52 Cited by many authors, a copy of the letter can be found, among other locations, in Archiv der sozialen Demokratie, Bonn, Helmut Schmidt Archiv, b. b. 6356, Henry Kissinger to Willy Brandt, 15 January 1976.
53 In addition to the above-mentioned Kissinger-Jørgensen meeting, see for example the meeting with Brandt of US Ambassador to the FRG Martin J. Hillenbrand: 1976STATE017800, "Meeting of European Socialists in Denmark – January 18–19, 1976", 23 January 1976.
54 TNA, FCO 33/2871, "The United States and the French Left".
55 TNA, PREM 16/1082, "Note of the Meeting of European Social Democratic Leaders in Højstrupgaard, Denmark".
56 Harold James, *International Monetary Cooperation since Bretton Woods* (Oxford and New York: Oxford University Press; Washington, DC: International Monetary Fund, 1996), 279–282 and 322–335; Kevin Hickson, *The IMF Crisis of 1976 and British Politics* (London: I.B. Tauris, 2005); Duccio Basosi and Giovanni Bernardini, "The Puerto Rico Summit and the End of Eurocommunism", in *The Crisis of Détente in Europe: From Helsinki to Gorbachev: 1975–1985*, ed. Leopoldo Nuti (New York and London: Routledge, 2008), 256–67.
57 Emmanuel Mourlon-Druol and Federico Romero (eds.), *International Summitry and Global Governance*.
58 See, for one, Kristina Spohr, *The Global Chancellor: Helmut Schmidt and the Reshaping of the International Order* (Oxford and New York, Oxford University Press, 2016).
59 See, as an example, the SI working groups on inflation and employment policies in IISH, SIA, b. 410, 1011, 1012.
60 GFL, NSC Europe, Canada and Ocean Affairs Staff: Files, 1974–1977, box 48, "Memorandum. Europe: In Search of Identity", 5 August 1976.
61 FES, AdsD, SPD-PV, b. 11921, Karsten Voigt 12.6.78, "Bericht über die Reise in die USA vom 12.5. bis 28.5. 1978."
62 Emma De Angelis and Eirini Karamouzi, "Enlargement and the Historical Origins of the European Community's Democratic Identity, 1961–1978", *Contemporary European History*, 25, no. 3 (2016), 439–458, here 455.
63 This resonates with Kiran Patel's call to "provincialise the European Union" and avoid considering it "as a kind of gold standard, with its alleged exceptionality serving as the yardstick of interpretation, while other forms of international and global co-operation are marginalised". See Kiran Klaus Patel, "Provincialising European Union: Co-operation and Integration in Europe in a Historical Perspective", *Contemporary European History*, 22, no. 4 (2013), 649–673, here 652.
64 See Christian Bayley, "Socialist Visions of European Unity in Germany: Ostpolitik since the 1920s?", *Contemporary European History* 26, no. 2 (2017), 243–260.

5 Logics of influence
European Social Democrats and the Iberian transitions to democracy

Stine Bonsaksen

The Socialist International today represents undoubtedly the strongest international political movement with 19 member parties in government and a total of 22 parties either [in government or] sharing government responsibility. The return of democracy in Portugal leading to a socialist government, the return of democracy in Greece as well as significant steps in the direction of democracy in Spain are largely the result of action by socialist parties in government as well as by moral pressure exercised by the Socialist International.[1]

As the quote above shows, the Socialist International (SI) had no qualms about taking credit for the democratisation of southern Europe. A part of the Bureau's report from 1976, it reflects how the organisation viewed its own role and that of its members in aiding and facilitating southern Europe's transition to democracy. While there is no doubt that the SI and its member parties did play an active role, many questions remain about the European social democrats and the Iberian transitions to democracy. In illuminating relations between social democrats from the peripheries of Europe, the North-South approach draws attention to a central issue; how did the European social democrats intend to erase the divide between the democratic north and the authoritarian south?

Increasing interest in the international aspects of democratisation and democracy promotion has led to a range of studies on the external dimension of the Iberian transitions. The argument that external actors tend to play marginal and indirect roles in democratisation processes has long since been modified, and social democratic influence on the Iberian processes is well established.[2] Overarching studies have showed us how the Europeans in general, and social democrats in particular, played a vital role in aiding and facilitating democracy in Portugal and Spain.[3] The role of the major powers is likewise clear, with a number of studies analysing the role of the United States, Germany and Great Britain.[4] Among the social democratic parties, the role of the German Social Democratic Party (*Sozialdemokratische Partei Deutschlands* or the SPD) and the British Labour Party has been the focus of much scholarly attention. These parties are highlighted for their efforts in building up the Iberian socialist parties and their leaders, thus enabling them to play vital roles in the democratisation of their countries.[5]

DOI: 10.4324/9781003181439-6

Building on these works, this study aims to provide a more complete picture of the social democratic approach to the Iberian transitions. The SI was not a monolithic organisation, and newly released archival sources suggest that the European social democrats had different ideas on how to promote democracy. This study provides a more nuanced picture, as it explores dissension among SI member parties on how they should approach the Iberian processes of democratisation. Furthermore, very little attention has been paid to the actual democratisation strategies behind the policies of the European social democrats. By examining these strategies and the inherent logic underpinning them, this study provides a new approach to the democratisation of the Iberian Peninsula.

The main argument is that while the SI had a more or less coherent democratisation policy, diverging views on how best to further democratisation did exist among its members. The different approaches advocated by the SI member parties do not imply a clear-cut divide between the northern established democracies and the southern transitioning into democracy. Rather, the SI member parties saw the transitions in Portugal and Spain as two separate processes that demanded different strategies, on which they did not always agree. Interestingly, the outcome of the transnational bargaining – the actual SI policies on Portugal and Spain – did not reflect the preferences of the historically most influential SI members, but that of its Scandinavian member parties.[6]

Analytical framework

In order to isolate and analyse the different components of the SI and its member states' approaches to democratisation, this study utilises Magen and McFaul's "logics of influence". In the introductory chapter to *Promoting Democracy and Rule of Law: American and European Strategies*, they identify four logics of influence through which an external actor may attempt to promote democratic change in a target country. Of these, three are relevant for the purpose of this study: material incentives, normative suasion and capacity building.[7]

Material incentives entail both threats of punitive measures and promises of positive rewards. The aim is to alter the cost-benefit calculations of domestic leaders, in order to encourage democratic reform in the target state. Negative material incentives are punitive political, diplomatic and economic sanctions. Such strategies are typically aimed at weakening or overthrowing autocratic regimes. Positive material incentives are policy instruments linking progress in democratisation with international entitlements. The aim is to nudge non-democratic regimes towards democratic reform. The underlying assumption of this logic of influence is that actors are rational and engage in cost-benefit analysis in the face of promises and threats from external actors.[8]

Normative suasion, on the other hand, is based on the assumption that actors are influenced by "a logic of appropriateness".[9] The interests of the actors are products of social structures and interactions, and external actors can therefore facilitate internalisation of democratic norms, policies and institutions. Strategies within this category can assume both positive and negative forms. Positive normative suasion tends to take the form of the establishment of different forums for socialisation, alongside intensification of diplomatic, political and economic linkages between the West and transitional countries. Negative normative suasion often takes the form of normative pressure, ranging from phone calls to leaders, to issuing public reports on human rights violations. The aim here is to "name and shame" target countries into compliance with democratic norms and practices.[10]

Finally, capacity building entails democracy promotion through knowledge sharing and the strengthening of domestic capabilities. The underlying assumption is that democratic progress is dependent on actors addressing human, institutional and financial shortcomings. By providing informational, financial and technical assistance, external actors can empower domestic actors to ensure democratic progress.[11]

Promoting Democracy and Rule of Law examines the strategies that Americans and Europeans have used to promote democracy, describing a European approach to democracy promotion. Magen and McFaul disregard the "Mars vs. Venus" caricature of differences and highlight the emergence of a transatlantic consensus on democracy promotion during the period after 9/11. They also point out historic differences, however. The American approach has been known for "pushing" democracy. US officials have tended to favour an uncompromising approach, including measures such as diplomatic and trade isolation, economic sanctions and active support of opposition movements seeking to overthrow dictatorships. The European approach, on the other hand, is characterised by a preference for engagement and integration, with the main instrument being the conditional offer for inclusion in the European Union (EU). It also includes a more expansive definition of what constitutes democracy promotion, utilising measures aimed at advancing equality, solidarity and peaceful conflict resolution.[12] As this study will demonstrate, a common European position on democratisation did not emerge on its own. How best to promote democracy was a source of disagreement within the social democratic community of Europe and the policies of the SI was the result of transnational negotiations. The analytical framework will not only help structure this debate but will also help uncover the underlying assumptions of the different strategies.

The SI is a worldwide organisation of social democratic, socialist and labour parties. Reconstituted in Frankfurt in 1951, the organisation's main purpose was to strengthen relations between the affiliated members and to enable rapprochement between different viewpoints and policies. The two most important institutions were the Congress, the supreme decision-making body, and the Bureau, the permanent executive. Organisations such as the SI have a limited policy-making capacity, but nonetheless the potential to influence processes of democratisation both directly and indirectly. Directly, they can issue declarations and resolutions, send fact-finding missions and provide financial assistance. Indirectly, they can influence democratisation through their member parties, particularly and perhaps most effectively, those in government.[13] In addition to the policies of the SI, the policies of the member parties in government therefore constitute the focal point of the analysis. The period in focus is primarily the most crucial years of the

Iberian transitions, from 1974 to 1978. In order to understand the opposing views on democratisation, however, it is also necessary to look at certain elements of the pre-transition policies towards Portugal and Spain.

Diverging views on democratisation

The 1970s was a decade of radical change on the Iberian Peninsula, as two of the oldest authoritarian regimes in the world disintegrated within a period of just a few years. In Portugal, the Carnation Coup of April 1974 swept away the 48-year-old Salazar-Caetano regime. Across the border, the passing away of Francisco Franco in November 1975 opened up for the democratisation of Spain after thirty-six years of dictatorship.[14] Meanwhile, political life in Western Europe was characterised by a turn to the left, as social democratic governments came into power in a majority of the northern European countries. This meant that the social democrats were a force to be reckoned with, and they have been ascribed an important role in aiding and facilitating the Iberian transitions to democracy.[15] Evidence suggests, however, that they were not all pulling in the same direction. The following section explores diverging views on democratisation amongst governing northern European SI members. It centres on the logics of influence, uncovering three main cleavages within the social democratic debate concerning the Iberian transitions: whether to make aid contingent on democratic progress, whether to employ democratisation by exclusion and whether condemnation or dialogue was the more effective strategy.

Qualified or unqualified aid?

While the European social democratic parties all embraced strategies that utilised the manipulation of material incentives, they did not always agree on which strategies or how to employ them. One of the conflicts centred on whether or not they should make financial aid to Portugal contingent on a certain political development. The Portuguese economy was in shambles, with rising unemployment, declining productivity and a lack of investment. The trade deficit was increasing, tourism was almost non-existing and thousands of Portuguese citizens were returning from the former colonies and in need of governmental aid.[16] This meant that Portugal was in desperate need of foreign aid, and demanding democratic progress in return for aid may have seemed like an excellent way to nudge the interim government towards democratic reform. According to the British Labour Party, this was not necessary, however. The Portuguese authorities would realise that the help from the Western world would come to a halt unless they continued on the path towards a democratic form of government.[17] This was a sentiment the SPD seemed to support. The main aim of the SPDs stated policy on Portugal was to promote democracy in Portugal through economic aid and cooperation, and through statements of support and sympathy aimed at supporting the democratic parties both politically and morally. The argument was that the difficult economic situation in Portugal could have unknown political consequences if they did not receive fast and efficient help from the outside.[18] The SPD highlighted that the present situation demanded moral, political and economic support for Portugal, rather than premature ideological condemnation.[19]

The SPD and British Labour both ended up advocating qualified aid however. In a debate in the House of Commons in August 1975, Prime Minister Harold Wilson gave his support to the idea of making EC aid to Portugal conditional upon a development towards pluralist democracy. During the same debate, foreign secretary Leonard James Callaghan was asked why the government made aid to Portugal contingent on a democratic development while they were providing aid to other non-democratic states. His answer was that his government regarded aid to Portugal within a European context. They would not provide such aid to European dictatorships.[20] The same approach was supported within the social democratic network. At a meeting of socialist leaders in Stockholm in August 1975, Prime Minister Wilson and German Chancellor Helmut Schmidt argued that a rapid transition to pluralist democracy should be a condition for economic aid.[21] A majority within the SPD apparently supported aiding Portugal despite the political turmoil. Willy Brandt emphasised that Portugal in all likelihood faced several years of struggle over political power, and that the democratic forces had not lost. Thus, it would be politically unwise and morally unconscionable to withhold aid. This view was not reflected in the official German stance however. Schmidt explicitly stated that his government did not want to support dictatorships. There is no doubt that this line also found support within the SPD. The party's weekly newspaper "Vorwärts" praised the EEC decision as commendable while emphasising that it was the only choice if the Nine wanted to live up to their own principles.[22]

Olof Palme, on the other hand, was a categorical opponent of making the financial aid dependent upon certain conditions.[23] The Swedish social democrats believed that withholding aid would increase the isolation of Portugal, with the inherent risk of forcing the Armed Forces Movement (*Movimento das Forças Armadas* or the MFA) towards even more extreme measures, while increasing their dependence upon support from the Soviet Union. The way to push Portugal in the right direction, according to the SAP, was to maintain close relations with the MFA. They believed they had a real chance of influencing the MFA towards democratic progress. Their foreign policy was acceptable to the Portuguese authorities, and importantly, they had not joined their European colleagues in lamenting the country's leftwards turn.[24] The Swedes found support in Norway, where the Labour government maintained a policy of economic assistance without making political demands. The diverging stances on economic aid did not go unnoticed by the Portuguese. During a visit to Lisbon in June 1975, the Norwegian delegation met with Jorge Sampaio, the Portuguese secretary of state for external cooperation. While commending the Norwegians for their unqualified aid Sampaio commented that many countries making a particular political development a requirement for assistance was becoming a source of irritation.[25]

We have to see the change in the German and British stance in context however. In Portugal, the failed coup of 11 March 1975 strengthened the hand of the extreme left and the radicals within the MFA. They now controlled the administration, the unions, the army and the media. Banks, insurance companies and major industries were nationalised, while the Portuguese Communist Party (*Partido Comunista Português* or the PCP) guided the collectivisation of occupied estates in Alentejo. Neither the MFA nor the PCP seemed to be willing to tolerate the emergence of a democratic regime, and Portugal started to look more and more like an East-European-style people's democracy.[26] As the "hot summer" of 1975 approached, the backlash came. An anti-revolutionary movement emerged, causing an intense polarisation. Conservative groups organised marches, and PCP headquarters were sacked and burned. By August, Portugal seemed to be on the verge of civil war.[27] Naturally, the situation caused increasing levels of concern among western European governments. At the Brussels European Council in July, the member states reached an agreement that EEC aid should be conditioned on progress towards pluralist democracy. The statement from the meeting declared that the EEC would cooperate more closely with Portugal, as long as the country became a democratic state. This was a matter on which the Commission was very clear. If Portugal did not pursue this goal, all arguments in favour of emergency aid would lose their legitimacy.[28] As such, the reversal of the British and German stance may have been a question of EEC unity. It is also an important point that the Portuguese socialist leader, Mario Soares, encouraged his European sister-parties to make such demands. Publicly, he maintained the need for economic aid without any form of ideological or political demands.[29] In more private settings, however, he stressed that he understood the demands very well. The official position of his party had to be that no such demands should be made, but they were right to propose certain democratic conditions.[30] In a meeting with the international secretary of the SAP, he stated quite plainly that European aid should be tied to democratic progress. The aid should be generous, but it should be connected to a guarantee of pluralism in Portugal.[31]

Exclusion or inclusion?

Another dimension, albeit more indirect, of material incentives involves the question of exclusion. The crux of the issue was whether they should exclude Spain from the Western community of democracies and, more specifically, their cooperative bodies, until she could demonstrate certain democratic credentials. Membership of organisations such as the EEC, the North Atlantic Treaty Organization (NATO) and the Council of Europe no doubt constituted international entitlements. Not only would membership entail prospects for economic growth and security guarantees, it would also give international prestige and influence. On this matter, there was obvious disagreement among the European social democrats.

When the SPD came to power in 1966, they followed a conservative government with a long record of supporting the integration efforts of Franco's regime. The belief was that close relations with Europe would bring about a slow democratisation, while the stability of the Franco regime would contribute to the stability of the West.[32] This idea found support among the leadership of the SPD. During the last decade of the Spanish dictatorship, SPD leaders believed that Spanish participation in the European integration process was vital for preparing Spain's transition to democracy. A pragmatic and constructive policy towards Spain was necessary, and declamatory statements and a strong ethical pose should be avoided. In the face of growing resistance from the left wing of the party, Willy Brandt's coalition government therefore refused to back initiatives intended to put real pressure on Franco. Likewise, meeting with the illegal opposition in Spain, including the Spanish Socialist Workers' Party (*Partido Socialista Obrero Español* or the PSOE), was unthinkable because it would be seen as interference in the internal affairs of the country. The SPD did not change its strategy and increase their support to their colleagues in Spain until the idea that Spain would evolve gently without external pressure was disturbed by the Portuguese revolution. By the spring of 1975, the SPD had concluded that the strength of the Spanish Communist Party (*Partido Comunista Español* or the PCE) meant that Spain faced a real risk of destabilisation. In order to avoid this, they had to support an alternative left-wing pole, and this had to be the PSOE. From this point forward, the SPD and the Friedrich Ebert Foundation provided the PSOE with economic and logistical support, with the aim of turning it into a mass party with a fighting chance in the first democratic elections.[33]

The Scandinavian countries did not share the SPD's views on this matter. As long as the Norwegian Social Democratic Party (*Det norske arbeiderparti* or the DNA) was in office, opposition to Spain's authoritarian regime was an enduring feature of Norwegian foreign policy. The possibility of Spanish membership in NATO even caused the Norwegian government to threaten to exercise its veto within the Alliance. The fact that this was the first and, for the time being, the only time a Norwegian government has made this threat emphasises the force of this question in Norwegian foreign policy.[34] This policy of isolation did not end with the demise of the dictator. The Norwegian policy on Spain during the early years of the transition was characterised by demonstrative distancing: by deliberate attempts to exhibit the most restrictive policy towards the Spanish regime. During a parliamentary debate in April 1976, Foreign Minister Frydenlund explicitly said that Norway had assumed and still held the most restrictive stance on Spain. There was a price to pay, he argued, to be accepted into the western European community. This price was the introduction of full democratic rights to the Spanish people.[35] The DNA also found support among its social democratic neighbours. There is no doubt that the Danish Social Democrats (*Socialdemokratiet* or SD) was in favour of excluding Spain until the country was a democracy. This stance was made perfectly clear both within the framework of the Council of Europe and the EEC. As long as the present conditions prevailed, the SD argued, there could be no question of Spanish membership of organisations where cooperation was based on the shared ideals and principles of democracy and human rights. This applied to NATO, to the European Community and certainly to the Council of Europe.[36]

Shaming or dialogue?

There seems to have been broad agreement on the merits of employing normative suasion. Whether positive or negative forms would be more effective was contested, however. During the period of renewed repression in Spain in the months leading up to Franco's death in November 1975, the British Labour government was concerned that international outrage might lead to a polarisation of the political forces in Spain. Moderate, centrist forces, they argued, were the ones most likely to lead Spain to democratic reform. Polarisation would exclude the democrats and the risk of open conflict would increase. The sharp international reactions to the recent executions had, they argued, offended the Spanish national feeling and strengthened Franco's position. Labour therefore endeavoured to maintain contact with the centrist reformers in Spain. They were also establishing "correct relations" with the current regime.[37] This approach was maintained during the first period of the Spanish transition, while it was still unclear in which direction the country was headed. Despite advice not to do so from the PSOE and in the face of opposition from large parts of the British Labour movement, the Labour government trusted the new Spanish government to bring democracy to Spain.[38] Again, the Germans were in line with the British. They did not want the international community to adopt a hard line on Spain. Such an approach, they argued, would strengthen the traditional Falangist's in Spain.[39] Like the British, the German government disagreed with the PSOE's negative view of the developments in Spain during the first years of the transition and were very cautious about passing judgement on the policies and reforms proposed by the transitional governments of Arias Navarro and Adolfo Suarez.[40]

Also with regard to Portugal, the SPD and the Labour Party had more or less the same views on the use of suasion. The British argued that a policy of condemnation would push the Portuguese regime in the direction of Communism. The best approach was to show the military junta a certain level of trust, extend relations and give aid and assistance where it was needed – while making the western view on development towards democracy perfectly clear. One of the main ideas in the British approach was to get directly involved through technical and financial aid, and thereby ensure that the country did not regress any further.[41] While the chance of establishing democracy in Portugal existed, they should respond as positively as possible when requests for assistance came from the new Portuguese authorities, even if communists were included in the ranks of those authorities. Wilson's government argued that collaboration with Lisbon would increase their ability to influence the decisions of the Portuguese government.[42] The SPD emphasised the need for moral, political and material support for Portugal, and for avoiding premature ideological condemnation. When the danger of a Communist coup seemed imminent, SPD argued in favour of establishing closer relations between Portugal and The Council of Europe. In principle, they were also in favour of closer relations between Portugal and the EEC than the trade agreement they had at the time. Economic aid to Portugal, they argued, was more important than the wish to protect one's own industry.[43]

With regard to Portugal, the Scandinavian parties also emphasised positive normative suasion. The DNA stressed that the best way to contribute to the Portuguese democracy was to give all possible support and assistance to the country during the difficult period they were going through. It was of great importance both for the democratic forces in Portugal and for the Council itself, that the European countries exhibited a positive and active attitude towards Portugal.[44] The SD emphasised that the moderate politicians in Portugal would not benefit from Western governments publicly expressing concerns about the future of Portuguese democracy.[45] Finally, the Swedish Social Democratic Party (*Sveriges socialdemokratiska arbetareparti* or SAP) argued that Portugal should be able to count on the solidarity of the democratic European states in the efforts to create democratic institutions. They stressed that this support and solidarity was needed. It would be wrong to take a passive and awaiting attitude. Such an approach would, should democracy in Portugal fail, leave them with more than a little blame. It was now, they argued, while the problems were great, that the demands for solidarity with the democratic forces were the strongest.[46]

The Scandinavian policies on Spain on the other hand clearly show a preference for negative normative suasion. Here, the SAP stands out. Olof Palme was known for a "hard line", a fact which made him a hero to the Spanish Left and a villain amongst the Conservatives.[47] The Spanish ambassador to Sweden accused him of "attacking Spain like a rabid dog".[48] According to the Swedes, however, it was the task of the international opinion to ensure that the demands for a transition to a democratic form of government were kept constantly alive.[49] When the Spanish regime accused them of interfering with internal affairs, they stressed that violations of human rights were the concern of all nations. The principle of non-intervention should not be used as an excuse for preventing insight, debate and criticism. Sweden had repeatedly criticised such violations, and this they intended to continue doing, with "consistency and firm resolve".[50] This promise was kept, even after the SAP lost the general election in 1976 and spent six years in opposition. Palme's speech at the PSOE congress in Madrid in 1976 clearly showed his lack of trust in the new Spanish government and his willingness to "name and shame" those who did not live up to his expectations. Democracy already existed in Spain, he emphasised. It was practised within certain political parties, unions and other popular movements where hundreds of thousands of people were breathing the air of liberty, living and coexisting in clearly democratic ways. He was not, he stressed, talking about the official Spain. He was talking about the real Spain. The *Spain* that was already building its democratic future.[51] While less outspoken than their Swedish colleagues, the DNA supported the hard line on Spain. Their argument was that premature acceptance of the new government in Spain might remove motivation for liberalisation.[52]

This examination demonstrates that the social democratic governments of Europe did not agree on the best approach to promote democratisation. Of the strategies discussed, the only one the governments in question all agreed on was capacity building. They all argued in favour of supporting their sister-parties in Portugal and Spain by all means possible.

The SI's policy on Portugal

By the early 1970s, Portugal was becoming a source of embarrassment for the European democracies. Its brutal colonial policy and undemocratic regime made its presence within Atlantic and European institutions increasingly unpopular. This caused the European social democratic parties to step up their efforts to support democratic forces in Portugal, both individually and together through the SI.[53] In September 1971, member parties established the Portugal Committee of the Socialist International. The purpose of the committee was to provide the Bureau with information about the situation in Portugal, and with ideas and suggestions as to how the SI and its members could support democracy and democratic socialism in Portugal. During the first meeting of the Committee, the members decided that support for democracy in Portugal would fall into three categories. The first was support through diplomatic and political channels. The second was information campaigns, where the aim was to make the public in democratic countries better informed about the conditions in Portugal, and to give publicity and prominence to the opponents of the Caetano regime. The third and last was practical, financial and organisational assistance to the Portuguese Socialist. This included measures to make the Portuguese immigrant workers in democratic countries more familiar with concepts of democracy, socialism and free trade unionism.[54]

When the Portuguese revolution broke out in 1974, the immediate response from the SI was a warm welcome. On 29 April, only four days after the rebellion of the armed forces, the chairman and general secretary of the SI sent a message to General António de Spínola, the leader of the revolution. They praised the Portuguese military forces for having destroyed the "fascist" and colonial government of Marcelo Caetano, and for the liberalising measures they had already taken. Especially they commended the declaration to hold free elections within a short period of time, the suspension of censorship and the freeing of political prisoners. Finally, the SI leadership expressed the hope that the revolutionary authorities might urgently undertake decolonisation and stressed their complete solidarity with the Portuguese Socialist Party.[55]

Two days later, the Bureau of the SI adopted a statement on Portugal. They stressed their support for the PS and expressed their hope that a democratic government might come to power in Portugal. A government that respected human rights and the principle of self-determination, they emphasised, might put an end to the growing isolation of Portugal on the international scene. They also made a strong appeal to the governments of member countries of NATO to exercise their influence in this direction.[56]

During the turbulent period in Portugal from 1974 to 1976, characterised by coups and counter-coups, three elements were recurring in the SI´s approach. First, they repeatedly reminded the ever-changing Portuguese governments of the liberties and rights central to any true democracy. Specifically, they emphasised freedom of speech, a free press and diversity of opinion and idea.[57] Second, the SI provided financial aid to the PS and to the Portuguese government, both directly and indirectly. In June 1974, they adopted a massive programme of support for the PS, including a £5,000 donation from the SI reserve fund.[58] Additionally, they repeatedly encouraged their member parties to give financial assistance to the PS and to improve the trade position of Portugal. It was absolutely necessary, they argued, for socialist governments to provide such assistance to help Portugal remain on the path to democracy. The situation in Portugal had implications for all of Europe. Should conditions for democratic life in Portugal deteriorate, it would be an impediment towards détente and dialogue in Europe.[59] Third, the SI continuously attempted to enhance the standing of the PS, both domestically and internationally.[60]

In sum, the SI's policy on Portugal emphasised capacity building and normative suasion. The continuous requests for financial aid to the PS and the Portuguese governments reveal an underlying assumption about a causal link between economic and political stability. In the case of the PS, the aid was not only financial but also practical and organisational. A strong, well-organised party organisation capable of taking democratic responsibility was seen as necessary to ensure democratic progress. Finally, the focus on giving the PS domestic and international prestige also constitutes a form of capacity building. International prestige could help convince the international community about the prospects for democracy in Portugal, and domestically the support of leading politicians and organisations could help win the PS public support and, later on, votes.

Normative suasion also seems to be a central point of the SI's democratisation policy. The repeated appeals to the Portuguese regime to adhere to democratic norms and practices point to a belief that the regime could be convinced to do what they considered appropriate. As we will see, however, this strategy was more prevalent in the case of Spain.

The SI's policy on Spain

Ever since the relaunch of the SI in 1951, the organisation had been consistently hostile to the Franco regime. The Spanish Civil War maintained a prominent place in the collective memory of the European Left, and any rapprochement with the regime was out of the question.[61] When reports came that Franco's regime would not survive his disappearance, the social democrats were quick to act.[62] In March 1974, the SI established the Spain Committee of the Socialist International. The purpose of the Committee was to study the situation in Spain, and to make recommendations to the Bureau as to what the SI and its member parties could do to aid the Spanish Socialist Workers' Party (*Partido Socialista Obrero Español* or the PSOE) and the cause of democracy in Spain.[63]

In November 1975, the Bureau adopted what they termed "Action for Democracy in Spain". It consisted of a series of recommendations to member parties, with the aim of restoring democracy in Spain. The first part was directed at all member parties and stressed the importance of supporting the PSOE. Public solidarity with the PSOE was an important point, alongside financial support and campaigns to increase the public knowledge of the Spanish party. The second part was directed at the member parties in government at the time and included three main points. Firstly, it encouraged the socialist governments to repeat their full solidarity with democratic objectives. Specifically, it highlighted freedom of speech and association, freedom for all political parties and trade unions, as well as universal suffrage. Secondly, the SI stressed that member governments should not accept a situation of "false democracy" in Spain. Lastly, they encouraged socialist governments to maintain the political isolation of Spain as long as there was no real democracy. On this point, the recommendations were quite specific. Socialist governments should not enter into any new bilateral agreement with Spain. The European Community (EC) should maintain its suspension of the trade negotiations with Spain. NATO should not establish relations with Spain until the Spanish people were free to decide in favour of this. Finally, governments were encouraged to put pressure upon the United States and France not to establish any new military or political relations with the new Spanish regime, and to avoid giving Juan Carlos prestige.[64]

Despite mainly focusing on what member states might do to promote democracy in Spain, the leadership of SI did not shy away from direct involvement. In January 1976, the Spanish Prime Minister Arias Navarro held a speech to the Cortes, presenting a plan for political reform. The following day, General Secretary Hans Janitschek issued a statement commenting on Arias' plan. According to him, it was "utterly insufficient and unacceptable". He urged the Spanish regime to free all political prisoners, to grant freedom of speech and assembly and to legalise all political parties and trade unions. He also encouraged all European governments to put pressure on the Spanish regime to restore full democratic rights to the people of Spain, and to refrain from establishing closer relations with the regime. Until a genuinely democratic government was established, the political isolation of Spain should be maintained.[65] Two months later, the Bureau adopted a new statement on Spain. It was time, they argued, to move from declarations of liberalisation to actual deeds. Spain had to release all political prisoners and restore basic democratic liberties. What the Spanish regime was currently doing, the Bureau argued, was nothing more than an attempt to create a democratic image without actually risking loss of political control.[66]

The Bureau also maintained staunch support for their Spanish member party, PSOE. The reasons why the SI chose the PSOE as the only Spanish member party has been well covered elsewhere.[67] The support went beyond pointing out the true representatives of socialism in Spain however, and constituted both moral and financial aid. Statements of supports emphasised the SI's solidarity with the PSOE, and praised the party for its tenacious efforts to achieve democracy in Spain.[68] The PSOE was also at the receiving end of both financial and practical, organisational assistance aimed at strengthening the PSOE's organisation inside Spain.[69] This included the SI establishing the Spanish Solidarity Fund.[70]

In the case of Spain, the SI used their entire arsenal of strategies and instruments. As with the case of Portugal, capacity building and normative suasion were key elements of the SI's democratisation strategy. Capacity building was directed at the PSOE. Financial, practical and organisational support aimed at enabling the party to help ensure democratic progress. We also observe the logic of capacity building in the way the SI attempted to strengthen the PSOE as an important actor both domestically and internationally. An important element of this was the attendance of influential European social democrats at events arranged by the PSOE.[71] Normative suasion is also evident in the SI's policy on Spain, but with clear differences from the approach on Portugal. Positive normative suasion was employed in more or less the same manner. Statements and recommendations emphasised democratic norms and practices to which the Spanish regime should adhere. In the case of Spain, however, the SI also employed negative normative suasion. Wording such as "false democracy" and "utterly insufficient" point to a belief the Spanish regime could be shamed into compliance with democratic norms and practices.

Finally, in the case of Spain, we see the SI employing material incentives. They had a clear preference for positive material incentives, with the main carrot being the inclusion of Spain in the cooperative bodies of the western community of democracies. According to the SI, Spain should not be associated with NATO or with the EEC until the country was a democracy. Several times the Bureau also urged its member parties to maintain a firm stand in order to "ensure that the present status of Spain vis-à-vis NATO and the EEC was not modified".[72] The wording make it seem like the SI considered exclusion as more of a punishment for not adhering to the values of democracy and human rights, but the logic behind the strategy is clearly that of positive material incentives. The policy links democratisation with membership in influential organisations, with the implicit rewards of economic progress and international prestige.

Concluding remarks

This study clearly illustrates three important points. First, the SI member parties viewed the transitions in Portugal and Spain as two different processes that demanded different strategies. On Portugal, the member parties in question were more or less on the same page. They all emphasised capacity building and positive normative suasion. They intensified their diplomatic, political and economic ties to Portugal, while reminding the new regime of democratic norms and practices. Additionally, they all agreed on the importance of financial aid, both for the PS and for the government. The assumption of a causal link between financial and political stability is obvious, and a central part of their approach to promoting democracy in Portugal. The member parties did disagree on whether or not to make the financial aid contingent on democratic development. This seems to have been more a question of EEC unity, however, than a question of diverging strategies on how to promote democracy.

The approach to Spain was another matter. Here, positive material incentives seem to have been a central part of their approach. The SI and the Scandinavian member parties repeatedly argued that Spain should be isolated, and not be allowed to join their cooperative organs until the country demonstrably was a democracy. The underlying assumption here is one of material incentives that the expected gains of membership would function as an incentive to democratic reform. The approach to Spain was also characterised by negative normative suasion. While the statements about Portugal stressed support, statements about

Spain emphasised the regime's shortcomings. It is clear that the member parties did not agree on this approach towards Spain, however. The German and British governments favoured positive normative suasion also in the case of Spain.

Second, the idea of a social democratic position on democratisation needs modification. Previous research emphasises the important role the European social democrats played in the Iberian transitions to democracy. This analysis demonstrates that they did not agree on the best way to promote democracy. The main dissension involves material incentives and normative suasion. Should undemocratic and transitional regimes be included in cooperative bodies, where external actors can facilitate the internalisation of democratic norms, policies and institutions? Alternatively, should they use membership of such organisations as an incentive to democratic reform, by demanding a democratic form of government before the regimes are allowed in? The actual policy of the SI reflects a belief in the latter.

Third, the analysis demonstrates that the SI's policy did not reflect the preferences of the historically influential members from Germany and Great Britain. Rather, the SI's actual policy was in line with the preferences of the Scandinavian countries. This highlights the fact that there was no coherent northern policy, while indicating that a distinct internal dynamic between the Scandinavian countries existed. Evidence suggests that the prominence of Olof Palme might have been key to Scandinavian influence.[73] This certainly seems to have been the case with regard to the *Committee of Friendship and Solidarity with Democracy and Socialism in Portugal*, established by a group of high-ranking socialist and social democrats after the meeting in Stockholm in August 1975. At the end of the month, Palme sent a proposal for the goals and strategy of the committee to Willy Brandt, who was to be its chairman.[74] When the goals and strategy of the actual committee were presented a month later, they were more or less identical to those of Palme's proposal.[75]

When the SI took credit for the democratisation of Southern Europe in their report, they were not wide of the mark. There is no doubt that the organisation and its ruling members did play an important part in securing Iberian democracy. We have also seen that the SI certainly did not shy away from exercising moral pressure whenever it had the chance. Unanswered questions still remain however. This study is a first examination of the transnational negotiations that determined the SI's policies towards the Iberian transitions to democracy. In order to answer how the SI's policy was determined and what motivated the national positions, further research is needed.

Notes

1 Socialist International Archives, 293, International Institute of Social History, Amsterdam, "Bureau's Report – Introduction" (21.05.1976).
2 Geoffrey Pridham, ed., *Encouraging Democracy: The International Context of Regime Transition in Southern Europe* (Leicester: Leicester University Press, 1991); Laurence Whitehead, ed., *The International Dimensions of Democratization: Europe and the Americas* (Oxford: Oxford University Press, 1996); Pilar Ortuño Anaya, *European Socialists and Spain: The Transition to Democracy, 1959–77* (Houndmills: Palgrave, 2002).

3 Mario Del Pero, "A European Solution for a European Crisis. The International Implications of Portugal's Revolution", *Journal of European Integration History* 1 (2009); Charles Powell, "International Aspects of Democratization. The Case of Spain", in *The International Dimensions of Democratization. Europe and the Americas*, ed. Laurence Whitehead (Oxford: Oxford University Press, 1996).
4 Del Pero; Oscar Jose Martin Garcia, "'The End of the Carnival': The UK and the Carnation Revolution in Portugal", *Contemporary British History* 29, no. 2 (2015); David Castaño, "'A Practical Test in the Détente': International Support for the Socialist Party in the Portuguese Revolution (1974–1975)", *Cold War History* 15, no. 1 (2015).
5 Ana Mónica Fonseca, "The Federal Republic of Germany and the Portuguese Transition to Democracy (1974–1976)", *Journal of European Integration History* 15, no. 1 (2009); Antonio Muñoz Sánchez, "The Friedrich Ebert Foundation and the Spanish Socialists During the Transition to Democracy, 1975–1982", *Contemporary European History* 25, no. 1 (2016); *El Amigo Alemán: El SPD y el PSOE De la dictadura a la democracia* (Barcelona: RBA Libros, 2012); Anaya.
6 For an overview of the power relations within the SI during the 1970s, see Christian Salm, *Transnational Socialist Networks in the 1970s: European Community Development Aid and Southern Enlargement*, Palgrave Studies in the History of Social Movements (Basingstoke, Hampshire: Palgrave Macmillan, 2016), 17–22.
7 The first category, control, involves a form of democratisation through coercion. It entails the abolition of a state's sovereignty and seizure of its institutions of government, after which the external power attempts to transform the controlled state's domestic structures. It is safe to say that no such measures were taken in Spain or Portugal during the period in question. This category is therefore not relevant for the purpose of this study. Amichai Magen, Thomas Risse, and Michael McFaul, eds., *Promoting Democracy and the Rule of Law: American and European Strategies* (New York: Palgrave Macmillan, 2009).
8 Amichai Magen and Michael A. McFaul, "Introduction: American and European Strategies to Promote Democracy – Shared Values, Common Challenges, Divergent Tools?", in *Promoting Democracy and the Rule of Law: American and European Strategies*, eds. Amichai Magen, Thomas Risse, and Michael A. McFaul (New York: Palgrave Macmillan, 2009), 12–13.
9 James G. March and Johan P. Olsen, "The Logic of Appropriateness", in *The Oxford Handbook of Political Science*, eds. M. Rein, M. Moran, and R. E. Goodin (Oxford: Oxford University Press, 2004).
10 Magen and McFaul, 14.
11 Ibid., 15.
12 Ibid., 16–17.
13 Wolf Grabendorff, "International Support for Democracy in Contemporary Latin America: The Role of the Party Internationals", in *The International Dimensions of Democratization: Europe and the Americas*, ed. Laurence Whitehead (Oxford: Oxford University Press, 1996), 201–02. Anaya, 18.
14 Nancy Bermeo, "Redemocratization and Transition Elections: A Comparison of Spain and Portugal", *Comparative Politics* 19, no. 2 (1987): 213–14.
15 Pridham; Whitehead.
16 Castaño, 17.
17 UD, 25.4/92, bind 22, JN 015859, Melding fra ambassaden i London, "Portugal. Britisk vurdering.", (05.06.1975).
18 25.4/92, bind 23, JN 020752, Melding fra ambassaden i Bonn, "Portugal. Tysk vurdering.", (28.07.1975).
19 25.4/92, bind 22, JN 014975, Innkommet melding fra ambassaden i Bonn, "Tysk syn på utviklingen i Portugal", (02.06.1975).
20 25.4/92, bind 23, JN 021486, Telegram fra ambassaden i London, "Portugal. Britiske synspunkter.", (11.08.1975).

21 25.4/92, bind 23, JN 021472, Melding fra ambassaden i Lisboa "Møte i Stockholm av sosialdemokratiske ledere.", (04.08.1975).
22 "Portugal. Tysk vurdering".
23 ARAB, SAP, 1889/F/2/A/13, Statsrådsberedningen, Pierre Schori "Portugalöverläggningen 10 Downing Street september 5, 1975", (09.09.1975); UD, "Møte i Stockholm av sosialdemokratiske ledere".
24 ARAB, SAP, 1889/F/2/H/3, Statsrådsberedningen, Pierre Schori "Rapport Från Besök i Lissabon Den 10–12 Juni -75", (16.06.1975).
25 UD, 25.4/92, bind 22, JN 021586, "Samtale Med Statssekretær Sampaio i Det Portugisiske Utenriksdepartment.", (10.07.1975).
26 Walter C. Opello, "Portugal: A Case Study of International Determinants of Régime Transition", in *Encouraging Democracy: The International Context of Regime Transition in Southern Europe*, ed. Geoffrey Pridham (1991), 94–95; Kenneth Maxwell, "Regime Overthrow and the Prospects for Democratic Transition in Portugal", in *Transitions from Authoritarian Rule: Southern Europe*, eds. Guillermo O'Donnel, Philippe C. Schmitter, and Laurence Whitehead (London: Johns Hopkins University Press, 1986), 121; P. Nikiforos Diamandouros, "Southern Europe: A Third Wave Success Story", in *Consolidating Third Wave Democracies: Regional Challenges*, eds. Larry Diamond, et al. (Baltimore: Johns Hopkins University Press, 1997), 6.
27 Lawrence S. Graham, "Redefining the Portuguese Transition to Democracy", in *Elites and Democratic Consolidation in Latin America and Southern Europe*, eds. John and Richard Gunther Highly (Cambridge: Cambridge University Press, 1992), 285–86.
28 Alice Cunha, "Underwriting Democracy: Portugal and European Economic Community's Accession", *Cahiers de la Méditerranée*, no. 90, vol. 45 (2015): 5–6.
29 Utrikesdepartementet, HP 1 Dp, Promemoria, Utrikesministerns Kansli, ds H. Dahlgren "Mario Soares om utländskt bistånd till Portugal", (04.09.1975).
30 ARAB, SAP, 1889/F/2/A/13, Statsrådsberedningen, Pierre Schori "Minnesanteckningar från överläggningarna om Portugal vid socialistledarmötet på Haga Slott den 2 Augusti 1975".
31 SAP, 1889/F/2/H/3, Pierre Schori "Samtal med Mario Soares i Lissabon Den 10 Juni 1975", (13.06.1975).
32 Birgit Aschmann, "The Reliable Ally: Germany Supports Spain's European Integration Efforts, 1957–67", *Journal of European Integration History* 7, no. 1 (2001): 47–51.
33 Muñoz Sánchez, *El Amigo Alemán: El SPD y el PSOE de la dictadura a la democracia*.
34 Stine Bonsaksen, "Guarding the Gates of Democratic Europe: Norway and the Spanish Accession to NATO", (Masters' thesis, NTNU, 2013).
35 Stortingsforhandlinger 1975–1976, 7c, Forhandling nr. 335, Sak nr. 4 "Interpellasjon fra representanten Berit Ås til Utenriksministeren: Hva har Norge gjort og hva mer kan Norge og nordmenn gjøre for å styrke de demokratiske kreftene i Spania?", (07.04.1976).
36 Rigsarkivet, 0002 Udenrigsministeriet, 5.D.73a, 238, Udkast til talepunkter til brug for Udenrigsministeren under Europarådets 57. ministermøde den 27. novemver 1975, "Spanien", (20.11.1975); 0002 Udenrigsministeriet, 5.D.73a, 238, P. I. Notits, "Det Europæiske Råds møde i Rom den 1.-2. december 1975. Aktuelle spørgsmål: Spanien og Portgual", (27.11.1975).
37 UD, 25.4/102, bind 30, JN 026922, Notat fra UD til ambassaden i London, "Spania. Britiske vurderinger", (10.10.1975).
38 Anaya, 113–15.
39 UD, 25.4/102, bind 33, JN 012237, Notat, "Forholdet mellom Forbundsrepublikken Tyskland og Spania, samt forbindelsen mellom SPD Og CDU og spanske opposisjonelle", (18.03.1976).
40 Anaya, 180–81.
41 UD, "Portugal. Britisk vurdering".
42 Garcia, 9.

43 UD, "Tysk syn på utviklingen i Portugal".
44 25.4/92, bind 21, JN 010892, Momenter til innlegg til Europarådet - Det 56. Ministerkomitémøte 17. april 1975, "Dagsordens Pkt. 2. Portugal", (14.04.1975).
45 Rigsarkivet, "Det Europæiske Råds møde i Rom den 1.-2. december 1975. Aktuelle spørgsmål: Spanien og Portgual".
46 Utrikesdepartementet, HP 1 Dp, Telegram, Utrikesministerns kansli, ds Dahlgren "Utkast til innlegg om Portugal", (11.04.1975).
47 HP 1 Ds, Telegram, Swedeleg New York, Rydbeck "Artikeln i New York Times om spanska Socialistpartiets kongress", (06.12.1976).
48 HP 1 Ds, Telegram, Svensk Madrid, Bernström "Besök hos Los Arcos", (12.11.1975).
49 HP 1 Ds, Telegram, Cabinet Stockholm, "Regeringsdeklaration", (31.03.1976).
50 HP 1 Ds, Telegram från Swedeleg New York, Pol III, Berner "Engelsk översättning av Lidboms tal", (03.11.1975).
51 HP 1 Ds, Svenska ambassaden Madrid, LD "Tal av Olof Palme", (09.12.1976).
52 UD, 25.3/82, JN 009968, Notat til nordisk utenriksministermøte i Stockholm 25. - 26. mars 1976, "Generelt", (22.03.1976).
53 Del Pero, 15–16.
54 Socialist International Archives, 169, International Institute of Social History, Amsterdam, "Minutes of the First Meeting of the Portugal Committee of the Socialist International", (06.04.1972).
55 264, International Institute of Social History, Amsterdam, "Socialist International Welcomes Overthrow of Caetano", (29.04.1974).
56 264, International Institute of Social History, Amsterdam, "Statement on Portugal", (31.03.1974).
57 264, International Institute of Social History, Amsterdam, "In Defence of Human Rights in Portugal", (28.05.1975).
58 176, International Institute of Social History, Amsterdam, "Bureau Meeting of the Socialist International, Rome June 8 1974", (08.06.1974).
59 264, International Institute of Social History, Amsterdam, "Statement on Portugal", (13.07.1975).
60 293, International Institute of Social History, Amsterdam, "Bureau Report to Congress 1976", (21.05.1976).
61 Powell, 300.
62 Antonio Varsori, "Crisis and Stabilization in Southern Europe During the 1970s: Western Strategy, European Instruments", *Journal of European Integration History* 15, no. 1 (2009): 11.
63 Socialist International Archives, 176, International Institute of Social History, Amsterdam, "Establishment of Spain Committee of the Socialist International", (22.03.1974).
64 293, International Institute of Social History, Amsterdam, "Action for Democracy in Spain" (30.11.1975).
65 "Bureau Report to Congress 1976".
66 193, International Institute of Social History, Amsterdam, "Minutes of Bureau Meeting, Suresnes March 28–29 1976", (18.06.1976).
67 See for instance Powell, 300-04; Anaya, 27-33; Salm, 104-05.
68 Socialist International Archives, 196, International Institute of Social History, Amsterdam, "Resolution on Spain Adopted by the Bureau of the Socialist International March 30 1977", (31.03.1977).
69 809, International Institute of Social History, Amsterdam, (30.07.1974).
70 812, International Institute of Social History, Amsterdam, "Spain - Decisions and Recommendations by Bureau of Socialist International", (10.10.1975).
71 AAB, ARK-1001-D/Dd/LO00224, "Psoe Congress 1976", (05–08.12.1976).
72 Socialist International Archives, "Spain - Decisions and Recommendations by Bureau of Socialist International".

73 According to Salm, the socialist triumvirate of Brandt, Kreisky and Palme came to dominate the policies of the SI during the 1970s. Salm, 106.
74 ARAB, Olof Palme, 676/4/2/121, "Working Paper Concerning the Portugal Committee", (27.08.1975).
75 AAB, ARK-1001-D/Dd/LO00258, Brev til Reiulf Steen fra Willy Brandt "The Committe of Friendship and Solidarity with Democracy and Socialism in Portugal", (18.09.1975).

Archives

Archives of the Norwegian Labour Movement (Arbeiderbevegelsens Arkiv og bibliotek, AAB)
Danish National Archives (Rigsarkivet)
Norwegian Ministry of Foreign Affairs (Utenriksdepartementet, UD)
International Institute of Socialist International Archives
Swedish Labour Movement's Archives and Library (Arbetarrörelsens arkiv och bibliotek, ARAB)
Archives of the Swedish Ministry of Foreign Affairs (Utrikesdepartementet)

Bibliography

ARAB. SAP, 1889/F/2/A/13, Statsrådsberedningen, Pierre Schori "Minnesanteckningar Från Överläggningarna Om Portugal Vid Socialistledarmötet På Haga Slott Den 2 Augusti 1975" 02.08.1975.
———. SAP, 1889/F/2/A/13, Statsrådsberedningen, Pierre Schori "Portugalöverläggningen 10 Downing Street September 5, 1975". 09.09.1975.
———. SAP, 1889/F/2/H/3, Statsrådsberedningen, Pierre Schori "Rapport från besök i Lissabon den 10–12 Juni −75". 16.06.1975.
———. SAP, 1889/F/2/H/3, Socialdemokraterna, Pierre Schori "Samtal med Felipe Gonzalez Den 28 januari 1978 i Alger". 01.02.1978.
———. SAP, 1889/F/2/H/3, Pierre Schori "Samtal med Mario Soares i Lissabon den 10 juni 1975". 13.06.1975.
———. Olof Palme, 676/4/2/121, "Working Paper Concerning the Portugal Committee". 27.08.1975.
Rigsarkivet. 0002 Udenrigsministeriet, 5.D.73a, 238, Notits, P.I., "Det Europæiske Råds møde i Rom den 1.-2. december 1975. Aktuelle Spørgsmål: Spanien og Portgual". 27.11.1975.
———. 0002 Udenrigsministeriet, 5.D.73a, 238, Udkast til talepunkter til brug for Udenrigsministeren under Europarådets 57. ministermøde den 27. novemver 1975, "Spanien". 20.11.1975.
Socialist International Archives. 809, International Institute of Social History, Amsterdam. 30.07.1974.
———. 293, International Institute of Social History, Amsterdam, "Action for Democracy in Spain". 30.11.1975.
———. 176, International Institute of Social History, Amsterdam, "Bureau Meeting of the Socialist International, Rome June 8 1974". 08.06.1974.
———. 293, International Institute of Social History, Amsterdam, "Bureau Report to Congress 1976". 21.05.1976.
———. 293, International Institute of Social History, Amsterdam, "Bureau's Report – Introduction". 21.05.1976.

102 *Stine Bonsaksen*

―――. 176, International Institute of Social History, Amsterdam, "Establishment of Spain Committee of the Socialist International". 22.03.1974.

―――. 264, International Institute of Social History, Amsterdam, "In Defence of Human Rights in Portugal". 28.05.1975.

―――. 193, International Institute of Social History, Amsterdam, "Minutes of Bureau Meeting, Suresnes March 28–29 1976". 18.06.1976.

―――. 169, International Institute of Social History, Amsterdam, "Minutes of the First Meeting of the Portugal Committee of the Socialist International". 06.04.1972.

―――. 196, International Institute of Social History, Amsterdam, "Resolution on Spain Adopted by the Bureau of the Socialist International March 30 1977". 31.03.1977.

―――. 264, International Institute of Social History, Amsterdam, "Socialist International Welcomes Overthrow of Caetano". 29.04.1974.

―――. 812, International Institute of Social History, Amsterdam, "Spain – Decisions and Recommendations by Bureau of Socialist International". 10.10.1975.

―――. 264, International Institute of Social History, Amsterdam, "Statement on Portugal". 13.07.1975.

―――. 264, International Institute of Social History, Amsterdam, "Statement on Portugal". 31.03.1974.

UD. 25.4/92, Bind 21, JN 010892, Momenter til innlegg til Europarådet – Det 56. Ministerkomitémøte 17. april 1975, "Dagsordens Pkt. 2. Portugal". 14.04.1975.

―――. 25.4/102, Bind 33, JN 012237, Notat, "Forholdet Mellom Forbundsrepublikken Tyskland Og Spania, Samt Forbindelsen Mellom Spd Og Cdu Og Spanske Opposisjonelle". 18.03.1976.

―――. 25.3/82, JN 009968, Notat til nordisk utenriksministermøte i Stockholm 25–26 mars 1976, "Generelt". 22.03.1976.

―――. 25.4/92, Bind 23, JN 021472, Melding fra ambassaden i Lisboa "Møte i Stockholm Av Sosialdemokratiske ledere". 04.08.1975.

―――. 25.4/92, Bind 22, JN 015859, Melding fra ambassaden i London, "Portugal. Britisk Vurdering". 05.06.1975.

―――. 25.4/92, Bind 23, JN 021486, Telegram fra ambassaden i London, "Portugal. Britiske synspunkter". 11.08.1975.

―――. 25.4/92, Bind 23, JN 020752, Melding fra ambassaden i Bonn, "Portugal. Tysk vurdering". 28.07.1975.

―――. 25.4/92, Bind 22, JN 021586, "Samtale med Statssekretær Sampaio i det Portugisiske Utenriksdepartment". 10.07.1975.

―――. 25.4/102, Bind 30, JN 026922, Notat fra UD til ambassaden i London, "Spania. Britiske vurderinger". 10.10.1975.

―――. 25.4/92, Bind 22, JN 014975, Innkommet melding fra ambassaden i Bonn, "Tysk syn på utviklingen i Portugal". 02.06.1975.

Utrikesdepartementet. HP 1 Ds, Telegram, Swedeleg New York, Rydbeck "Artikeln i New York Times om Spanska Socialistparties Kongress". 06.12.1976.

―――. HP 1 Ds, Telegram, Svensk Madrid, Bernström "Besök hos Los Arcos". 12.11.1975.

―――. HP 1 Ds, Telegram från Swedeleg New York, Pol III, Berner "Engelsk översättning av Lidboms tal". 03.11.1975.

―――. HP 1 Dp, Promemoria, Utrikesministerns Kansli, ds H. Dahlgren "Mario Soares om utländskt bistånd till Portugal". 04.09.1975.

―――. HP 1 Ds, Telegram, Cabinet Stockholm, "Regeringsdeklaration". 31.03.1976.

―――. HP 1 Ds, Svenska ambassaden Madrid, LD "Tal av Olof Palme". 09.12.1976.

———. HP 1 Dp, Telegram, Utrikesministerns kansli, ds Dahlgren "Utkast till inlägg om Portugal". 11.04.1975.
AAB. ARK-1001-D/Dd/LO00258, Brev til Reiulf Steen fra Willy Brandt "The Committe of Friendship and Solidarity with Democracy and Socialism in Portugal". 18.09.1975.
———. ARK-1001-D/Dd/LO00224, "PSOE Congress 1976". 05–08.12.1976.
Anaya, Pilar Ortuño. *European Socialists and Spain: The Transition to Democracy, 1959–77*. Houndmills: Palgrave, 2002.
Aschmann, Birgit. "The Reliable Ally: Germany Supports Spain's European Integration Efforts, 1957–67". *Journal of European Integration History* 7, no. 1 (2001): 37–52.
Bermeo, Nancy. "Redemocratization and Transition Elections: A Comparison of Spain and Portugal". *Comparative Politics* 19, no. 2 (1987): 213–31.
Castaño, David. "'A Practical Test in the Détente': International Support for the Socialist Party in the Portuguese Revolution (1974–1975)". *Cold War History* 15, no. 1 (2015): 1–26.
Cunha, Alice. "Underwriting Democracy: Portugal and European Economic Community's Accession". *Cahiers de la Méditerranée* 90 (2015): 47–58.
Del Pero, Mario. "A European Solution for a European Crisis. The International Implications of Portugal's Revolution". *Journal of European Integration History* 1 (2009): 23.
Diamandouros, P. Nikiforos. "Southern Europe: A Third Wave Success Story". In *Consolidating Third Wave Democracies: Regional Challenges*, edited by Larry Diamond, Marc F. Plattner, Yun-han Chu, and Hung-mao Tien, 3–25. Baltimore: Johns Hopkins University Press, 1997.
Fonseca, Ana Mónica. "The Federal Republic of Germany and the Portuguese Transition to Democracy (1974–1976)". *Journal of European Integration History* 15, no. 1 (2009): 35–56.
Garcia, Oscar Jose Martin. "'The End of the Carnival': The UK and the Carnation Revolution in Portugal". *Contemporary British History* 29, no. 2 (2015): 199–221.
Grabendorff, Wolf. "International Support for Democracy in Contemporary Latin America: The Role of the Party Internationals". In *The International Dimensions of Democratization: Europe and the Americas*, edited by Laurence Whitehead, 201–26. Oxford: Oxford University Press, 1996.
Graham, Lawrence S. "Redefining the Portuguese Transition to Democracy". In *Elites and Democratic Consolidation in Latin America and Southern Europe*, edited by John and Richard Gunther Highly, 282–99. Cambridge: Cambridge University Press, 1992.
Magen, Amichai, and Michael A. McFaul. "Introduction: American and European Strategies to Promote Democracy – Shared Values, Common Challenges, Divergent Tools?" In *Promoting Democracy and the Rule of Law: American and European Strategies* edited by Amichai Magen, Thomas Risse, and Michael A. McFaul, 1–33. New York: Palgrave Macmillan, 2009.
Magen, Amichai, Thomas Risse, and Michael McFaul, eds. *Promoting Democracy and the Rule of Law: American and European Strategies*. New York: Palgrave Macmillan, 2009.
March, James G., and Johan P. Olsen. "The Logic of Appropriateness". In *The Oxford Handbook of Political Science*, edited by M. Rein, M. Moran and R. E. Goodin. Oxford: Oxford University Press, 2004.
Maxwell, Kenneth. "Regime Overthrow and the Prospects for Democratic Transition in Portugal". In *Transitions from Authoritarian Rule: Southern Europe*, edited by

Guillermo O'Donnel, Philippe C. Schmitter, and Laurence Whitehead, 109–37. London: Johns Hopkins University Press, 1986.

Muñoz Sánchez, Antonio El Amigo. *Alemán: El SPD y el PSOE de la dictadura a la democracia*. Barcelona: RBA Libros, 2012.

———. "The Friedrich Ebert Foundation and the Spanish Socialists During the Transition to Democracy, 1975–1982". *Contemporary European History* 25, no. 1 (2016): 143–62.

Opello, Walter C. "Portugal: A Case Study of International Determinants of Régime Transition". In *Encouraging Democracy: The International Context of Regime Transition in Southern Europe*, edited by Geoffrey Pridham, 84–102. Leicester: University Press, 1991.

———. *Portugal: From Monarchy to Pluralist Democracy*. Oxford: Westview Press, 1991.

Powell, Charles. "International Aspects of Democratization. The Case of Spain". In *The International Dimensions of Democratization. Europe and the Americas*, edited by Laurence Whitehead, 285–315. Oxford: Oxford University Press, 1996.

Pridham, Geoffrey, ed. *Encouraging Democracy: The International Context of Regime Transition in Southern Europe*. Leicester: Leicester University Press, 1991.

Salm, Christian. *Transnational Socialist Networks in the 1970s: European Community Development Aid and Southern Enlargement* [in English]. Palgrave Studies in the History of Social Movements. Basingstoke, Hampshire: Palgrave Macmillan, 2016.

Stortingsforhandlinger 1975–1976. 7c, Forhandling nr. 335, Sak nr. 4 3105–19, "Interpellasjon fra representanten Berit Ås til Utenriksministeren: Hva har Norge gjort og hva mer kan Norge og nordmenn gjøre for å styrke de demokratiske kraftene i Spania?" 07.04.1976.

Varsori, Antonio. "Crisis and Stabilization in Southern Europe During the 1970s: Western Strategy, European Instruments". *Journal of European Integration History* 15, no. 1 (2009): 5–14.

Whitehead, Laurence, ed. *The International Dimensions of Democratization: Europe and the Americas*. Oxford: Oxford University Press, 1996.

6 Radicalism and reformism in Post-war Italian socialism

A comparative view

Paolo Borioni

This chapter focuses on the political culture of Italian socialism during and right after the phase of centre-left coalitions (around 1962–1976) using a comparative method. It offers an interpretation based on two fundamental points: (1) the weaving of the organisational nature of the Italian left into its political culture and (2) the degree of Italian development compared to other advanced democracies, and the overlap between socialist reform and national modernisation. To do this, the interaction between political culture, socio-economic history and programmatic/ideological solutions will be taken into account. Economic and social history – especially the relationship between the labour movement, economics and the position of the national economy in the international division of labour – acquires special significance. A more complete idea of the difference between Italian socialism and European social democracy could emerge as a result of this. This necessarily requires an investigation into what the specificity of the social democratic element is. Which is where we must begin.

The specificity of social democracy: a comparison

P. H. Jensen specifically chooses Italy as an "opposite" term of comparison when contrasting it with a typical trait of the Nordic and Belgian labour movement: the Ghent system, which was organised by the union and later regulated and co-financed by public authorities.[1] Jensen highlights how, at its founding in 1906, the Italian union Cgl (or CGdL) discussed the Ghent model but refrained from adopting it on social and structural grounds. Instead, a mix of professional federations and trade unions came into being with regard to Italian labour, i.e., the opposite of the Ghent system. An attempt was thus made to obviate the fragmentation of the labour market: a horizontal trade unionism, and a strong labour confederalism aimed at bringing together working classes that were still not very compact. To this very day, Italian trade unionism, and especially the CGL / CgdL / Cgil, still seem distant from the Ghent system, which determines, where brought to bear, the highest rate of unionisation in the world. The "Ghent" organisational model would go on to extend from Denmark, Belgium and later Norway (until 1938) to other Nordic countries, resulting in a self-sufficient union, which is not atomistic though still capable of standing on an equal footing with the pro-Labour party,

DOI: 10.4324/9781003181439-7

while also establishing capital-labour parity. It is above all this twofold parity that typifies a hegemonic type of social democracy.

As Procacci points out, the "horizontal" trade unionism of the Camere del Lavoro,[2] unifying workers according to a horizontal geographical area principle, strives to make up for the relatively low density of professional and industrial unionism, and does this among other things by aggregating radical cultures (republican, anarchists and post-Risorgimento radicalism) typical of Southern Europe. Conversely, a less dense organisation, whose internal radical cultures may be less influenced by modern socialism – whether inspired more by Kautsky or by Bernstein is of little importance here[3] – will tend to build around "clusters" of another type ("movement-driven"), rather than by relying on the strength consolidated as part of conflict resolution. Such conflict, rest assured, persists in the social democratic organisational culture, thanks to the organisational strength of the class: going on strike, due to its potentially disruptive nature, plays an implicit major role in the "regulated" negotiation, even when strikes are not called. Mentioning the two German theorists leads us to another socio-economic model: the *Soziale Marktwirtschaft* within Ordoliberalism. Although it derives from Eucken's school (University of Freiburg), it nevertheless finds its basis in social legislation and in the highly competitive Bismarckian project. It places the project within strict rules regarding cartels and especially with regard to trade balance and government budget, to overcome both the economic instability that led to Nazism and the Nazi *Wehrmarktwirtschaft* based on debt, which resulted in the subjugation of non-German resources in order to sustain it.

This model differs not only (it goes without saying) from Keynesian economics but also from neoliberal theories, in that the state plays a prominent role in it, though not as a regulator of the economic trend nor through a high percentage of public ownership.[4] The Ordoliberal state is a "Gardener State": unlike (tendential or ideal-typical) Anglo-Saxon neoliberal scenarios, it is very significant, actively managing social legislation (relying on government insurance programmes ushered in between 1883 and 1889 that were inclusive and ahead of their time), and as the primary norm-giver of a once and for all fixed balance. The latter, for example, is achieved by ensuring that irreversible budget and debt rules are strictly adhered to, and letting then the "garden" (the market economy) grow accordingly, just as a gardener would.[5] The state therefore sets up a highly competitive project in which both social legislation and social players are involved.

Social democracy, with the establishment of its trade unions, plays an important part in it in at least two ways: (1) in its role as negotiator and labour organiser (2) in the phase going from 1966 to 1976 (first the *Grosse Koalition*, and then from Willy Brandt's to the early years of Helmut Schmidt's chancellery), the roles and benefits of the social democratic trade union establishment are expanded within the model itself. This takes place by increasing welfare spending (so much so that this will be referred to as Germany's only Keynesian period)[6] and an enlargement of the *Mitbestimmung* (1976).[7] This is the era in which, within the German model, it is not *partnership* that advances, but capital-labour *parity*, which, however, will be downsized from 1982, thus re-establishing the Ordoliberal qualities of "technocratic" – rather than "democratic" – competitiveness.[8]

Let us now return to the definition: democratic socialism implies building organisational, trade union, political, constitutional and legal equality between capital and labour. However, this constitutes a necessary, albeit insufficient, premise. In fact, starting from this premise, social democracy aims to criticise and reform capitalism, foregrounding (especially in the most hegemonic national cases and periods) the socio-economic, as well as democratic, regulation of the market. This takes place by encouraging – in a democratic and non-technocratic manner – innovation and competitiveness, which become "obligatory" roads to follow as more precise and effective conditions brought about by high wages come into being as the outcome of a stronger organisation of the "democratic"-class dialectics and its related rights.[9]

The welfare state and its role in capital-labour parity

Against this background, welfare can be described as an important part of the wage and social rights floor that allows for a relatively lesser degree of competitiveness (progressively less so) through labour exploitation. Therefore, if we move on to the more strictly political and social sphere, according to social democracy, this simultaneously means: (a) the introduction, including beyond the workplace and the trade union, of instruments of equality with capital (specific welfare institutions); (b) the enlargement beyond the wage labour classes of a social alliance that supports this parity (i.e., with the middle classes, or, especially in the case of Nordic countries, with some agricultural classes). These two components then lead to the economic and structural element, i.e., the consolidation of a production that does not rely, if not decreasingly or marginally, on the low cost of labour to produce, export and compete. It is evident how this social entrenchment and the social democratic political culture of capital-labour parity progressively affect and consolidate a new social model in the mid-20th century, and, on the other hand, social democracy gains real advantages from this competitive system. Even so, the reverse is also true: from a political and organisational culture perspective, the less a single country is able to achieve these conditions, the less a social democratic culture of parity can assert itself – a kind of parity which, as we have seen, is not merely about conflict or compromise, but a recognised and hegemonic form of both. Clearly, the cultures of Italian socialism when the centre-left coalitions (1962–1970) ruled were attempts to find alternative solutions both for modernising the country and for developing a political culture well suited to it.

Not only a wage floor but also an elevator

The welfare state "wage floor" role in terms of capital-labour parity generally interacts with what we might call "elevators", that is to say, with the propulsive side of productive and economic development. Figuratively speaking, the "wage floor" represents the range of factors that prevent us from growing through an exploitation-driven labour market, whereas the "elevators" are those production, investment and planning factors driving up innovation, prices and competition.

For example, one can start from agricultural exports in Denmark, which, partly thanks to the Ghent system and its political and organisational culture, gradually turned into industrial capital-labour parity between the 1930s and the 1960s. Denmark, too, came to a development crossroads, and in the late 1920s, a blatant attempt was made by liberal-conservative governments to cause an internal wage deflation to boost the price competitiveness of its export-led agriculture. Indeed, in the 19th century, Denmark had relied on this factor of production and development to exit poverty well before Sweden and other Nordic countries. However, although the agrarian sector and its parties (typically Venstre) held a consolidated position of power in the socio-political system of the country, the strength and the social democratic political and organisational culture made it possible to choose a diametrically opposed exit from the crisis of interwar years. Social democracy succeeded in taking advantage of the fall in foreign demand linked to the great post-1929 crisis and turned it into a counterargument, i.e., to not accept a wage devaluation that would safeguard export quotas, but rather to enhance domestic wage demand and not be taken hostage by agricultural exports alone.

This, in turn, prevented welfare from being cut, thus causing wage devaluation as the liberal-agrarian governments of the 1920s wanted, but rather to be maintained and expanded thanks to both agricultural exports and domestic demand. Hence, according to our figure of speech, a "wage floor" was strengthened under the increasingly inclusive and therefore increasingly effective labour market.[10] In the years that followed shortly afterwards, Sweden's exportation of forest, mining and semi-finished products played a similar role to the Danish agricultural export. Given the extreme poverty in Sweden and the ensuing serious conflicts in the world of work, however, the construction of parity (through the organisational strength of the party-trade union-welfare complex, e.g., the Ghent model) did not take place until 1934.[11] Since then, however, Sweden's reliance on agricultural exports would exert less pressure than on its Danish neighbour, allowing for even more extensive industrialisation.

Another example of an "elevator" is the strength of industrial exports and the military-industrial complex in Germany. Before long, it equipped itself with social insurance which, at first, in Bismarck's designs was meant to empty the socialist movement of its consensus and social base. This military factor of development (which as we have seen is both socio-economic and political-democratic) will be curtailed or altogether stamped out by the events of the two world wars and Nazism. In any case, a remarkable potential for labour-capital parity was still present: capital-labour parity becomes clearly progressive in the post-war period, with the *Mitbestimmung* and the adoption of a democratic system – both electoral and constitutional – specially designed to embolden mediation between political and social forces.[12]

Let us now focus on Italy: the industrial development here generally lagged behind in many geographical areas and was mostly uneven. This gap was bridged by state-funded intervention programmes, the only way to provide long-term investments and to invest permanently in systemic innovation. Then, in the immediate post-war period, the so-called De Gasperi-Einaudi pact would play a decisive role where liberal culture – which probably disavowed the very notion of programming and Keynesian demand – allowed the survival, and even the expansion of state investment and consequently of state ownership in this and other areas. A compromise between two worlds was thus worked out: on the one hand, the liberalism and private property that did not allow interference (and would first try to obtain very advantageous wage conditions and labour costs) and, on the other hand, the sphere of *dirigisme* and public property.[13] Compared to what has been summarily reconstructed above, the "elevator" component in Italy – more than elsewhere – and that of the imperfect "wage floor" (comparatively limited so as not to prevent the private sector from competing through extensive downward wage pressure) coexist, thereby generating a less systemically integrated complex than elsewhere.[14]

The "social democratic wholeness", i.e., elevator/investment/competitiveness *together with* floor-welfare, therefore gives rise to the capital-worker parity within the labour market, the economy and democratic political system in a more systematic way than in Italy. The research assumption put forth herewith is that this structural element affects retroactively – and at least in three ways – the material context for socialist economic reform:

a) Perpetuating more than necessary the conditions of uneven development between backward and advanced areas/sectors, i.e., for all its undeniably crucial role, planning becomes nonetheless more complicated.
b) Perpetuating cultures of the transformation of capitalism that rely somewhat more on (superstructural) materials of distinction and of ideological otherness. Conversely, a fully social democratic hegemony is based on a distinction drawn more through the real (structural) power of entrenchment (and is consequently *also* ideological). Thus, as it strives to come to a compromise – that is, while reforming capitalism – the social democratic political culture knows how to/can act in a wholly parity manner even without excessive recourse to ideological otherness.
c) Thus perpetuating through the party (specifically the PSI of the early centre-left) a strategy which, for historical and structural reasons that mutually feed back into ideological ones, is shifted to political action (coalitional, superstructural, etc.) and which pertains to the enlargement of public property – already widely present – developing it, though, as an approximation to socialist programming.

The complex social democratic parity thus favours, as a structural element, an economy tending to compete more cohesively through long-term investments. This is often the result of a concerted measure between labour and capital, but, according to a purely socialist idea of democracy, it is based on an equal relationship between interests (class interests or, at any rate, social interests) which, in and of themselves, would tend to be divergent if not downright conflicting.

Another important point is the nature and composition of compromise. Compromise, both in real and ideological terms, takes place between distinct and as a tendency diverging poles, so it can never exhaust itself into indistinctness. However, this distinction is less ideological, less party-oriented and less superstructural in the case of social democracy. In other words, within this parity, ideology, party and conflict are more in keeping with social entrenchment, welfare institutions, negotiation mechanisms, co-decision procedures (MBL, *Mitbestimmung*) and, overall, the strength of the labour movement.

In contrast, wherever this system is less entrenched or less effectively engineered, there occurs: (a) a more conspicuous fluctuation between advancing and retreating, with a lower net balance in gains, and consequently in the consolidation of the system of capital-labour parity; (b) this lower net balance depends on – and in turn reinforces – the fact that there is a tendency to compensate for the lower degree of organised labour parity through the party's superstructural "political" action.

In the Italian communist party case, there has often been talk of a "Leninist" residue (the party leading the social movement). In the PSI, however, insufficient structural and organisational parity has been offset by the resources of a coalitional/governmental nature. This combines a structural element, that is, the role of public enterprise in development, with Italian socialism, which (more so than in European social democracies) tends to hybridise with the former.

This means an ambition to put pressure on ownership and public planning to then proceed towards socialism (especially Riccardo Lombardi and initially Antonio Giolitti). In other cultures (namely, Nenni-Mancini), the presence of the party in centre-left governments is central to prevent any regression, while bolstering progress instead. In both cases, it emerges, somewhat blurredly, that welfare institutions appear thereby to be a less central element of PSI programmatic believes. Lombardi's invaluable contribution in clearing the way for the state to act as a means of socialist reform.

Lombardi's invaluable contribution in clearing the way for the state to act as a means of such reform (and not as a pure means of capitalist domination), however, does ultimately underestimate the welfare/wage floor. Lombardi highlights

> two fundamental trends: one aimed at reforms that abide by the legal order governing the bourgeois state and essentially at equity in the distribution of income, that is, the tendency to create and consolidate [...] the *welfare state* [...]. The other trend [...] relying on the tools of political democracy, focuses on revolutionary reforms [...] aimed at breaking the framework of the existing proprietary order, to create not a welfare state but a classless society.[15]

In short, the interaction between the two tools (welfare/parity/wage floor vs. state/planning/elevator) is underestimated in PSI socialist reform as progress towards an increasing reduction in class imbalance is made.

This helps us understand how, in Italian socialism, social democracy is seen as a compromise in surrendering to capitalism. Interestingly, the same applies to French socialism. According to Pierre Rosanvallon, the denunciation of social democracy by French socialism exprime [...] une sorte de mauvaise conscience. Même s'ils sont réformistes, les partis sociaux-démocrates européens restent en effet des partis ouvriers structurellement lies aux organisations syndicales et puissamment enracinés dans la société civile à travers de multiples réseaux coopératives et mutuellistes. Rien de tout cela n'existe en France [...] il [French socialism. A/N] occulte ainsi la question même du fondement structurel et politique d'un mouvement qu'il n'a jamais été capable d'édifier [...] La peur de la social-démocratie traduit également l'incertitude du socialisme français sur son propre avenir et sur son propre projet.[16]

As Rosanvallon himself notes a little further on, the manifestos of Swedish Social Democracy and British Labour show no lack of references to industrial democracy and the public ownership of certain companies and the public management of the economy. Their aims, even if difficult to achieve, are not seen as against, but rather in keeping with entrenchment-welfare-equality. In South European socialism, on the other hand, it is assumed that more ambitious objectives can be pursued with the resources made available, such as ideological and superstructural resources from planning/public enterprise or (as a reflection that is both ideological and, on closer inspection, pragmatic and functional) in addition to coalitional/governmental power. That welfare can strengthen the parity of socially organised labour towards capitalism tends to become an elusive concept, thus strengthening the tendency to utilise other and more "political" resources.

This last form of power was rendered fungible in France first with the coalition governments of the fourth republic and then, in the fifth republic, with the two-round majoritarian system and presidentialism, while in Italy, it was accessible thanks to the indispensability of the PSI for any centre-left government (being centre-right coalitions excluded for the post-fascist and monarchist nature of the Right, and the Communist PCI unfit for government given the Cold War context).

In both cases, the extent of party politics is overarching with respect to that of parity structural positioning, which again reflects the level of distrust in welfare as a central element of this positioning.

Variations of socialism

We have briefly outlined the "pragmatic" point of view in Nenni's vision (i.e., the importance of the coalition "in and of itself", always mindful of the tragic inability to unite popular forces which, after 1919, led to Fascism)[17] and that of Lombardi's revolutionary reformism.[18]

A different orientation, though never officially Social Democratic in the terms mentioned above, is found in the work of Giacomo Brodolini, inspired by the more general political directions of Francesco De Martino, and in that of Antonio Giolitti. Giolitti's programme is integrated into the foreseeable potential and long-term structural investment by the industrial sector as well as public planning. The latter expresses its own nature of programming and takes its rightful place in the economic history of the country, or in the undeniable need to accelerate, through planning and a centre-driven impulse, the exit from backwardness and imbalances. Giolitti, however, would very soon distinguish himself from the Lombardi-Socialism's "revolutionary reformism", orientated towards an anti-capitalist rupture very much wary of mediations, though he would remain loyal to the idea of a linear and consistent array of reforms that clearly differs from the pre-eminence of the political formula, typical of Nenni's autonomism.

On the one hand, Giolitti would continue to conceive the centre-left in a more programmatic and less politicised manner than Nenni, thus remaining faithful to the philosophy of programming, for example, by publishing the 1965–1969 Five-Year plan on the very day of his resignation as budget minister (then taken over and approved in 1967 by the new Budget Minister Pieraccini). He would later break with Lombardi, believing, however, that one of the socialist government's tasks meant acting even in adverse circumstances such as the slowdown of the post-1963 economic situation, the Colombo-Carli monetary policy and the difficulty in pursuing an income policy and revision of wage dynamics across territorial disparities.[19] It was precisely his experience in government that helped Giolitti to expand and diversify the concept of reform of capitalism through strengthening the positions of workers and socialist organisations. Two facts can be cited: (a) the conspicuous presence, in the document for the five-year planning, of the construction of a European welfare state as never before in any socialist elaboration;[20] (b) in his interview with "La Stampa" in July 1976 Giolitti will make clear his approach to European social democracies.[21] The practice of government led him to understand how the cohesion and function of socialism should not necessarily contend with the systematic expropriation of capitalism.

As for De Martino, he confirms that, in Nenni, the political formula acquires an autonomous value, more than the programmatic content and the "programmatic beliefs",[22] claiming that, even without denying the results achieved, this approach soon reached its limits.

The socialist presence in the government at the end of the 1960s aimed primarily at interpreting and representing social movements, the "thrusts" coming from a society and a workers' movement that was particularly active and strong in those years. De Martino rejected the approach of Lombardi-socialists, since it would require a constructivism that already strived to be an alternative to the system while still in power (as if socialism should already be built in the coalition with the Christian Democrats). For the Lombardi-socialists, the "whole" of the maximum programme (i.e. the most radical hence maximalist) must be totally consistent with every stage of the reforming government and, according to De Martino, this approach resembles of a sort of "Enlightenment", that is, it acts in the name of a superiority of intent considered self-evident but does not make sufficient efforts in creating much-needed consensus.[23] Lombardi later replied by claiming that the lively season of political commitment and movements of the 1970s (with their widespread participatory will, and thanks to participatory decision-making in the workplace, schools and universities) could be a movement-driven added value in order to preserve the "revolutionary" content and direction of politically enacted reform.[24]

Brodolini is the maker and driving force behind De Martino's approach, through not only the continuous and effective contact with the trade union movement but also the many reforms carried out: the pension reform, the end of regionally diversified salary caps (lower in the South, higher in the developed North), the enormous contribution to health-care reform and the statute of the right of workers. This host of achievements is mirrored in the context outlined so far because (a) it imposes on the executive the "thrusts" of the movements of those years according to the idea of De Martino; (b) it seeks to strengthen the PSI in the area of waged work; (c) it aims to reinforce, in keeping with the Statute of the workers, but also with the rules of the welfare state, the position of "parity" of the labour movement as a structural element. In conjunction with the reform introduced "from above" by public, politically controlled ownership, and beyond the immediate political outcome. A reformism starting with worker emancipation and transforming it into an "upward moving" factor for the reform of capitalism.[25] Indeed, this approach is made even more real by the intense experience of 1968–1970.

Having classified the various socialist approaches to reforms, we can now turn to a more general historical perspective. The conclusion reached by De Martino provides some food for thought. In fact, De Martino spent his years as the leader of PSI preaching the principle whereby the division – primarily operational and functional, but ultimately also organisational – between the PSI and the PCI should have been resolved in order to unlock the political and institutional impasse. Indeed, the PSI had achieved its utmost when, thanks to Brodolini, it welcomed the social impetus of those years, but this could be rendered systematic only through a new convergence between PCI and PSI.

Furthermore, this period, which De Martino experiences as a historically groundbreaking event, perfectly embodies the fundamental historical and strategic problem of the Italian left, i.e., the division between the PSI (which entirely managed the resource of the political and coalition movement) and the PCI (rooted in the majority of unionised workers, but not completely expendable politically). This division has a lot to do with the delayed and incomplete implementation of the instrument of "parity" between capital and labour, and therefore with the use of this element for greater grassroots "upward" conditioning – that is to say, not only political and superstructural – of capitalism.[26] The bipartition of these two functions in two different parties fully represents the lack, or the paucity, of a social democratic culture in Italy. In fact, it is no coincidence that these roles in Europe are merged into social democracy. For this reason, it is necessary to highlight in the following paragraph how in fact even the PCI often used its labour entrenchment as an element of political negotiation rather than because it was aware of the structural and strategic consequences of achieving parity between capital and labour. Its main aim was instead to acquire the other missing element: its own governmental or, in any case, parliamentary and institutional expendability. Without a "social democratic" integration between social/trade union entrenchment and government expendability, there appears to be *also* an excessive emphasis on the political superstructure rather than on a more profound social and structural reform among the promoter of this entrenchment (the PCI). Let us now see how this can be further understood.

The PCI and the superstructurality of legitimisation

Let us complete what has been said thus far by further explaining the terms of social democracy's socio-political apparatus and, consequently, the outcomes of its lack or incompleteness in Italy. Let us start from the assumption that the social democratic system consists of the following:

Impetus from the established social base and union: the movement gives rise to the urge to grant as little as possible, and programmatically increasingly less, a development based on labour exploitation and its ramifications (weak innovation in many sectors, informal economy, low rate of employment, poor employment, etc.).

The contribution of the political and institutional level (party): the transmission within the institutional framework of grassroots demands (with De Martino's idea in the 1968–1970 phase approximating this) and the implementation of the necessary political mediations. Through this, the party also succeeds in preserving or expanding the established power itself, in a progressive virtuous circle that would last for many decades.

Double parity: it should be noted that the relationship between these two elements generates not only a significant and indeed prevalent function of capital-labour parity in influencing the framework for development but also a substantial parity between the socio-trade-unionist entrenchment and the main pro-labour party. Neither reality is subordinate to the other as in the Italian (not only Communist) model of "transmission belt". This implies that the party's political-parliamentary mediation role takes place, albeit with the necessary degree of compatibility and compromise, as little as possible according to the terms of the "sacrifice" of workers and their reasons. Hence, the fact that the political aim of the party, rather than trying to obtain the superstructural political compromise in itself, lies instead in its bid for "high" competitiveness policies, while avoiding forfeiting the reasons for good and growing wages as little as possible.

It is interesting to see how the lack of the parity factors listed here fully involved the PCI, a more intransigent party, in theory, than the centre-left PSI. The PCI's political exchange, without having prepared the groundwork for a culture of parity, demonstrates its limits at the end of the period being scrutinised (i.e. the era of the governments of national solidarity 1976–1979) and is well summarised by Paggi and D'Angelillo. The latter make a useful comparison with social democracy as it acted in those years and not as it was simply perceived, especially by the so-called Einaudi wing of the PCI, the "gradualist" one. Here, social democracy was in fact mostly understood as a culture of responsibility and respect for its compatibility, the way capitalism presented them at a given moment. In fact,

Amendola argued that: "Sacrifices are required by the state of things, and in this sense they are not the object of a negotiable option, but rather a state of necessity that transcends the interests of the individual social partners". It should be emphasised in our discourse that this occurs in ways that, pessimistically, do not believe in the potential of promoting, in the Italian context, a different type of growth in the face of wage concessions.[27]

In this connection, the debate between Augusto Graziani and Claudio Napoleoni regarding Cespe's *Rapporto sull'economia* (1976) is noteworthy. The former hoped that the containment of wages would be balanced by an increase in public spending, the latter, in his reply *Risposta ad un critico di sinistra*, which was in line with what the party was able to conceive and achieve at that time, remarked that a strengthening "of the role of enterprises in the process of recovery of the Italian economy" was needed. In essence, the PCI would see inflation as the greatest danger, accepting the government's austerity measures (increase in petrol prices, postal and railway tariffs, abolition of five holidays, forced underwriting of government bonds for the highest salaries, etc.) albeit thereby earning the right, however, to make them more equitable.[28] Paggi and D'Angelillo note, consistently with what we have stated throughout this paper, that the result of all this is that in Italy

> the traditional exposure to the trends of the world economic situation [...] is not taken as an element of national weakness to be attacked with intervention on the industrial structure, but is instead used as a further argument to force the workers' movement into a defensive stance, through a deflationary balance of foreign accounts.

Thus, as the authors of this useful comparison noted, social democracy has two meanings: in Austria, Sweden and Germany during the crisis management of the 1970s, it is a question of

> managing a capitalist economy at an advanced technological level, while substantially defending the centrality of wages from the point of view of all redistributive policies. In Italy, the same term becomes [...] the acceptance as a whole of a type of development in which the elements of modernisation are pursued through the constant search for a marginalisation of the workers' movement, both in terms of distribution and political representation.[29]

For this reason, those countries characterised by a strong social democratic system of capital-labour parity are also capable of greater international trade integration, where higher import-export shares of GDP, however, are combined with a high rate of employment. The choice of high competitiveness, high employment, high wages means that their export capacity due to the parity-competitiveness mechanism is then combined with a high potential for demand for foreign goods, hence a stronger international trade integration. The latter, given the socio-economic and political regime (the structural habit of competing with high wages and full labour rights, and consequently with strong productivity and innovation), is therefore less feared.

Furthermore, Paggi and D'Angelillo point out, by means of two appropriate charts, that in the three countries being examined (with a strong social democratic imprint), a "non-dirigiste industrial policy" is actually adopted, as well as policies of strong "*quid pro quo* for trade unions and workers" in exchange for wage moderation. These *quid pro quo* mechanisms in fact determine "policies to support income, employment and welfare" together with "further legitimacy of Unions". In essence, Paggi and D'Angelillo confirm the underlying assumption: there is a mechanism at work that affects productivity, high wages and employment which, due to its strength, requires fewer dirigiste industrial policies. The diagram, then, which in the book by Paggi and D'Angelillo describes the Italian case (management of the crisis by the PCI) lists a "vicious circle" of policies that are inadequate for any further development of the Italian system, i.e., not apt to trigger a new balance between labour parity, reduction of labour exploitation and productivity. This also entails "attempts to delegitimize Unions and labour movement" aimed at getting rid of its conditioning force, the one Brodolini had previously taken on board as a stimulus and yardstick for his own government.[30]

Clearly, the same idea of the supremacy of the party over the trade union, in the years in which Berlinguer distanced himself/was removed from the government, also brought about a reverse swing: the abandonment of wage moderation imbued with "Einaudian" communist culture, while urging the return to a more radical line.

By contrast, social democracy – although, especially in the Nordic case, never excluding explicit or implicit conflict – is less subject to this fluctuation than the PCI. This occurs to a large extent because of double parity – on the one hand, between capital and labour and, on the other hand, between the party and its social and trade union establishment. Furthermore, the complete political expendability of the two parities allows for more constant pressure, which, in turn, produces a considerable average increase in the level of the compromise that can be reached and that has been reached. All this according to a mechanism *that is first about distinction,* i.e., between ideologies, represented interests, suggested solutions, between "programmatic beliefs", between liberal democratic forces and democratic socialism *and then about compromise*, i.e., between social democratic reform and market liberal option, and between capital and labour.

Conversely, grassroots labour in the hands of the PCI plays out as conditioning mainly on a political and superstructural level: (a) as looming antagonism when the PCI is removed from the government (thus in the season in which the era of national solidarity ends, caught in between the 1980 Fiat dispute and the 1985 wage escalator referendum, and on many other occasions); (b) to promise "wage moderation" (with certainly fewer protections than those in the hands of European Social Democracy) in exchange for its support to the government (which will be the case both in 1976–1978 and in 1993–1994).

The move from the opposition to government, i.e., the already-achieved government fitness of the PSI, in this context finds its action less effective as well.

In fact, what it achieves on the level of governmental and superstructural action, including planning and direct investment of the state in the economy, has less hold since this political "elevator" is not supported as elsewhere by a labour "floor" and by its parity with capital. The government action thus brings about a comparatively lesser structural transformation in the Italian economy.

The reason for this is identified by Roberto Schiattarella in an ideological attitude of the PCI (but partly also of the PSI), which is essentially pessimistic towards development opportunities of capitalism in general and of Italian capitalism in particular.[31] This attitude, in the case of the PCI, was due, among other things, to the long subjection of economic culture to an excessively "pessimistic" Marxist historicism (thereby inclining to accepting the given framework for compromise), or rather characterised by an interpretation of capitalism that was not inclined to take note of the major Italian economic development in its initial phase ("economic miracle") and its resilience in a later phase (after the 1970s). According to Schiattarella, the ideology of mistrust was due to the persistence of the paradigm according to which the Italian economy was still completely in the grip of monopoly capital, which stifled its development. However, there are differences between the two parties even when looked from this perspective.

An optimistic line will also emerge in the PSI, and this, far from being artless, believes in the possibility of finding resources in the Italian economy to allow for a different type of development thus endorsing a new wave of reforms. However, this optimistic trend is, in key areas of thought within the PSI, mixed with an urgency for immediate and very profound reforms, which, even in the midst of an economic miracle, is entrenched in a negative idea of the Italian economy. Riccardo Lombardi, during a conference on state shareholdings (Partecipazioni Statali) in 1960, deemed inconceivable "a Keynesian policy in a system that does not already have its own development mechanism and is particularly inconceivable in a society that has not already reached a high degree of industrialization". According to Lombardi, despite the record decade-long growth rate, our economy was still "highly underdeveloped".[32]

These are certainly typical considerations of a socialist ideology whose highly positive and useful aspect is that of aiming, unlike most Keynesian thought, not so much to restart the economy but to reform capitalism (rather than supporting the demand, to reshape the supply side, i.e., how and what to produce). However, a negative element does emerge if these statements are placed within the framework of Lombardi's political history. His judgement on the state of the economy tends to be particularly unfavourable since it reinforces the reasons supporting his well-known intransigence, or the refusal to eschew profound structural reforms unless ostensibly directed towards socialism. Prioritising structural reforms (e.g., in the case of the more leftist party PSIUP, of workers' control) to such an extent as to deem any other reform insignificant or even deceptive, thus constitutes the specific PSI "ideological pessimism", which differs from the communist one, but is certainly not inconsequential.[33] Furthermore, it is worth noting that this absolute priority also denies the importance of the expansion of demand, at least in the sense that, under certain conditions, supporting demand strengthens employment and therefore the parity ratio between capital and labour. This application of Keynesian policies, on the other hand, would fall within the scope of European socialist "programmatic beliefs", safe in the knowledge that, even through this application of expansive demand, important effects could be obtained in terms of capitalist reform. In other words, demand could be used to shape supply, or to reform the way in which capitalism generates production: in short, an objective shared by socialists.[34]

In any case, however, we wish to interpret this aspect of Lombardi's thought, in the PSI, with the centre-left, a tendency to trust reform strategies prevails over the "pessimistic" one, while in the PCI, even after the ground-breaking novelty of the "economic miracle", "the two lines [...] overlap, coexist without the need to clear the air". This overlap and this "mostly pessimistic attitude towards the state of the Italian economy" can be explained by "the relative isolation of the PCI in its role as opposition". Alongside the cultural problem, a problem of role and self-perception in the history of Italy is identified: that of a party which, due to its social prominence, would like to be called upon to play a role in the government to solve crises without probing its own identity. This requires a state of emergency or a crisis "that alone can create the conditions for the PCI to rise to power". It is on this basis that the PCI, at the onset of the 1970s, begins "the long march towards the institutions", but the overlap of the two lines and its unresolved identity is reflected in its action. "The result is ambivalent: on the ideological level one believes in the crisis of capitalism and one longs for a momentous transformation, on the concrete level the party is too accommodating and [...] proposes and accepts laws that would be considered moderate from even a social democratic stance".[35]

PSIUP: an unsuccessful alternative form of labour representation

The experience of the PSIUP (Italian Socialist Party of Proletarian Unity) is important mentioning in this context. Since politics knows no voids, it stood to reason that a part of the workers' movement sought a third possibility of representing labour with respect to the two consolidated solutions: reformism through coalitional/superstructural practice (PSI), or supremacy of the party over labour entrenchment for political legitimacy (PCI). The PSIUP path would have been to bring the question and the need for action based on "workers' control" to the fore. However, its electoral impact remained limited (never higher than 4.5%), although the "season of movements", i.e. the particularly powerful Italian convergence between the 1968 generation and the worker's movement (1969–1974 approximately) showed the project indeed was rooted in the Italian society and history of the time.[36]

As to the balance between organised labour and the political direction entrusted to the parties, the clearest discourse on the temporary and limited impact of the PSIUP came from Silvano Andriani. According to him, PSIUP, after becoming involved in the "Hot Autumn" clash,[37] had essentially dissolved due to the persistent tendency we have not to see the relationship between the strategy of advancing power in the factory and [...] the rising controlling powers of the general trends of social change. Hence our difficulty in establishing a consistent link between the strategy of growth of social counter-powers and our political initiative within the institutions, without being reduced to ineffectiveness or subjected in a subordinate way to the tactics of the PCI, only to complain about it later on.[38]

Andriani describes quite enlighteningly how the season of movements, even at its peak of vitality, had not consolidated into a more advanced representation system and connection between worker subjectivity and political synthesis. The trade union force, whether organised or as a movement, evidently did not really succeed in imposing itself on its party representatives, who continued to use it as the political cultures at their disposal best suggested. The solution of the De Martino-Brodolini group (welcoming the social "thrusts" within the executive power) had in part notably obviated this lack, reaching its peak of success precisely at the time of the great movements of 1968–1970. Something therefore happened, but not everything was permanently resolved.

Missing parity and its structural aftermath

We have outlined some of the reasons why, according to a comparative approach (with the European Social Democratic Left) and economic history (definition of the elements rendering European socio-economic models more progressive), Italian socialist cultures tend towards strategies in which radical finalism and superstructural manoeuvre coexist and combine without leading to real hegemony.

The failure by these cultures to provide a strategy to systematically and completely lead the country out of its newcomer nature (which would also have required completing the "wage floor", for example, with more solid unemployment benefits – less discretionary than the CIG and more endowed with greater power of income substitution – or real *Mitbestimmung* institutions rather than forms of uncertain and movement-driven industrial democracy) have then probably caused it to swing in the opposite direction with an "extinction at the centre". Hence, the progressive pullback from 1980 onwards of the PSI and, from 1992 onwards, of the PCI and its successors[39] into a coalition manoeuver, while ensuring a considerably non-critical reliance on European precepts. On balance, the ideological and organisational structure of the Italian Historical Left produced a huge oscillation between (few) flare-ups of demands and (prolonged and very deep) compressions of rights and wages.

In terms of a reform agenda, that structure achieves an expansion of its more valuable work sectors lower than potentially possible, due to the absence of a consequent strategy of welfare-parity-inclusive floor combined with public initiative. Thus, the modernising and reforming thrust of socialist politics remains less hegemonic than necessary, while marginality and informality in the labour market remain larger than planned and hoped. In short, emancipation from the latecomer identity is never fully achieved.

This confirms a quadri-partition of society and the national labour market as identified by Massimo Paci in 1982.[40] Indeed, according to Paci, there is coexistence – and at least partial collaboration – in an area called "Centrality" between a guaranteed manufacturing sector and a very large peripheral manufacturing sector, which Paci calls intra-sector dualism. The quadri-partition consists of (1) a marginal and informal part, which, however, is connected with the "guaranteed" part (2) and allows it to be competitive by assuring it margins of low production cost even through informal work or informal supply. There is also a socio-economic zone in which there is a relatively productive state-owned or semi-public sector (3) together with an assisted marginal sector. (4) Sapelli,[41] too, allows us to see how the scheme developed by Paci affects the Italian economy and labour market. In the 1991–2005 period, wage work fell, percentage-wise, much more in Italy than elsewhere. In Germany, it went from 90.5% to 87.7%, with self-employment increasing from 8.1% to 11.2%. In Sweden in the same period, traditional wage labour fell from 92.1 to 90.2%. In Italy – it should be noted the starting point was already lower and as such showed a greater degree of pulverised workforce than elsewhere – wage labour decreased from 71.2 to 55%. Furthermore, Italy was the only country with 25.9% of "unclassified", or presumably "sham" self-employment. On balance, the share of illicit work, i.e., the originally higher degree of marginality, increased.

Even with regard to the salary and wages, which have suffered everywhere, Italy shows a more negative dynamic trend. Taking 1990 as a point of reference, the actual income of a salaried employee in Italy in 2012 shows an overall *decrease* of 2.9%, while the average figure for the Eurozone is an increase of 14.2%, while that of Germany is slightly lower at 13.7%, despite the fact that the German economy tends to compress wage potential substantially. In short, the economies of the Eurozone have allowed the income from employment to grow in real terms in the past 22 years, albeit below the level of potential inherent in the wealth produced, while even this poor European result has failed to occur in Italy. Even excluding 1990–1994, when Italian wages were held back by the elimination of wages indexation and the new industrial relations model, the growth in the purchasing power of wages was, in Italy, always lower than that of the Eurozone and often even in comparison to the German one, despite the fact that the latter was significantly cut back between 2004 and 2008.

In contrast, Italian prices, according to Eurostat grew by 94% between 1990 and 2012, while in Germany by 52%, and by 69% in the Eurozone average. A commodity that in 1990 cost more or less the same in Italy and in other Euro countries, in 2012, it cost over 40% more than in Germany and 25% more than in the Eurozone.[42]

Conclusion

The "wage floor" of the Italian labour market, for structural reasons the culture of the PSI (but also of the PCI and the PSIUP) was unable to change, did not have a deep or definitive impact. It is partly because of this reason that the "dirigiste" type of reform and innovative investment approach, while relevant and necessary given the historical characteristics of the Italian economy, was less penetrating than it could have in its rising phase, and in any case yielded to neoliberal hegemony in its descending phase. With the shift towards neoliberal hegemony around 1980, the intensity in labour exploitation advanced by leaps and bounds, damaging innovative competitiveness. This, of course, was also due to a number of other reasons, including the fact that European rules penalised Italian-style public intervention more than other methods of innovation. Italy was therefore a victim, like others less immediately compatible with the Ordoliberal ideology, of deficiencies of European unification and especially of the Eurozone government. To be sure, the characteristics of the political, ideological and economic culture of the Italian left did play a part in it, as they were unable to create solutions in the way the social democracy of the type described above could, i.e., deeply rooted, parity driven in various directions and proactive (as against being merely defensive). This political culture was thus unable to determine a virtuous circle that would include high-wages-long-term innovation systems of co-management-welfare state and that (in hegemonically favourable times) would therefore help to further reform capitalism. For the very same reason – and in hegemonically unfavourable times – the socio-economic and democratic decline a capitalist system can tend towards was particularly evident and left an indelible mark in Italy.

Notes

1 Per H. Jensen, "Grundlæggelse af det danske arbejdsløshedsforiskringssystem i komparativ belysning", in *Arbejdsforsikringsloven 1907–2007*, edited by Jesper Hartvig Pedersen and Aage Huulgaard (København: Arbejdsdirektoratet, 2007), 33–67.
2 Giuliano Procacci, *La lotta di classe in Italia agli inizi del secolo XX* (Roma: Editori Riuniti, 1978), 64–68; 97–100.
3 Kautsky, like Bernstein, differs from anarchist and unionist (later Leninist) antagonism: democracy for the labour movement is: "un terrain de culture aussi indispensable que l'est le mode de production capitaliste". Cited in Alain Bergounioux and Bernard Manin, *La socialdemocratie. Ou le Compromis* (Paris: PUF, 1979), 86–88.
4 C. S. Allen, "Ordo-Liberalism Trumps Keynesianism: Economic Policy in the Federal Republic of Germany and the EU", in *Monetary Union in Crisis. The European Union as a Neo-Liberal Construction*, edited by Bernard H. Moss (Basingstoke: Palgrave McMillan, 2005); Sebastian Dullien and Ulrike Guerot, *The Long Shadow of Ordoliberalism: Germany's Approach to the Euro Crisis*, ECFR/49, February 2012.
5 On this balance throughout German history, Allen writes: "Both Bismarck and the 'fathers' of the Social Market Economy, Adenauer and Erhard, realized that such social dislocation required protective social policies. These leaders did not offer such policies altruistically, rather, they were preventive policies aimed pragmatically at minimizing social tension and political opposition while the economy grew. Bismarck's creation of the first social insurance schemes (while simultaneously banning [...] SPD) was one mechanism. Another was the less draconian implementation of the Social Market Economy [...] the postwar welfare state in Germany's first stable democracy". C. S. Allen, "Ideas, Institutions and Organized Capitalism: The German Model of Political Economy 20 Years after Unification". Paper in International Affairs, University of Georgia. *German Politics and Society* 28, no. 4, 199–221, 2011.

6 Allen, "Ordo-Liberalism Trumps Keynesianism". Social spending doubles by reallocating the resources ensured by the post-war miracle (it is no coincidence that the Spd reaches its voting majority: 45% in 1972): G. Bingham Powell, Russel J. Dalton, and Kaare Strøm, *Comparative Politics Today* (New York: Pearson Longman, 2012), 250–251.
7 Rebecca Page, *Co-determination in Germany – A Beginner's Guide* (Berlin: HansBöckler Stiftung, 2011, Arbeitspapier 33), 22–23.
8 Through the Hartz IV and the threat of relocating to newly acceded EU states L. Tronti, Perché la Germania è diventata super, "Eguaglianza&Libertà", www.eguaglianzaeliberta.it.
9 Colin Crouch, *Making Capitalism Fit for Society* (Cambridge: Polity Press, 2013), 107, 112.
10 Paolo Borioni and Niels Finn Christiansen, *Danimarca* (Milano: Unicopli, 2015), 73–95.
11 Bo Stråth, "Sweden", in *The Organisation of Labour Markets*, edited by Bo Stråth (London: Routledge, 1996).
12 Paolo Borioni and Salvo Leonardi, "Modelli di partecipazione a confronto: Germania e Svezia", in *La partecipazione incisiva*, edited by Mimmo Carrieri, Paolo Nerozzi, and Tiziano Treu (Bologna: Mulino, 2015).
13 Carmine Pinto, *Il riformismo possibile* (Soveria Mannelli: Rubettino, 2008), 39–40.
14 Lucio Baccaro and Massimo D'Antoni, "Has the "External Constraint" Contributed to Italy's Stagnation? A Critical Event Analysis", *MPIfG Discussion Paper* 20/9, 2020, noted the following about IRI, the renowned (now privatised and downsized) Italian state concern: "In 1982, the year of its maximum size […] operated in 40 per cent of sectors and directly produced 3.6 per cent of Italy's GDP (5 per cent including indirect linkages). Furthermore, it exported more than 20 per cent of its production, double the figure of private enterprises in the same sectors […] IRI companies were more capital intensive than private companies, more likely to be present in high-tech sectors – such as telecommunications, electronics, informatics, robotics, aeronautics, and electronics – invested more in R&D, and had higher labour productivity levels and productivity growth". Adding that: "The common image of state-owned enterprises as economic basket cases is misplaced".
15 Giovanni Scirocco, *Politique d'Abord* (Milano: Unicopli, 2010), 189–90. This excerpt comes from Riccardo Lombardi, "Dopo il rapporto Krusciov. Rivalutazione della politica", *Il Mondo*, 7 August 1956.
16 Pierre Rosanvallon, "Introduction", in Michel Rocard et al (eds.) *Qu'est-ce que la social-democratie?* (Paris: Seuil, 1979), 7–8.
17 Enzo Bartocci, "I riformismi del Psi nella stagione del centro-sinistra (1957–1968)", in *I riformismi socialisti al tempo del Centro-Sinistra*, edited by Enzo Bartocci (Roma: Viella, 2019).
18 Riccardo Lombardi, *Dopo il rapporto Krusciov*, cited in Giovanni Scirocco, "Lombardi, la politica internazionale e la guerra fredda (1948–1957)", in *Lombardi 2013, riforme di struttura e alternativa socialista*, edited by Enzo Bartocci (Roma: Fondazione Giacomo Brodolini, 2013).
19 Gianluca Scroccu, "Lombardi e Giolitti: le riforme di struttura, l'alternativa e il socialismo possibile", in *Lombardi 2013, riforme di struttura e alternativa socialista*, edited by Enzo Bartocci (Roma: Fondazione Giacomo Brodolini, 2013).
20 Manin Carabba, *Un ventennio di programmazione 1954/1974* (Roma-Bari: Laterza, 1977).
21 Antonio Giolitti, *Lettere a Marta* (Mulino: Bologna, 1992), 195–96.
22 This expression indicates an area in which programme, historical achievements and political claims coincide with political identity and ideology. Eric Shaw, *Losing Labour's Soul?* (New York: Routledge, 2007).

23 Enzo Bartocci, "Il sogno dell'alternativa socialista", in *Lombardi 2013, riforme di struttura e alternativa socialista*, edited by Enzo Bartocci (Roma: Fondazione Giacomo Brodolini, 2013).
24 Riccardo Lombardi, "Riforme e rivoluzione dopo la seconda guerra mondiale", in *Riforme e rivoluzione nella storia contemporanea*, edited by Guido Quazza (Torino: Einaudi, 1976), 321–323.
25 Enzo Bartocci, "Francesco De Martino e Giacomo Brodolini: continuità evoluzione e declino del riformismo socialista (1960–1969)", in *Francesco De Martino e il suo tempo una stagione del socialismo*, edited by Enzo Bartocci (Rome: Fondazione Giacomo Brodolini, 2009).
26 Paolo Borioni, "De Martino, la socialdemocrazia, il riformismo", in *Francesco De Martino e il suo tempo una stagione del socialismo*, a cura di Enzo Bartocci (Roma: Fondazione Giacomo Brodolini, 2009).
27 About Luigi Einaudi and his free-market liberalism, see also above. For this wing of PCI, the communist Party had to educate the masses to accept the realities of free market as given in the Italian context. This led to a particularly pessimistic view concerning Italian economy in the late 1970s: any progress towards socialism had to realistically taken place within this framework. Especially PCI had to show its fitness for the government by convincing workers that more power and impact could be achieved if they accepted to share the burden of economic crisis with the always ruling Christian Democrats and the employers.
28 Leonardo Paggi and Massimo D'Angelillo, *I comunisti italiani e il riformismo* (Torino: Einaudi, 1986), 11–12, 24 footnotes 12 e 13.
29 *Ibidem*, 55–56.
30 *Ibidem*, 48–49.
31 Roberto Schiattarella, "La sinistra e l'economia italiana", *Democrazia e diritto* 1 (2008): 46–48.
32 In Guglielmo Ragozzino, *Lombardi e la nazionalizzazione dell'industria elettrica*, in Bartocci, *Lombardi 2013*, p. 104.
33 Lombardi, *Riforme e rivoluzione*, 234, claims no major reforms were adopted during the centre-left governments.
34 The link between demand policy, high employment rate and strength of organised workers is essential, see M. Kalecki, *Political Aspects of Full Employment*, which can be found at https://onlinelibrary.wiley.com/doi/abs/10.1111/j.1467-923X.1943.tb01016.x
35 F. Carmignani, "Pci, sinistra e mercato del lavoro: note dal passato", *Democrazia e diritto* 1 (2008): 163.
36 According to Agosti, PSIUP had to "bring new waters into the river then called 'the labour movement' and to question its relationship with its historical referent, 'the working class'", Aldo Agosti, *Il partito provvisorio* (Roma-Bari: Laterza, 2013), 285; Marica Tolomelli, *L'Italia dei movimenti* (Roma: Carocci, 2015).
37 In autumn 1969, a particularly pronounced class struggle started and continued, with varying intensity, several years.
38 Agosti, *Il partito*, 237.
39 With a much faster retreat in the latter case.
40 Massimo Paci, *La struttura sociale italiana* (Bologna: Mulino, 1982), 40–46, 237.
41 Giulio Sapelli, *Storia economica dell'Italia contemporanea* (Milano: Bruno Mondadori, 1997–2008), 220.
42 P. Borioni and L. Tronti, "Patto trilaterale per rilanciare il sistema economico", *l'Unità* 6, no. 5 (2014): 7.

7 Cultural affinity and small-state solidarity

Sweden and Global North–South relations in the 1970s[1]

Andreas Mørkved Hellenes and Carl Marklund

The Nordic social democratic parties and labour movements have since long promoted international humanitarianism and global solidarity. While certainly not unique among European social democratic parties in doing so, the political impact of Nordic social democracy domestically during the Cold War has also resulted in a continuous "Nordic" commitment to various humanitarian causes in the context of the decolonisation of the Global South, ranging from development collaboration, emergency assistance, peacekeeping, conflict management, poverty reduction, human rights and national liberation as well as – more recently – support for refugees, gender equality, sustainability and transparency. As this commitment has over the past decade come under pressure from internal/external critics, shifts in ideals as well as resource crunch, historians and political scientists have recently begun to take a greater interest in the practices and discourses of Nordic North–South relations, often concentrating upon either development assistance, humanitarian aid, or economic contacts, in what amounts to a modest turn towards "Nordic global history".[2]

While most of these studies address specific cases of outreach, there is also a more longstanding scholarly debate on the reasons why these minor powers – especially Norway and Sweden and to a lesser degree Denmark, Finland and Iceland – have committed support to the material and political development of what was then known as the "Third World", despite their comparatively limited contacts, experiences, interests and resources available for outreach to the Global South. Explanations have typically wavered between altruism/idealism and egotism/realism, either interpreting this Nordic internationalism as a reflection of the humanitarianism and solidarity of the national welfare state,[3] or as the international reflection of domestic/national political and economic priorities, or a pragmatic combination thereof.[4] In the peculiar security constellation of Cold War "Nordic balance", with three NATO members and two neutrals, Global North–South issues represented risks to the sensitive East-West balance in the north, but also presented an opportunity to offset or even displace East-West tension, which the so-called like-minded countries were to address during the 1970s.[5]

These debates and subsequent scholarship can be traced in all Nordic countries, due to the centrality of development aid and norm entrepreneurship in

DOI: 10.4324/9781003181439-8

Nordic political culture and nation branding. The issue has been highly politicised at least in the Swedish case, where much needed basic research is still in the process of being produced. Arguably, the puzzle is complex, as the Nordic countries have been deeply integrated into the wider Western regime vis-à-vis the emerging Global South, a relationship which is increasingly receiving critical scholarly attention and which mostly focuses upon Nordic development aid, humanitarian action and, eventually, norm entrepreneurship. In this chapter, we analyse how Sweden responded to the rise of the Global South and the call for a New International Economic Order (NIEO) – far-ranging negotiations for a more equitable and fair exchange of resources and technology between North and South, launched at the United Nations General Assembly in November 1974 – in two different spheres: public diplomacy and knowledge production.

The chapter is divided into two parts. The first part studies how the Swedish Institute, a public foundation charged with producing and disseminating information about Sweden overseas, sought to establish new interfaces and contacts through cultural outreach towards key audiences in the decolonising Global South. To some extent, these efforts were low key and followed simply the trajectory of traditional "Sweden information" disseminated in world languages such as English and French in other parts of the world. Gradually, however, a more programmatic theme can be detected in these outreach efforts, seeking to establish and confirm a cultural affinity between Sweden and selected Third-World countries. This tendency seeks its origins in the increasingly ambitious cultural policy and focuses on exchange from the late 1960s and onwards. Cultural affinity, for all of its vagueness, proved a flexible notion, which sometimes implied shared past and future experiences in moving "from poverty to affluence", as exemplified in material cultural production more generally. The second part studies how the prospect of NIEO and its impact upon Sweden's role in future North–South relations were processed in a key Swedish knowledge production institution, the Secretariat for Future Studies. A key theme in these debates is the notion of small-state solidarity, an imperative which requires Sweden – as well as possibly other minor or middle powers in the Global North – to solidarise itself with the needs and demands of the structurally and economically disadvantaged nations of the Global South in not only overcoming global poverty and inequality but also addressing environmental degradation, global development and bipolar East–West rivalry.

Swedish cultural affinity with the Third World?

Amidst growing tension between the leading Western power and the increasingly assertive, if highly diverse Global South, internationally oriented Swedish social democrats, such as the radical circle of young diplomats around incoming Prime Minister Olof Palme,[6] identified a need for Sweden to pave its own way into Western European and North American North–South diplomacy.[7] Both the messages of small-state solidarity and of cultural affinity were central elements of Sweden's communication overtures directed at the Third World publics in the 1970s. For example, in a special issue produced by the *tiers-mondiste* monthly *Afrique Asie* and the Swedish MFA entitled "La Suède et le tiers-monde", Palme emphasised the importance of solidarity between small states in working towards shared international interests.[8] In the same publication, the Swedish prime minister identified an *affinité historique*, a historical affinity between the Nordic social democracy and the new nations of the Third World: Sweden had also been a poor, underdeveloped land of peasants.[9] Such ideas, together with non-alignment and democratic socialism, formed a rhetoric which placed Sweden in a natural league together with developing countries, working against the bipolar order of the Cold War. In the following, the message of the Swedish-Third World affinity will be studied through the case of the travelling exhibition *De la pauvreté au bien-être* (*From poverty to welfare*), which represented a tool for pilot projects of cultural and political outreach deployed in Tunisia and the Democratic Republic of Vietnam – two countries where Sweden for various reasons enjoyed a good reputation – in 1975 and 1976, respectively. First, however, it is necessary to briefly outline the broader development of Swedish public diplomacy in the 1970s.

The early 1970s saw an organisational transformation of Swedish public diplomacy which had a clear impact on the nature of its outreach. The Swedish Institute, which had been established in 1945 as a private-public organisation whose funding originally depended on its usefulness for strengthening Swedish exports, became in 1970 a public foundation fully funded by the MFA.[10] Reflecting this turn away from the 1960s visions of uniting various kinds of Sweden information abroad to splitting it up into different sectors, the responsibility of promoting Swedish business and exports through commercial information was given to the new Swedish Trade Council. These shifts ushered in a new paradigm in the activities of the Swedish Institute, centring on the concept of cultural exchange, whose importance had been established by the UNESCO from the mid-1960s, and on the cultural sphere as separated from the economy – mirroring the ongoing reconceptualisation of (social democratic) cultural policy in Sweden.[11] In its Swedish interpretation, thus, cultural and experiential exchange (*kultur- och erfarenhetsutbyte*) and the ideal of reciprocity was placed centre-stage in the country's international cultural relations.

The increased role of the state and organisational separation between cultural exchange and export promotion within Swedish public diplomacy ran parallel with Sweden's first organised efforts at systematic cultural outreach towards the Global South. Historian Andreas Åkerlund has shown how Swedish academic internationalisation and the Swedish Institute's exchange and scholarship programmes in this period became re-conceptualised as "an aspect of international solidarity", as special grants were created for the Third World students to study at Swedish universities.[12] More generally, the Third World publics represented a new audience for the Swedish Institute – publics which were considered to have predominantly sympathetic attitudes towards Sweden. For a Swedish industry exhibition in Beijing in 1972, for example, ten tons of printed materials with general information about Sweden were shipped to China for distribution.[13] Moreover, cultural exchange was an area of activity that partly lay outside of the field of development aid, which was oriented towards themes chosen to a large extent by the recipient countries. *Kulturellt bistånd* (cultural development aid) thus came to be interpreted as sorting under the Swedish Institute, rather than SIDA.[14]

In 1972, the Swedish Institute thus launched a pilot project, the Africa project, with the ambition to widen the scope of its activities to African countries.[15] While the first efforts were directed at Léopold Sedar Senghor's Senegal, they were soon followed by more comprehensive projects in Tunisia, a country with which Sweden enjoyed longer and deeper bilateral relations. Importantly, in the perspective of the Swedish Institute, Tunisian public cultural policy made a more varied and widely disseminated cultural outreach possible, including outside of the elite circles of the capital, by making use of the French-inspired cultural infrastructure. The new, decentralised *maisons du peuple*, cultural centres, offered possibilities both for public talks, debates, movie screenings and travelling exhibitions.[16] Furthermore, the cultural exchange put in place with Tunisia would include a scientific component, with Swedish archaeologists participating in the large-scale, UNESCO-supported project of excavating old Carthage.[17]

The main tool for informing foreign publics about Sweden, not only in the Africa project's manifestations but also more generally, was travelling exhibitions. This was far from unique to the Swedish case – exhibitions emerged as a prominent genre within cultural diplomacy in the era of détente – used by countries belonging to both great power blocs – and with them museums rose to a position of brokers of foreign relations: "The core premise of these exhibitions' cultural diplomatic missions was that the objects within them would serve as ambassadors, embodiments of political identities, on one hand, and bridges across these entrenchments, on the other", according to exhibition historian Alice Goff.[18]

At the centre of the first Swedish manifestations in Tunisia in 1975 was an exhibition titled *De la pauvreté au bien-être* (From poverty to welfare). It was an abridged, international version of Nordiska museet's 1973 centennial exhibition *Svenskens 100 år – känn dig själv* (The Swede's 100 years – know thyself), which in its English language version bore the title *And So They Became Welfare Swedes...* . The theme was explored in detail in an ambitious publication produced for the Swedish Institute concomitantly, namely the anthology *Sweden's Development from Poverty to Affluence, 1750–1970*, edited by historian Steven Koblik.[19] The volume comprised articles by some 13 leading Swedish historians and social scientists, all of them introduced by Koblik: it was a work that also had explicit scientific ambitions, namely to bring out the analysis of Sweden's development trajectory as an alternative history of modernisation from those of the great powers. In *De la pauvreté au bien-être*, Sweden's national development trajectory was visualised through a historical narrative that followed five generations of a Swedish family from 1870 to 1970, which focused on five dates at 30 year intervals. It stated that Sweden's current welfare state was founded in long unbroken peace, natural resources, stable economic expansion, good commercial relations, and, in particular, numerous social reforms: "The evolution of Sweden during the last hundred years is the history of the transformation of a poor, agricultural country to a highly industrialised welfare society", as the exhibition catalogue spelt out.[20] In Tunisia, the exhibition was displayed in both Kairouan and Sfax, along with the capital Tunis.

The notion of cultural affinity, present also in other examples of outreach in the period, was highly present in the accompanying cultural manifestations that took place in Tunisia in 1974–1975. The exhibition *Images du Nord* in Dakar in 1973, for example, had made a point out of the communalities between Swedish contemporary modernism and African art. Along similar lines, smaller exhibitions about naivist art and the conditions of the indigenous Sami population were considered particularly suited for Tunisian publics, respectively due to the French cultural influence and the presence of Nomadic cultures in the North African country. Be that as it may, in the evaluation report of the Tunisian project made by the head of the Swedish Institute's exhibition division, *De la pauvreté au bien-être* was singled out as by far most successful of the Swedish manifestations in attracting the attention of the visiting Tunisian publics – mostly male students – not least due to its depiction of how Sweden had overcome problems along the way to creating a better society.[21] The "non-boastful" presentation of Sweden's way to welfare and industrial modernity proved useful in "a partly developed, but still underdeveloped country" like Tunisia, where the perceived hunger for information about Sweden inspired continued activities in the future.[22]

While the Tunisian project could take place in a country where bilateral relations were comparatively well-developed, the exhibition's ensuing destination, the Democratic Republic of Vietnam represented an altogether different and highly political case. The year 1973 represented a watershed year for publicity about Swedish positions on Third-World developments in international press. This was to a large extent a result of Palme's so-called Christmas Eve Declaration, where he condemned in unusually strong words the American Operation Linebacker II.[23] The echoes resounded in the press, for example, in an approving editorial of *Le Monde*,[24] and a three-page exclusive interview in *Le Nouvel Observateur* in its first issue of the year carried the title "Being neutral does not mean staying silent", a phrase used with slight modifications in many interviews to resume Palme's definition of Swedish active neutrality.[25] In a letter to the Vietnamese Prime Minister Pham Van Dong, Palme wrote that he hoped, "without exaggerating its importance", that his own and the Swedish people's protests could influence the global public opinion against the war.[26] Indeed, in the interview too, Palme claimed to have spoken on behalf of all of Sweden, but not only that, other countries had followed by using more discreet and diplomatic channels, and together this represented the protests of the international opinion against the terror balance of the great powers. The same day that the interview with *Le Nouvel Observateur* was printed, Simon Malley wrote an editorial in *Afrique Asie* where he paraphrased Palme's declaration.[27] And *Jeune Afrique* noticed that not only Palme, but also the Swedish people, through a petition signed by a million Swedes, took position against the United States.[28]

While this thus contributed to raising Sweden's standing around the Third World, it also gave more specific opportunities for outreach in North Vietnam.

Sweden had in 1969 been the first Western country to recognise North Vietnam, and established an embassy there, with the Social Democratic diplomat Jean-Christophe Öberg as its first ambassador.[29] When the Swedish Institute soon after evaluated the future possibilities of cultural exchange with North Vietnam, the goodwill that the country's criticism against the United States had created led to the conclusion that "Sweden and the Swedes" had now "a special position before all other countries including the socialist states" – a position that warranted information about Swedish society.[30] Moreover, Sweden was in the lucky position of being a "people with which one feels great sympathy but never has seen!" The position was considered all the more interesting for this reason, as an opportunity for *tabula rasa* public diplomacy; it was literally the first time Sweden information could be the first information about Sweden to a receiving public. In Hanoi, *De la pauvreté au bien-être* was displayed in exhibition rooms located on one of the capital's main streets, and accompanied with an exhibition that portrayed Swedish-Vietnamese friendship, both on people-to-people level and through the main political leaders.[31] According to the Swedish Embassy's enthusiastic report, the exhibition was visited by more people than usual (ca 12,000 in ten days), and an enquête revealed that visitors had particularly appreciated the historical perspective on Sweden's evolution.[32]

Both in North Vietnam and Tunisia, the Swedes acknowledged that the French cultural hegemony could hardly be challenged, but that there was a window of opportunity for a Western country that was neither a former colonial power nor part of the two superpower blocs both in Indochina and the Maghreb. Although it was the French version of the exhibition that was placed centre-stage in the manifestations both in Tunisia and in North Vietnam, its texts were in both instances translated to the vernacular to communicate more directly with the non-elite and non-Francophone members of the audience.

Notwithstanding the fact that the exhibition's historical narrative was identical to that referred to in later Swedish historiography as the "Social Democratic narrative of Swedish modernity", a map of its deployment also offers an interesting perspective on Swedish public diplomacy outreach in the mid-1970s.[33] The exhibition was used in quite different ways in Western Europe and the Third World – as well as between countries – illustrating the differentiation of Swedish outreach in the 1970s. It is illuminating in this respect to follow the tracks of the French version of the exhibition on its *tour* in 1975–1976. Starting at the Centre culturel suédois in Paris, where it accompanied a high-level seminar on labour relations in France and Sweden and was closed with an open debate on the topic "Sweden: a paradise lost?" it continued to Marseilles by lorry and crossed the Mediterranean by boat. From Tunisia, it was shipped back to France, and flown via Sweden to Hanoi. Following this oriental adventure, the exhibition returned to France, destined for display in several provincial cities. At this point, in September 1976, a minor diplomatic controversy erupted, as the Socialist mayor of Draguignan impromptu cancelled the exhibition – which was to be inaugurated by the Swedish ambassador – as a direct result of the parliamentary elections that ended Social Democratic rule for the first time since 1936.[34] No longer representing a kindred regime in the North, Sweden's historical trajectory suddenly seemed less appealing to "the ancient despotic Socialist", as the Cultural Centre's director Pontus Grate called him, noting that he "obviously only intended to use *The Welfare Swedes* as a weapon in his own electoral propaganda".[35]

While the exhibition in France was an example of a (relatively) parallel trajectory of welfare state construction, it became in Third-World outreach a model for how to successfully develop from a poor agricultural nation to successful industrial modernity. Put differently, the exhibition and its theme of modernisation from poverty to welfare served in Western Europe as a historical exhibition, outlining how Sweden represented an alternative, yet also similar, way to industrial modernity and a position where Swedish society struggled to overcome challenges shared by all modern industrial countries. As such, it informed contemporary discussions about the so-called Swedish model – frequently contested by the Swedes themselves – and its potential for exportability. At the same time, the exhibition, similar to Koblik's book, sought to counter anti-Swedish writings such as Roland Huntford's *The New Totalitarians*, published in English in 1971, German in 1973 and French in 1975.

Conversely, in the Third World, the exhibition functioned by means of analogy. If Sweden had successfully transformed from underdevelopment and poverty to affluence and welfare as a result of "in particular, social reforms", then this was an alternative model of modernity to those offered by the great powers. While Swedish public diplomacy in Western Europe struggled hard to counter exaggerated claims of Swedish exemplarity, it was precisely the contrary strategy that was deployed in the Third World through the notion of cultural affinity.

Swedish small-state solidarity on the world market?

While the exhibition certainly was a typical expression of cultural diplomacy, it also played directly into the intricate connection between *cultural* life and *socioeconomic* order at the critical centre of the global cultural Cold War and debates on alternate paths towards development and modernity.[36] As classic modernisation theory increasingly came under criticism for ignoring the structuring of the world market into centres and peripheries and for misjudging the possibilities for the developing countries in following the path towards modernity already paved by developed countries, the juxtaposition of Swedish culture and political economy took on a new meaning in the context of the rising Global South. With the multifaceted demands as posed by the Afro-Asian bloc at successive UN summits on the environment, food and population, culminating in the calls for NIEO at the UN General Assembly in May 1974, the future relation between North and South emerged as a top preoccupation during the next decade. The United States took a critical view of the relation between European – especially British – social democracy and the NIEO,[37] devising a long-term strategy focused on human rights based on the individual as a counter-weight to the economic rights of states as promoted under the NIEO.[38]

Cultural affinity 131

In the Swedish social democrats' North–South diplomacy, long-term knowledge production with a view of the future would be central: in response to the global shifts caused by the rise of the Third World and especially the dramatic consequences of the oil crisis, four projects were initiated at the newly formed Secretariat for Future Studies in 1975. These projects were "Energy and Society", "Resources and Raw Materials", "Working Life in the Future" and "Sweden in the World Society". The same year, in recognition of the domestic and international importance of its work, the Board of the Secretariat was given parliamentary representation, international expert groups were invited, and a reference group of Swedish governmental agencies was formed.[39]

The futures study "Sweden in the World Society" was to analyse "the ways in which the international system may evolve over the coming years" as well as "to determine to what extent Sweden and the Swedes will be able to shape their own future and to realise their own values and goals" as stated in the eponymous final report.[40]

The latter offered a meta-analysis of Palme's take on Swedish active foreign policy which was presented as an explicit "small-state doctrine".[41] According to this analysis, the balance of terror resulted in overall East-West détente which could be viewed as positive. Palme, however, had according to the authors identified the risk of a superpower "duopoly", controlling the affairs of the "small states" across the world, thus infringing upon national sovereignty, violating national liberation and stalling development. Here, there was a community of interest between all small countries – rich or poor, Northern or Southern – in acting in concert against great power dictatorship of global affairs.[42] Obviously, not all the countries in the Global South supporting the NIEO agenda could be classified as "small states" – Algeria, Brazil and Iran were among its more prominent protagonists. Yet, most of the members of the Group of 77 at the time had small populations and low GDP, lending credence to the discourse of a North–South small-state solidarity.

To Swedish social democrats, however, it was also obvious that the economic rise of the Global South – whether by NIEO or any other process – would in fact pose serious problems to Western European economies as embedded in the lopsided world market, and hence also to Sweden. The challenge would lie in turning the eventual risks into future opportunities: in a speech in Piteå in August 1974 – often considered as the public launch of the Swedish small-state doctrine – Palme solved the conundrum by presenting the NIEO agenda as precisely an example of such small-state solidarity – a community of interest between non-aligned and neutral countries, North and South – while urging his audiences to consider the reach of such solidarity.[43] During the autumn of 1974, the interconnection between the small-state doctrine and the NIEO agenda was further underscored by Palme during his travels to the Netherlands, Canada and – most symbolically – his November 1974 visit to Algeria's leader Houari Boumediene, Secretary General of the NAM and a prominent exponent for the NIEO agenda.[44] Francophone Third World Press hailed Stockholm as the capital of solidarity, in reference to Palme's and Sweden's contributions to the Stockholm conference in

1972, and Algiers as the capital of non-alignment, in recognition of Boumediene's and Algeria's efforts vis-à-vis the NIEO. Subsequently, Swedish support of the NIEO agenda was officially pronounced in the Statement of Government Policy in the Parliamentary Debate on Foreign Affairs in 1975.[45]

Confirming the centrality of this commitment on the part of Swedish social democracy, an entry on the NIEO was also included in the new Party Program of the Swedish Social Democratic Party (SAP), adopted at the Party Congress in September 1975.[46] The question of fusing economic and ecological concerns paralleled the issue of aligning Swedish domestic and international policies, as underscored by Palme speaking at the UN General Assembly in November 1975.[47]

Aside from these diplomatic initiatives, also more pragmatic forms of global outreach were extended to the Global South from Sweden during this time, especially in the shape of export credits, educational exchanges, technology transfers and development aid, which reached the Swedish government's target of allocating one-per cent of GDP to development aid in 1975.[48] In the elections of 1976, the SAP lost to a centre-right coalition led by the Centre Party, which nevertheless tended to follow Palme's line, if somewhat less articulated, indicating the centrality of the small-state doctrine at the time.[49] As the negotiations on NIEO continued inconclusively at the CIEC and within UNCTAD, a steady flow of motions and interpellations in Parliament – as well as exchanges between Minister of Foreign Affairs Karin Söder and Olof Palme, in opposition but fundamentally agreed on NIEO – vouch for the continued relevance of North–South dialogue as an important reference object in Swedish political debate.[50] While both the Centre Party and the People's Party included references to the NIEO in their new party programmes in 1979 and 1982,[51] respectively, it is unlikely that these centre-right parties would have accepted the prospect of the NIEO if not for the widespread identification between Sweden and the Third World as evidenced in not only social democratic political discourse, but also in development aid information efforts which both reflected and promoted a strong interest in the Third World issues and support for development aid in Swedish public debate at the time.[52]

By 1977, the pressures of oil crisis and the rise of the Third World in the shape of OPEC, NIEO as well as the emergence of the Newly Industrialized Countries (NICs), combined with post-materialism, recession and stagflation in the West, continued to add renewed urgency to the matters under study in the "Sweden in the World Society" futurology project. In recognition of this fact, as well as the explicit support of the NIEO as voiced by successive Swedish governments, the Secretariat for Future Studies launched a three-year project on "Sweden in a New International Economic Order" to provide "a review of the demands and proposals put forward by the developing countries and of international future studies with a similar focus" as well as "a discussion of the effects of the New International Economic Order on Sweden and the demands which such an order can make on Swedish policy".[53]

Noting that an active foreign policy and "a concerted policy towards the developing countries" could not any longer be confined to development policy and "UN policy" (e.g., disarmament, environment), the project was to study how Swedish domestic policy fields – e.g., trade, exchange, agriculture, industry, science and defence – could be reoriented in line with NIEO.[54] The project also invited key civil society organisations to present their views of Sweden in the NIEO. Their reports were generally positive or even enthusiastic on the prospects of adapting Swedish society to the NIEO, noting the interest of Swedish business in "internationalising" its activities, its growing awareness of the importance of environment in general and in North–South commercial contacts and its embrace of the "trade not aid"-focus of the early NIEO proposals. But the reports also voiced concerns regarding the "self-reliance" track of the later NIEO negotiations as well as competition with the NICs over natural resources, energy supply and labour costs, if Swedish economy and society was to be scaled down in the interest of environmental preservation and global solidarity with the Third World.[55]

The report of the Labour Movement's International Center (Arbetarrörelsens internationella centrum, AIC) reiterated SAP support for the NIEO agenda, suggesting that Swedish society could possibly be divided into an open, competition-oriented export sector and a protected, publicly supported public sector based on small-scale production and bilateral agreements with certain developing countries.[56]

The (Christian) religious communities of Sweden turned the problem upside down by asking: "Can the world afford Sweden?"[57] Here, the demands of the NIEO were rather regarded as an opportunity to enact necessary changes in Swedish society, troubled by soulless bureaucracy, capitalism and consumerism.[58] Similarly, the representatives of the alternative movement sketched an eco-political programme for Sweden, emphasising Swedish economic self-reliance, replacing dependence upon the West with regional cooperation with the Third World countries, for mutual win-win.[59]

However, by the time of delivery of the final report of the future study in 1982, not only the hope and fears of the NIEO had faded. Also, the very idea that a country could have a "choice" appeared decidedly less credible. Instead, international interdependence spelt a need to adapt to global trends. Nevertheless, the organising principles of the NIEO debate still reverberated in Swedish politico-scientific knowledge production and "opinion formation", long after NIEO had ceased to be a reference object of internationalism. Now, however, the notion of choice pertained less to Sweden's *foreign policy* or its ideal role in terms of future North–South relations and solidarity. Rather, it was fundamentally concerned with the introspective issue of how Swedish *domestic policy* should be reformed to better prepare Swedish economy and society for the inevitable globalisation and the rising competition between countries and trading blocks, East and West, North and South – a prospect which the NIEO debate had acknowledged, but explicitly turned against.

Conclusion

Detailing these two key spheres allow us to identify and analyse discourses and rhetorics in play when Swedish stakeholders and policy professionals addressed the issue of Sweden's ideal role in a future world – possibly less dominated by East-West bipolar issues, but critically shaped by North–South global challenges. In studying Swedish responses to rising North–South tensions, it seems clear that an inordinate amount of resources and efforts were spent, not only to present Sweden to the emerging Global South but also to prepare Swedes to the emergence of the Global South, in a manner of circulation. On the one hand, the rise of the Global South was presented as a risk to contemporary Swedish standards of living and patterns of life. On the other hand, its rise posited unique opportunities to a minor and neutral, but also prosperous and technologically advanced country such as Sweden.

However, for these risks to be turned into opportunities, both public diplomats and knowledge producers engaged in procedures of "framing", i.e., presenting the supposedly distant and other Global South as in some ways close. In our study, we have identified two sets of such rhetoric at work – cultural affinity and small-state solidarity, respectively. The cultural affinity argument based itself primarily upon the modernisation thesis that the avenue from poverty to affluence as experienced by Swedish society in 1870–1970 could and would be paved also by many so-called Third World countries in a shared experience of progress, neither due to unfettered capitalism or to communist dictatorship, but to democratic socialism and pragmatic reform. The small-state solidarity argument nuanced and qualified the apparent difference between a wealthy, if minor, country in the northern periphery and the preconditions of numerous new states across the Global South, some of which were key holders of globally strategic resources and some of which were hardly in control of their own territory, if not for the continuously fluctuating bipolar Cold War (in)balance.

The factual foundation and argumentative scope of these two types of rhetoric as found in these two spheres as studied here can certainly be called into doubt on various grounds. First, politically, economically and technologically, Sweden definitively belonged to the West during the Cold War for all practical purposes. Second, these two spheres are limited and need to be complemented with studies of different forms and arenas of diplomacy and international collaboration as well as public and parliamentary debate for a full assessment of Swedish North–South commitment. Third, it is difficult from these rhetorics to ascertain what for example Swedish social democrats *really* thought that Sweden's own experience could import – as a future "model" for the modernisation of Tunisia and Vietnam or merely as a parallel in the past – and whether they *really* acted on this consideration or on some other grounds. Finally, the materials surveyed for this chapter does not provide us with much insight into how the rhetoric of affinity and solidarity were viewed and interpreted by audiences and observers in the Global South.

Yet, it is at least clear that these dual rhetorical repertoires apparently did command interest in *tiers-mondiste* press as shown above. Moreover, they apparently fulfilled an important role in structuring Swedish social democratic self-perceptions and self-identity in the global Cold War as representing and at times playing part in a mid-way movement, in between the two super power blocs. These perceptions and identities may in hindsight appear exaggerated or unrealistic. However, it is also evident from the material surveyed for this chapter that they were not only taken seriously at home, as well as abroad, but also shaped political priorities during a key phase of the bipolar Cold War regarding Global North–South issues, issues which are current still today, and now steeped in the overarching problem of globalisation. As such, the underlying logic of these rhetorical moves transcends the simple dichotomy of either idealist solidarity or realist geopolitics, current in much of the contemporary scholarship on Swedish, as well as Nordic, North–South relations.

Notes

1 This research has been undertaken within the scope of the research project "Nordic Model(s) in the Global Circulation of Ideas, 1970–2020", funded by Independent Research Fund Denmark (Project 8018-00023B).
2 For a useful overview, see Thorsten Borring Olesen, Helge Pharo and Kristian Paaskesen (eds.), *Saints and Sinners* (Oslo: Akademika, 2013).
3 See for example Hans Lödén, *För Säkerhets Skull* (Stockholm: Nerenius & Santérus, 1999).
4 The keyword here is "moral" or "humanitarian great power". For Sweden, see Ann-Sofie Nilsson, *Den moraliska stormakten* (Stockholm: Timbro, 1991); for Norway, see Øyvind Østerud, "Lite land som humanitær stormakt?" *Nytt Norsk Tidsskrift* 23, no. 4 (2006), 303–316.
5 Olav Stokke (ed.), *Western Middle Powers and Global Poverty* (Uppsala and Oslo: NAI and NUPI, 1989); Cranford Pratt and Bo Södersten (eds.), *Internationalism under Strain* (Toronto: University of Toronto Press, 1989); for the role of the Nordic balance, see for example: Aryo Makko, *Ambassadors of Realpolitik* (New York: Berghahn Books, 2017); for the global Cold War context, see Odd Arne Westad, *The Cold War* (London: Penguin Books, 2018).
6 Gunnar Åselius, "Revolutionen under kristallkronorna: Den svenska utrikesförvaltningen och 1968", *Aktuellt om historia*, n. 1 (2016), 113–135.
7 Kjell Östberg, *När vinden vände: Olof Palme 1969–1986* (Stockholm: Leopard, 2009); Pierre Schori, *Minnet och elden: En politisk memoar med samtida synpunkter* (Stockholm: Leopard, 2014), 93ff.
8 Olof Palme, "Pas de détente sans la libération totale de toutes les nations", *Afrique Asie*, n. 48 (1974), 29.
9 Simon Malley, "Aider le tiers monde face à l'hégémonie des 'Grands'", *Afrique Asie*, n. 26 (1973), 22–23.
10 Nikolas Glover, *National Relations* (Lund: Nordic Academic Press, 2011); Nikolas Glover, "A Total Image Deconstructed", in Louis Clerc, Nikolas Glover and Paul Jordan (eds.), *Histories of Public Diplomacy and Nation Branding in the Nordic and Baltic Countries* (Leiden: Brill Nijhoff, 2015), 123–144.
11 Andreas Mørkved Hellenes, *Fabricating Sweden. Studies of Swedish Public Diplomacy in France from the 1930s to the 1990s* (Paris and Oslo: Sciences Po Paris and University of Oslo, 2019).
12 Andreas Åkerlund, *Public Diplomacy and Academic Mobility in Sweden* (Lund: Nordic Academic Press, 2016), 84.
13 Marie Norgren, "Rapport från kontaktresa till Peking 29 mars – 15 april och Moskva 16–17 april 1972", undated report, 1. RA, SI(2), F12:8.
14 Per-Axel Hildeman, "Rapport över Per-Axel Hildemans tjänsteresa till Tunisien 12–20 november 1973", report dated December 11, 1973, 1. RA, SI(2), F12:7.
15 Andreas Mørkved Hellenes and Carl Marklund, "Sweden Goes Global", *Histoire@ Politique*, no. 35 (2018), 11ff.

16 Per-Axel Hildeman, "Rapport över Per-Axel Hildemans tjänsteresa till Tunisien 12–20 november 1973", report dated December 11, 1973, 2. RA, SI(2), F12:7.
17 Ibid., 1.
18 Alice Goff, "Introduction: The Object as Ambassador", *Representations* 141, no. 1 (2018), 1.
19 Steven Koblik (ed.), *Sweden's Development from Poverty to Affluence, 1750–1970* (Minneapolis: University of Minnesota Press, 1975). The book first appeared in a Swedish version, see Steven Koblik (ed.), *Från fattigdom till överflöd* (Stockholm: Wahlström & Widstrand, 1973). However, it was from the outset conceived mainly towards an English language audience, according to Koblik.
20 Birgitta Conradson and Hans Medelius, *De la pauvreté au bien-être* (Stockholm: Nordiska museet, 1974), 1.
21 Birgitta Lönnell, "Kulturveckor i Tunisien, 19 november–16 december 1975. Reserapport från Sfax och Kairouan", report dated January 7, 1976, 4–5; 7; 9.
22 Ibid., 9.
23 Utrikesdepartementet, *Sverige i utländsk press 1973* (Stockholm: UD:s pressbyrå, 1974), 1.
24 "La Suède dit tout haut", *Le Monde*, 29.12.1972.
25 Josette Alia, "Être neutre ne signifie pas rester muet", *Le Nouvel Observateur*, 8.1.1973. The phrase was also used by Jerrold Schechter, "Sweden's Olof Palme: 'Neutral but Not Silent'", *Time Magazine*, 29.1.1973, and earlier in "Olaf (sic) Palme: 'Être neutre ne signifie pas renoncer à ses opinions'", *Jeune Afrique*, 5.5.1970.
26 Olof Palme to Pham Van Dong, letter dated 3.1.1973. ARAB, OP, 3.2:90.
27 Simon Malley, "Mobilisation!…", *Afrique Asie*, 8.1.1973.
28 "Un peuple prend position", *Jeune Afrique*, 27.1.1973. In fact, no less than 2.7 million Swedes signed the petition, out of a population of 8.1 million.
29 Öberg, who had been an advisor both to Palme and foreign minister Torsten Nilsson, took a pro-North Vietnamese stance in public, castigating, for example, on the front page of *Le Monde diplomatique* the Americans, and urging the Western democracies to reconsider their inactivity and passivity when faced with the realities of the situation in Vietnam. See Jean-Christophe Öberg, "Un défi aux démocraties", *Le Monde diplomatique*, January 1973.
30 "Reserapport från Bo Jonssons vistelse i Demokratiska Republiken Vietnam (DRV) 15.2 – 9.3.1973", report dated March 16, 1973. RA, SI(2), F12:8.
31 Bo Kjellén, "Sverigeutställning i Hanoi", report dated May 10, 1976, attached to letter from Kjellén to Lönnell, dated May 17, 1976, 1. SIP, F2:1.
32 Ibid.
33 On the social democratic modernity narrative, see for example: Martin Wiklund, *I det modernas landskap* (Eslöv: Östlings bokförlag Symposion, 2006) and Åsa Linderborg, *Socialdemokraterna skriver historia* (Stockholm: Atlas, 2001).
34 The Socialist *senateur-maire* Édouard Soldani, nicknamed respectively "le vieux lion" ("the old lion") by friends and "le Parrain" ("the Godfather") by foes, had been a senator since 1946 and mayor of Draguignan since 1959.
35 From Grate to Lönnell, letter dated September 29, 1976. SIP, F2:1. Conservative daily *Svenska Dagbladet* gleefully put the story on the front page under the heading "Here culture and elections go hand in hand!", see "Här hör kultur och val i hop!", *Svenska Dagbladet*, September 22, 1976.
36 Gaia Caramellino and Stéphanie Dadour (eds.), *The Housing Project: Discourses, Ideals, Models and Politics in 20th Century Exhibitions* (Leuven: Leuven University Press, 2020).
37 Daniel P. Moynihan, "The United States in Opposition", *Commentary* 59, no. 3 (1975); see also Kathleen Teltsch, "Moynihan Calls on U.S. to 'Start Raising Hell' in U.N.", *New York Times*, February 26, 1975.

38 Guiliano Garavini, "From Boumedienomics to Reaganomics: Algeria, OPEC, and the International Struggle for Economic Equality", *Humanity* 6, no. 1 (2015), 79–92; on the US position, see Michael Franczak, *Global Inequality and American Foreign Policy in the 1970s* (Ithaca: Cornell University Press, forthcoming 2022); Samuel Moyn, *Not Enough: Human Rights in an Unequal World* (Cambridge: The Belknap Press of Harvard University Press, 2018); Quinn Slobodian, *Globalists: The End of Empire and the Birth of Neoliberalism* (Cambridge, MA: Harvard University Press, 2018); see also Rasmus Sinding-Søndergaard's forthcoming work on the Scandinavians' human rights diplomacy in the context of the NIEO.
39 Sekretariatet för framtidsstudier, *Sveriges internationella villkor* (Stockholm: Sekretariatet LiberFörlag, 1975).
40 Bo Huldt, *Sweden in World Society* (Oxford: Pergamon Press, 1980), 1.
41 Bo Huldt, *Sweden, the United Nations, and Decolonization* (Stockholm: Esselte Studium, 1974); Bo Huldt, *Sverige och Förenta nationerna* (Stockholm: Sekretariatet för framtidsstudier, 1976), 130–131, 136–137; Bo Huldt, *Sweden in World Society* (Oxford: Pergamon Press, 1980), 88ff.
42 The origins of the small-state doctrine can be traced to Palme's so-called Gävle speech in 1965, but Bo Huldt also finds parallels in Prime Minister Tage Erlander's (1946–1969) 1961 argument that the small-state development aid cannot be accused of "colonial demands, great power dreams, or side interests". Erlander's view would be challenged by New Left scholars, see: Lennart Berntson and Gunnar Persson, *U-hjälp och imperialism* (Stockholm: Aldus/Bonnier, 1968); for a discussion, see Olav Stokke, *Sveriges utvecklingsbistånd och biståndspolitik* (Uppsala: NAI, 1978).
43 Olof Palme's Archives, ARAB, "Speech at the Congress of the Union of Christian Social Democrats in Sweden in Piteå, August 4, 1974".
44 Olof Palme's Archives, ARAB, "Discours pronocé par le Premier Minstre Olof Palme à l'occasion du diner offert par le Président Boumediènne en l'honneur du Premier Ministre le 12 novembre 1974".
45 Olav Stokke, *Sveriges utvecklingsbistånd och biståndspolitik* (Uppsala: NAI, 1978); Magnus Jerneck, "Olof Palme – en internationell propagandist", in Bo Huldt and Klaus Misgeld (eds.), *Socialdemokratin och svensk utrikespolitik* (Stockholm: Utrikespolitiska institutet, 1990), 121–142.
46 Sveriges socialdemokratiska arbetareparti, *Partiprogram och stadgar* (Stockholm: Socialdemokraterna, 1975).
47 "Speech by Prime Minister Olof Palme in the United Nations General Assembly, November 11, 1975", ARAB, OP.
48 1977 års industribiståndsutredning, *Sveriges utvecklingssamarbete på industriområdet* (Stockholm: LiberFörlag/Allmänna förl., 1977), 9; Norbert Götz and Ann-Marie Ekengren, "The One Per Cent Country", in Thorsten Borring Olesen, Helge Pharo and Kristian Paaskesen (eds.), *Saints and Sinners* (Oslo: Akademika Publishing, 2013), 21–49.
49 Bo Huldt, *Sweden in World Society* (Oxford: Pergamon Press, 1980), 88.
50 For additional favourable statements on the NIEO by other Swedish politicians, acknowledging the need for Swedish society to adapt, see Sekretariatet för framtidsstudier, *Sweden in a New International Economic Order* (Stockholm: Sekretariatet för framtidsstudier, 1979), Appendix 3. For examples of the parliamentary debate in the *Riksdag*, see Riksdagens protokoll, 1975/76:35, 99–105, 127–130, 133–134, 135, 136; Riksdagens protokoll, 1977/78:96–97, 7–8, 13, 19–20, 26–28, 30–31.
51 Centerpartiet, *Partiprogram* (1979); Folkpartiet, *Liberalismen* (1982).
52 Lars Diurlin, "'Att vidmakthålla och stärka allmänhetens intresse och stöd" SIDA:s attitydförändrande informationsstrategier', in Fredrik Norén and Emil Stjernholm (eds.), *Efterkrigstidens samhällskontakter* (Lund: Mediehistoria, Lunds universitet, 2019), 317–360; see also Ebba Dohlman, *National Welfare and Economic Interdependence:*

The Case of Sweden's Foreign Trade Policy (Oxford: Clarendon Press, 1989); Antony J. Dolman, "The Like-Minded Countries and the New International Order: Past, Present and Future Prospects", *Cooperation and Conflict* XIV (1979), 57–85; Ann-Marie Ekengren and Henrik Oscarsson, *Solidaritet med omvärlden? Biståndsviljan i Sverige 1956–1998* (Göteborg: Statsvetenskapliga institutionen, Univ., 1999).

53 Sekretariatet för framtidsstudier, *Sweden in a New International Economic Order* (Stockholm: Sekretariatet för framtidsstudier, 1979), Appendix 3.

54 This policy shift, away from development policy (*biståndspolitik*), to a more comprehensive "developing country policy" (*u-landspolitik*) was explicitly motivated by reference to the NIEO and the need to align global and national policy agendas – i.e., Swedish domestic policies and Swedish foreign policy which was prevalent in the government reports prepared on Swedish development policy underway in parallel with the "Sweden in a New International Economic Order" project. Biståndspolitiska utredningen, *Sveriges samarbete med u-länderna* (Stockholm: LiberFörlag/Allmänna förl., 1977).

55 Marian Radetzki, *Sverige och den tredje världen* (Stockholm: Studieförb. Näringsliv och samhälle, 1980).

56 Arbetarrörelsens internationella centrum, *Handlingsutrymme, samhällsbalans, rättvisa* (Stockholm: Arbetarrörelsens internationella centrum, 1981); see also discussion in Ruth Link, *Gränslös utveckling* (Stockholm: Sekretariatet för framtidsstudier, 1982), 113–123.

57 The so-called Ecumenical U-week was formed in 1972 on the initiative of the Christian National Assembly in Gothenburg, which recommended that an "annual u-week would be organized with the aim of creating public opinion for the responsibility of Christianity and society to reduce the gap between rich and poor in the world". Three principal organisations stood behind the formation of this initiative: the Swedish Mission Council, the Swedish Ecumenical Committee and the Swedish Christian Youth Council.

58 Carl-Henric Grenholm and Håkan Wall, *Handla för frihet* (Uppsala: Ekumeniska u-veckan, 1980).

59 Bengt Gustafsson, Mats Kihlberg and Gunnar Sundberg, *Ambassadör med tjänstecykel* (Stockholm: LiberFörlag, 1981); see also discussion in Ruth Link, *Gränslös utveckling* (Stockholm: Sekretariatet för framtidsstudier, 1982), 172ff.

References

Archival sources

Riksarkivet (Arninge)
Svenska institutet, Huvudarkivet II / Svenska institutet (2) SI(2)
Svenska institutet i Paris (SIP)
Arbetarrörelsens arkiv och bibliotek (Flemingsberg)
Olof Palmes arkiv (OP)

Printed sources

Newspapers

Afrique Asie
Commentary
Jeune Afrique
Le Monde
Le Monde diplomatique

Le Nouvel Observateur
New York Times
Svenska Dagbladet
Time Magazine

Other published sources

1977 års industribiståndsutredning, *Sveriges utvecklingssamarbete på industriområdet* (Stockholm: LiberFörlag/Allmänna förl., 1977).
Arbetarrörelsens internationella centrum, *Handlingsutrymme, samhällsbalans, rättvisa* (Stockholm: Arbetarrörelsens internationella centrum, 1981).
Berntson, Lennart & Gunnar Persson, *U-hjälp och imperialism* (Stockholm: Aldus/ Bonnier, 1968).
Biståndspolitiska utredningen, *Sveriges samarbete med u-länderna* (Stockholm: LiberFörlag/Allmänna förl., 1977).
Centerpartiet, *Partiprogram* (1979).
Conradson, Birgitta & Hans Medelius, *De la pauvreté au bien-être* (Stockholm: Nordiska museet, 1974).
Folkpartiet, *Liberalismen* (1982).
Grenholm, Carl-Henric & Håkan Wall, *Handla för frihet* (Uppsala: Ekumeniska u-veckan, 1980).
Gustafsson, Bengt, Mats Kihlberg & Gunnar Sundberg, *Ambassadör med tjänstecykel* (Stockholm: LiberFörlag, 1981).
Huldt, Bo, *Sverige och Förenta nationerna* (Stockholm: Sekretariatet för framtidsstudier, 1976).
Huldt, Bo, *Sweden in World Society* (Oxford: Pergamon Press, 1980).
Huldt, Bo, *Sweden, the United Nations, and Decolonization* (Stockholm: Esselte Studium, 1974).
Koblik, Steven (ed.), *Från fattigdom till överflöd* (Stockholm: Wahlström & Widstrand, 1973).
Koblik, Steven (ed.), *Sweden's Development from Poverty to Affluence, 1750–1970* (Minneapolis: University of Minnesota Press, 1975).
Link, Ruth, *Gränslös utveckling* (Stockholm: Sekretariatet för framtidsstudier, 1982).
Radetzki, Marian, *Sverige och den tredje världen* (Stockholm: Studieförb. Näringsliv och samhälle, 1980).
Riksdagens protokoll, 1975/76:35.
Riksdagens protokoll, 1977/78:96–97.
Sekretariatet för framtidsstudier, *Sveriges internationella villkor* (Stockholm: Sekretariatet LiberFörlag, 1975).
Sekretariatet för framtidsstudier, *Sweden in a New International Economic Order* (Stockholm: Sekretariatet för framtidsstudier, 1979).
Sveriges socialdemokratiska arbetareparti, *Partiprogram och stadgar* (Stockholm: Socialdemokraterna, 1975).
Utrikesdepartementet, *Sverige i utländsk press 1973* (Stockholm: UD:s pressbyrå, 1974).

Secondary sources

Åkerlund, Andreas, *Public Diplomacy and Academic Mobility in Sweden* (Lund: Nordic Academic Press, 2016).

Åselius, Gunnar, "Revolutionen under kristallkronorna: Den svenska utrikesförvaltningen och 1968", *Aktuellt om historia*, no. 1 (2016), 113–135.

Borring Olesen, Thorsten, Helge Pharo, and Kristian Paaskesen (eds.), *Saints and Sinners* (Oslo: Akademika Publishing, 2013).

Caramellino, Gaia, and Stéphanie Dadour (eds.), *The Housing Project: Discourses, Ideals, Models and Politics in 20th Century Exhibitions* (Leuven: Leuven University Press, 2020).

Diurlin, Lars, "'Att vidmakthålla och stärka allmänhetens intresse och stöd" SIDA:s attitydförändrande informationsstrategier', in Fredrik Norén and Emil Stjernholm (eds.), *Efterkrigstidens samhällskontakter* (Lund: Mediehistoria, Lunds universitet, 2019), 317–360.

Dohlman, Ebba, *National Welfare and Economic Interdependence: The Case of Sweden's Foreign Trade Policy* (Oxford: Clarendon Press, 1989).

Dolman, Antony J., "The Like-Minded Countries and the New International Order: Past, Present and Future Prospects", *Cooperation and Conflict* XIV (1979), 57–85.

Ekengren, Ann-Marie, and Henrik Oscarsson, *Solidaritet med omvärlden? Biståndsviljan i Sverige 1956–1998* (Göteborg: Statsvetenskapliga institutionen, Univ., 1999).

Franczak, Michael, *Global Inequality and American Foreign Policy in the 1970s* (Ithaca: Cornell University Press, forthcoming 2022).

Garavini, Guiliano, "From Boumedienomics to Reaganomics: Algeria, OPEC, and the International Struggle for Economic Equality", *Humanity* 6, no. 1 (2015), 79–92.

Glover, Nikolas, "A Total Image Deconstructed", in Louis Clerc, Nikolas Glover, and Paul Jordan (eds.), *Histories of Public Diplomacy and Nation Branding in the Nordic and Baltic Countries* (Leiden: Brill Nijhoff, 2015), 123–144.

Glover, Nikolas, *National Relations* (Lund: Nordic Academic Press, 2011).

Goff, Alice, "Introduction: The Object as Ambassador", *Representations* 141, no. 1 (2018), 1–2.

Götz, Norbert, and Ann-Marie Ekengren, "The One Per Cent Country", in Thorsten Borring Olesen, Helge Pharo, and Kristian Paaskesen (eds.), *Saints and Sinners* (Oslo: Akademika Publishing, 2013), 21–49.

Hellenes, Andreas M., *Fabricating Sweden: Studies of Swedish Public Diplomacy in France from the 1930s to the 1990s* (Paris and Oslo: Sciences Po Paris and University of Oslo, 2019).

Hellenes, Andreas M., and Carl Marklund, "Sweden Goes Global", *Histoire@Politique*, no. 35 (2018), 1–17.

Jerneck, Magnus, "Olof Palme – en internationell propagandist", in Bo Huldt and Klaus Misgeld (eds.), *Socialdemokratin och svensk utrikespolitik* (Stockholm: Utrikespolitiska institutet, 1990), 121–142.

Linderborg, Åsa, *Socialdemokraterna skriver historia* (Stockholm: Atlas, 2001).

Lodén, Hans, *För säkerhets Skull* (Stockholm: Nerenius & Santérus, 1999).

Makko, Aryo, *Ambassadors of Realpolitik* (New York: Berghahn Books, 2017).

Moyn, Samuel, *Not Enough: Human Rights in an Unequal World* (Cambridge, Mass.: The Belknap Press of Harvard University Press, 2018).

Nilsson, Ann-Sofie, *Den moraliska stormakten* (Stockholm: Timbro, 1991).

Östberg, Kjell, *När vinden vände: Olof Palme 1969–1986* (Stockholm: Leopard, 2009).

Østerud, Øyvind, "Lite land som humanitær stormakt?", *Nytt Norsk Tidsskrift* 23, no. 4 (2006), 303–316.

Pratt, Cranford, and Bo Södersten (eds.), *Internationalism under Strain* (Toronto: University of Toronto Press, 1989).

Schori, Pierre, *Minnet och elden: En politisk memoar med samtida synpunkter* (Stockholm: Leopard, 2014).
Slobodian, Quinn, *Globalists: The End of Empire and the Birth of Neoliberalism* (Cambridge, MA: Harvard University Press, 2018).
Stokke, Olav (ed.), *Western Middle Powers and Global Poverty* (Uppsala and Oslo: NAI and NUPI, 1989).
Stokke, Olav, *Sveriges utvecklingsbistånd och biståndspolitik* (Uppsala: NAI, 1978).
Westad, Odd Arne, *The Cold War* (London: Penguin Books, 2018).
Wiklund, Martin, *I det modernas landskap* (Eslöv: Östlings bokförlag Symposion, 2006).

8 Looking South

The role of Portuguese democratisation in the Socialist International's initiatives towards Latin America in the 1970s

Ana Monica Fonseca

The purpose of this chapter is to analyse the role that the Socialist International (SI) and Western European Socialist and Social-democratic parties had during the Portuguese democratisation process. Simultaneously, we also wish to understand how Iberian democratic transitions impacted on the *modus-operandi* of the SI in other areas of the world, namely in Latin America. However, it is impossible to analyse the SI's perspective in this process without focusing on the role that some socialist and social-democratic European parties played during the 1970s. In this case, the Social Democratic Party of Germany (SPD) is particularly relevant. In fact, the SPD was the leading party in support of the Portuguese socialists, something that was part of its strategy of engagement with the democratisation of Southern Europe.[1]

The specific characteristics of non-state actors and their transnational activities, namely their ability to overcome the governmental framework and interact transnationally without the constraints of state actors, turned them particularly interesting when analysing political regime change and democracy promotion.[2]

The Socialist International was one of the many non-state transnational actors of the Western bloc in the second half of the Cold War, and its relevance is clear if we understand that it combined some of the most influential West European socialist and social democratic parties. Founded in its modern form in 1951, the main guiding principle of the Socialist International was, as stated in the Frankfurt manifesto, to express "solidarity with all peoples suffering under dictatorship, whether fascist or communist, in their efforts to win freedom".[3] This means that the SI "was as fearful of Communism as it was opposed to Fascism", something that will be determinant in the SI's position regarding the transition of the Iberian countries, particularly in the Portuguese case.[4]

The Socialist International and the Iberian dictatorships

In the 1970s, the Socialist International lived through a period of growing political influence, mainly because the majority of its member-parties were in government.[5] Willy Brandt was elected West German chancellor in October 1969, the same year as Olof Palme was elected Sweden's prime minister; Bruno Kreisky reached the Austrian Chancellery in 1970; Joop den Uyl, from the Dutch Labour Party

(PvdA) was elected in 1973; and Harold Wilson, from the British Labour Party, took office in 1974. All these were leaders of Socialist and Social-democratic parties that would reinforce the SI visibility. As will see in the West German case during the Portuguese process of transition to democracy, this allowed for a combination of international support from both state and non-state actors.[6]

However, another reason lies behind the SI's increasing relevance in this period: the developments in the international system. Indeed, the evolution of the Cold War into a phase of détente, in the 1960s and 1970s, created a window of opportunity for other actors, both at the state and non-state level, to develop autonomous initiatives in the international politics.[7] As James Callaghan, of the British Labour Party, recognised in January 1973, "there was now an opportunity [for the democratic socialists] to escape from the sterile exchanges of the Cold War".[8] The West Germans, in particular, were especially successful in increasing their own autonomy in world affairs. The initial steps in this direction were taken by the Social Democratic Party of Germany's (SPD) government, from 1969 onwards, both by developing its Eastern policy (Ostpolitik) and by reinforcing its connection to Western Europe and favouring the enlargement of EEC.[9] In this particular aspect, the leadership of Willy Brandt in Bonn is determinant, during and after his chancellorship. Willy Brandt's leadership of the SPD was determinant for the visibility of SI's international activity, mainly because he had access to a very powerful resource for its international activity: the Friedrich Ebert Foundation (FES).[10] All these elements combined resulted in a strong West German leadership in the Socialist International.[11]

Nonetheless, the main West German / European trend while dealing with the Iberian dictatorships (despite some important exceptions) was giving prevalence to the anti-Communist dimension of the two regimes. In this sense, and combining the strategy of "change through rapprochement" used in *Ostpolitik* (i.e. the best way to liberalise the Spanish and Portuguese regimes was to foster their approximation to Europe, to a more developed economic and political centre, and not by their isolation or even by demising the authoritarian regimes), the West German social-democratic governments always tried to keep good relations with Lisbon and Madrid in order to be able to rely on the strong existing ties if the occasion for the liberalisation of their authoritarian regimes arose.

In 1969, the new head of the Portuguese government, Marcelo Caetano,[12] allowed the participation of opposition lists to the legislative elections. Despite this permission, the opposition parties / political groups would remain illegal in the regime, being only authorised during the electoral period. Additionally, he allowed the return to Portugal of Mário Soares, in a clear gesture of political opening, carried out relevant reforms in the social field and extended voting rights to women, with the same conditions in which these were conceded to men – which nonetheless were somehow limited. All these initiatives nurtured a rising belief, in Portuguese society and internationally, that Caetano might "bring about a genuine liberalizing reform" of the New State.[13] However, as it turned out, the elections proved to be the turning point for the expectations regarding the likelihood of a "Marcelist" liberalisation. Not only their outcome failed to reflect any kind of political opening as, from this point onwards, it was made clear that Caetano was not able to carry forth any in-depth reform of the regime.[14]

The Socialist International's attention on the Portuguese socialists was further boosted in the early 1970s, especially after Mário Soares was again forced into exile in the summer of 1970, with the creation of a working group on Portugal. The first meeting of the Portugal Committee was on 3 March 1972 and had in its agenda issues related with the relations between Portugal and the European countries and with the EEC, as well as the representation of the Portuguese clandestine political forces in the Council of Europe.[15] It was in the aftermath of the meetings of the Portugal Committee that Soares requested full membership of the ASP to the Socialist International, which was concluded in June of 1972. This amounted to a significant step forward in the path of Portuguese Socialists' international recognition.

In fact, the cooperation between the Portuguese Socialist Action (ASP) and the SI had increased since the elections in 1969, when the SI sent a team of observers to follow the electoral process in Portugal. The members of the team were Tom McNally (British Labour Party), Pierre Schori (Swedish Social Democratic Party), Luciano de Pascalis (Partito Socialista Italiano), Maria Vitoria Mezza (Partito Socialista Unitario Italiano) and Brendan Halligan (Irish Labour Party). The Commission was accompanied by Hans Janitschek, SI's general secretary.[16] This mission was closely prepared with the assistance of Mário Soares and other exiled Portuguese socialists, and their goal was to "observe the electoral campaign and study all the aspects of the situation", as it was explained to Marcelo Caetano.[17] However, the members of the SI's Commission were threatened to be arrested and were kicked out from Portugal only a couple of days after their arrival.[18] The SPD had refused to be a part of this mission on the grounds that it would likely be counter-productive given Caetano's promises of liberalisation.[19]

On the other hand, the admittance to the SI entailed the partidarisation of the ASP. The Portuguese Socialist Party (PSP) was then founded on 19th April 1973 during a congress of the ASP at the FES Academy in Bad Münstereifel. Mário Soares was chosen as the new party secretary general. However, the political support granted by German Social Democracy in this foundational moment of the PSP was largely symbolic. In fact, the German representatives, Elke Esters (FES) and Hans-Eberhard Dingels (SPD), had little or no intervention in the Congress, being present merely as observers.[20]

Until the end of the New State, the West German and West European leaders were manifestly interested in keeping in touch with the Portuguese socialists. Yet, their persistent hope that Marcelo Caetano might still prove able to liberalise the Portuguese regime prevented the leaders of the SPD, the majority of whom held offices in the government, from engaging in a closer and more blatant communication with the Portuguese Socialist opposition.[21]

However, during 1973 and the first months of 1974, there was a shift in the approach to Portugal by German Social Democracy. On the one hand, on a formal governmental level, the bilateral relations remained stable and constant.[22] On the other hand, in so far as the stance of the informal actors was concerned, namely the Social Democratic party and the Ebert Foundation, there was a strengthening of the support granted to the Portuguese Socialist opposition, which materialised firstly in the aforementioned foundation of the Socialist Party at an FES academy near Bonn, and culminated in frequent contacts throughout the first trimester of 1974.[23] Throughout the months prior to the coup of 25th of April of 1974, there was a constant tension between these two sides that vanished only on the eve of the coup, when the SPD finally agreed to openly receive a delegation of the Socialist Party. This high-level invitation, requiring the presence of the PS leader, was the reason why Mário Soares was in Bonn on the 25th of April, when the Portuguese dictatorship was finally overthrown.

"Watering the carnations": West European Social-democracy support to Portuguese and Spanish democratic forces

The Portuguese transition to democracy that began in April 1974 was characterised by a period of intense fighting between the democratic forces (in particular by the Socialist Party) and the forces at the extreme left. Until the approval of the democratic constitution, in April 1976, there was a constant presence of West European social-democratic parties (and governments), which were profoundly engaged with Soares' Socialist Party. On the left spectrum of the political scenario in Portugal, there were also important international solidarities. The Soviet Union and the GDR strongly supported the Communists and some other extreme left tendencies in Portugal. The Western engagement was embodied by the Federal Republic of Germany's Social-Democratic Party, headed by Willy Brandt. The SPD, taking "advantage of the resources of the Friedrich Ebert Foundation and skilfully appealing to the Government of Helmut Schmidt", was able to develop a comprehensive support strategy to the socialists (and, in a lesser extent, to the Popular Democratic Party of Sá Carneiro and Rui Machete).[24]

This strategy encompassed several types of support. Financial support, for example, by assisting the PS in buying office supplies, paper and cars to sustain the party organisation, or by paying the salaries of some party staff. There was also important organisational inputs given by the Ebert Foundation experts, namely when was necessary to define the party's national, regional and local structure, or when it was necessary to establish a successful electoral campaign (something which the PS and all the other political parties experienced the first time in the spring of 1975); political and moral support were particularly felt in times of growing tension, as, for example, in the fall of 1974, when General Spinola left his position as head of state (president of the Republic) and Willy Brandt made his first visit to Lisbon. Or, by the fact that there was always an Ebert or SPD representative (point of contact) in Lisbon, who would eventually work as a direct channel to Bonn.[25]

However, despite the major internal impact that this support had in the Portuguese scenario (as it would definitively position the PS as one of the best prepared parties to capture the attention of the population), the most important element of the strategy of engagement with the Portuguese democratisation came through the mobilisation of the European socialist and social-democratic parties through the Socialist International. This allowed for a growing material support to the PS but also the reinforcement of the visibility of the party's international connections, mostly with the northern European countries, which seemed so distant from Lisbon just a few months ago.[26]

Through all these levels of action, we can have an overview of the interconnected strategy behind the support of the European Social-democratic parties to the Portuguese Socialist Party of Mário Soares and, therefore, to the democratisation of Portugal. There was a combined effort, which added a particular international presentation of the Portuguese case as a real threat to the developments in terms of détente. Brandt himself was concerned in explaining his position both in Washington and in Moscow. In the United States, he and his SPD fellows (particularly Chancellor Schmidt) concentrated in demonstrating that the Western European parties would not accept any type of military intervention "à la Chile" and strongly defending that Soares should be supported unconditionally; in Moscow, Brandt personally told Brejnev that any communist takeover in Lisbon would endanger the whole process of détente – let's not forget that Helsinki's final Act was signed precisely during the Portuguese "Hot Summer" (July/August 1975). As we all know, despite the radicalisation of the Portuguese process, in particular during the summer of 1975, Portugal eventually became a pluralist and representative democracy, with the first constitutional government being headed by Mário Soares. This might just be the most obvious image of the success of the Social Democrat strategy towards Portugal.

The case of the Spanish transition, which began later but which was, by this time, already expected (Franco was very old and sick), was a little bit different. The transition was not made by any revolutionary means nor it was as radicalised as the Portuguese one; instead it was a *transicion pactada*, meaning that there was an agreement between almost all of the political forces to reach an understanding in order to establish a democratic regime. This would take its time, and it was in December 1978 that the democratic constitution was approved. Nonetheless, the Spanish example was also very important and reflected clearly the lessons learned with the Portuguese process. Because of the Portuguese revolutionary transition, all eyes were in Spain as the time for the transition approached.

Franco's chosen successor, Prince Juan Carlos, had already assured the European leaders that he would try to liberalise and democratise the regime – it was just a matter of seeing how long and at what pace it could be done. The major fear regarding the Spanish transition was the risk that it would easily turn into a violent civil conflict (one must not ignore the profound impact that the Spanish Civil war had in the memories of most of the political leaders of this time, and most particularly in Willy Brandt's mind and political formation). The Communist Party of Santiago Carrillo was (as in the Portuguese case), the better organised of the opposition forces and most European leaders looked at it with deep distrust, associating it with Moscow and as similar to the Portuguese PCP. In order to avoid a renewal political radicalisation in the Iberian Peninsula, the Socialist and Social democratic parties of Western Europe – again, under the leadership of Brandt and the SPD (never forgetting the incredible material support given by the Ebert Foundation) – took measures to create the conditions as to have an progressive party which could work as an alternative to the Communists both to the electors and to the political authorities. In this sense, the newly elected PSOE General-Secretary Felipe Gonzalez emerged as the ideal man to be supported by the SPD and the other European forces. Indeed, it was in Lisbon, in October 1974, that Gonzalez met Brandt for the first time, beginning a very close and fruitful relationship almost immediately. Gonzalez transformed the PSOE into a balanced and pro-European party, with a clear and intelligent strategy to force the government to negotiate with the opposition, through a cautious approach to the development of close relations with the other socialist tendencies (which were dispersed in the Spanish political panorama).[27]

Again, the support given to the PSOE by the West German and West European sister-parties was well succeeded. Reaching government only in 1982 (mostly due to the internal characteristics of the *transicion pactada*), Felipe Gonzalez was already a respected and international recognised political leader before that.

Lessons learned? The Iberian democratisation and its impact on the SI strategy towards Latin America

Bearing this in mind, we can say that the main consequences of the Iberian democratisation processes to the future strategy of the Socialist International were twofold: first, the Portuguese and Spanish transitions could work as examples of successful processes of regime change, both from right wing authoritarian regimes to pluralist democracies. They were two cases where the democratic moderate left forces were the winners, having defeated not only the authoritarian resistance but also powerful communist tendencies. A second and very important consequence, especially in the case of Latin America, was that the Iberian democratisation gave the SI the front men for its missions. Both Soares and Gonzalez were respected and recognised internationally, and they would make good use of the historical, linguistic and cultural connections between the Iberian and the Latin American countries. As Willy Brandt himself said in the opening remarks of the Estoril Conference, there were "already useful experiences in Latin *Europe*, which hopefully will constitute grounds for hope for Latin *America*".[28] There was clearly the idea that the Iberian experiences should play a decisive role in the expansion of the IS strategy towards Latin America.

In any way, Soares had already a reputation in Latin America. Already since 1970 that Soares visited the region sent by Ebert Foundation. Indeed, during his exile, the Ebert Foundation paid to Soares in exchange for "technical advice" precisely on Latin America and in the end of 1973, he made an important journey to Brazil, Peru and Chile, where he contacted the "progressive forces in these countries". This journey was also very important to the Soares image with the West German social democrats, reflecting a man compromised with democracy and willing to collaborate on the same ideological principles as Willy Brandt.[29] In the countries he visited, Soares did lectures, met people and tried to speak of the European social democracy and its usefulness as a natural ally in the struggle against military dictatorships. He then developed friendships and contacts that were then explored by the Socialist International.[30]

In this sense, there were already some contacts and a growing interest of the European social-democratic parties towards Latin America. The journal Nueva Sociedad was first published in 1972 as an initiative of the Friedrich Ebert Foundation of Venezuela (although today its headquarters are in Buenos Aires) and its objective was to "advocate the development of political, economic and social democracy in the region" – in fact, Mário Soares was part of the first editorial committee of the journal.

This growing attention of the IS towards the South American continent gained momentum in May 1976, with the Caracas Conference. We have heard already what this event meant for the evolution of the SI strategy in that region. Between the Caracas conference and the Estoril Conference, the SI was very active in establishing a common ground for the relations with the parties of the region.

Still during the Caracas conference Brandt, together with Mário Soares, Gonzalo Barrios (AD, Venezuela) and Porfírio Muñoz Ledo (PRI, partido revolucionario institucional, México) established a contact group. The main goal of this group was to tighten the contacts between its representatives of both continents and to find solutions for a greater cooperation between the European and Latin American parties. This group met in several occasions during the Caracas Conference (several times a day, as the schedule of the agenda allowed) and during these meetings, the ideas and goals of the group become more organised. In this sense, the first and most immediate objectives of the "Group of the 4" (as the German Social-democrats called it, Vierergruppe) was to organise further meetings of the group and of the Latin American representatives, to establish a relief fund to support the Latin American parties (which should not be used against the governments) and to create some sort of institution (a foundation or documentation centre) which could reflect externally the organisation of such a cooperation between the European and Latin American parties. The most discussed objective was the relief fund, which would then remain an open question as it raised significant political reserves. The presidency of the Group was on Gonzalo Barrios, from the Venezuelan AD, to symbolise the decentralisation of the traditional relations.[31]

The Caracas meeting was a kick-off from the broader strategy of the SI to overcome Eurocentrism, considered by Brandt as the institution's major weakness – in particular, considering that it should play a role in the international developments. In that sense, three major missions were organised in 1977 and 1978: first, a delegation headed by Olof Palme visited southern Africa; the Austrian Chancellor Bruno Kreisky was sent to the Middle East and Mário Soares was the leader of the SI Mission to Latin America, which took place in March 1978. There were also other meetings of the SI structures in Asia and Africa, and in 1978, the SI Congress met in Vancouver, Canada.

However, we will focus on the Latin American mission of March 1978. This mission, headed by Soares, was proposed in the Bureau meeting of the International gathered in Rom, in the beginning of June 1977. The historical leader José Peña Gomez, from the Dominican Revolutionary Party, was who advocated such a mission, calling the attention "to the spread of dictatorships in Latin America in the recent years" and considering that "the mission was necessary because of the support which it would give to democratic political parties" in the region.[32] The mission, which includes visits to Mexico, Costa Rica, Venezuela, the Dominican Republic and Jamaica, took place between 15 and 25 March 1978. This was mainly a good-will and information mission. It was not the mission's purpose to "give any solutions or instructions" to the partner parties – instead, it should deepen the knowledge on both sides and contribute to the networking and development of contacts between the representatives of the European and Latin American similar parties. Obviously, behind these general goals, there was the objective of showing "active solidarity with the people and similar parties living under dictatorship and underdevelopment". The main recommendations of the Mission showed that there was an increasing need for a deeper knowledge of and engagement with the problems of the region. There was growing openness from the democratic parties in Latin America to receive support from the SI, but there was also a need for greater integration of the Latin American parties in finding their own solutions for some of their problems. Of the concrete proposals presented in the mission report, I point out the urge for a clear and coherent position of the democratic socialist parties in SI in defence of the human rights and against the dictatorships, particularly showing their support to those parties with similar ideological principles fighting these regimes. This support should be even more relevant in those cases where there were electoral competition, which was the case of several countries in this period – the Latin America Committee should play a determinant role in this sense and the mission recommended that it should be "initiated immediately". The expansion of the IS membership to more parties in Latin America was also seen as something very positive, as the rising number of applications already showed.[33]

The mission was a success and had great international visibility. However, it was necessary to give a greater demonstration of interest from the European parties in Latin America – and to explore the willingness of those parties to become closer to the SI. In this sense, and by a proposal of Mário Soares, the Portuguese Socialists organised an International Conference to take place in Lisbon, which should be the European response to the Caracas Conference. Having received immediate support from Willy Brandt, according to his chief-of-staff, and former Ebert Representative in Venezuela, Klaus Lindenberg,[34] Soares decided to summon the first meeting of Latin American and European representatives of the Democratic socialism in Europe. This conference gathered between 30 September and 2 October 1978 in Estoril and brought together representatives of 28 countries.

However, and as a preparation for the Estoril Conference, a mission to the countries that were not previously visited by Soares was organised. This time, it should be done in greater discretion and only two men would take part: Klaus Lindenberg, Friedrich Ebert representative in Venezuela, and Bernardino Gomes, close aid to Mário Soares in the Socialist Party. These two men visited eight countries between 18 August and 14 September 1978: Venezuela, Brazil, Paraguay,

Uruguay, Argentina, Bolivia, Peru and Ecuador, contacting with representatives of several political forces. There was no press and no grand receptions. This mission was paid and organised by the Friedrich Ebert Foundation and it was the decisive moment for the study of the current situation in Latin America and for the planning of the perspectives for its further development. It was also important to have a clearer idea of who should be the partners in each particular country (especially if there were several political forces who allegedly were close to social-democratic values).[35]

The Estoril Conference gathered more than 40 party representatives and had a major impact, either in the public opinion, as in the international role played by the PS and Mário Soares. It was very important for the definitive launch of the Latin America Offensive by the Socialist International. The Lisbon Declaration, approved in the end of the Conference and later adopted by the SI Congress in Vancouver, became the SI's official document regarding Latin America for that period. In this declaration, it was recognised that the Conference had a major goal of bringing together parties and political forces that shared the principles of "liberty, democracy and social progress". Besides this, the Iberian countries, which were presented as being in transition between Latin America and developed Europe, were the grand examples of the possibility of success that the progressive forces of Latin America should follow. Both Portugal and Spain showed that it was possible to obtain the victory of progressive forces, thus defeating any form of dictatorship, either to the right or to the left. And the Latin American forces should follow this. Finally, the Lisbon Declaration stated that there should be a more active and conscious support by the European and North American parties and governments, to the forces in the region, to help them fight against the authoritarian regimes and promote democratisation.[36]

Conclusion

The contacts between the Portuguese Socialists and German Social Democracy, both the Ebert Foundation and the SPD alike, were established in the mid-1960s, but only after 1970, with Mário Soares' exile and the ensuing corroboration that all hopes regarding a "Marcelist Spring" had been unfounded, did these contacts become of any consequence. The admission of the ASP to the Socialist International in 1972, the foundation of the Portuguese Socialist Party, a year later, at the Friedrich Ebert Foundation Academy, and the presence of Mário Soares in the West German capital on the 25th of April of 1974 are instances that demonstrate the intensification of the relationship between Portuguese Socialists and German Social Democrats. All these episodes, punctuated by the constant contact with Mário Soares and other Portuguese Socialists, mirror the rising West German interest in the creation of a strong Socialist opposition that might play an important role in a setting of political transition. However, as the reactions to the information conveyed by Mário Soares on the 24th of April of 1974, in Bonn, demonstrate, no one in FRG expected the fall of the longest dictatorship in Western Europe to happen on such short notice.

When the coup of the 25th of April of 1974 took place, it was German Social Democracy that held the contacts with the Portuguese opposition and the instruments to deal, as no other political force in West Germany and in the Western bloc, with the political instability that was foreseeable in the process of political transition in Portugal. The presence in Portugal of a number of representatives from the Ebert Foundation made it possible to delineate a strategy of engagement with the Portuguese Socialists with a view to the establishment of a pluralistic democracy. The evolution of the political situation yielded a diversification in the SPD initiatives for the promotion of Portuguese democratisation. The support given to the organisation and growth of the Socialist Party was a main goal, so that it might become the dominating party in the Portuguese political scene. To this end, the FES provided material backing to the party, while the SPD contributed with ideological guidance and moral and political support. At the same time, the German Social Democracy did not hesitate to summon the highest authorities to give their support to the Portuguese moderate forces, leading a number of international initiatives. The clearest examples of that are Willy Brandt's meeting in the Soviet Union and the creation of the "Friendship and Solidarity Committee for Portuguese Democracy and Socialism". These international activities assured the support of Western Europe to the Portuguese moderate forces in the struggle for the establishment of a pluralistic parliamentary democracy, which came to actually happen during the first semester of 1976.

Thus, the Socialist International was another instrument available for the West German Social-Democracy's solidarity with the Portuguese democratic forces. Although it combined several West European socialist and social-democratic parties, who were, all of them, supporting the Portuguese socialists, the leading figures and the wide range of resources available in the SPD make it the most important party to assist the PS and Mário Soares, before and after the Carnations Revolution. SI's main role was, as referred to earlier, the constant call for attention for the needs of the Portuguese socialists and the triangulation between the PS and the other European countries. Also, because of the SI's growing importance in the international system, it was another voice of international pressure regarding the evolution of the Portuguese situation, in particular in the summer of 1975.

But the Portuguese democratisation process also taught significant lessons for the European socialists. Understanding the importance of having good contacts within the political oppositions as a way for easing the influence of regime change, the Socialist International and the individual socialist and social-democratic parties developed strategies of supporting the sister-parties from other dictatorships. This is particularly clear regarding the Spanish transition (although there were already many contacts before 1974), but it is also evident when we observe the Socialist International's activity in the second half of the 1970s. Clearly influenced by Willy Brandt's presidency and his beliefs on the North-South dialogue, the Socialist International will develop a strategy of close contacts with several parties in Latin America. Mário Soares and Felipe Gonzalez, the highest examples of the success of international party solidarity, were important assets in this strategy.

Notes

1 Ana Monica Fonseca, "«*É Preciso Regar os Cravos!*» A Social-democracia alemã e a transição para a democracia em Portugal (1974–1976)" (PhD diss., ISCTE-Lisbon University Institute, 2011).
2 Thomas Risse-Kappen, ed., *Bringing Transnational Relations Back In. Non-State Actors, Domestic Structures and International Institutions* (Cambridge: Cambridge University Press, 1995). Wolfram Kaiser, ed., *Transnational Networks in Regional Integration. Governing Europe, 1945–1983* (London: Palgrave MacMillan, 2010); Anne-Marie le Gloannec, ed., *Non-State Actors in International Relations. The Case of Germany* (Manchester: Manchester University Press, 2007).
3 Declaration of the Socialist International adopted at its first congress held in Frankfurt-am-Main on 30 June–3 July 1951, accessed April 14, 2021. https://www.socialistintern ational.org/congresses/i-frankfurt/.
4 Pilar Ortuño Anaya, *European Socialists and Spain. The Transition to Democracy, 1959–1977* (London: Palgrave, 2002), 19.
5 Lawrence Whitehead, "International Aspects of Democratization", in *Transitions from Authoritarian Rule*, edited by Guillermo O'Donnell et al. (Baltimore: Johns Hopkins University Press, 1986), 3–46. According to the SI Bureau Report 1972–1976, there were "22 parties in government or sharing government responsibilities" in this period. See "Bureau's Report – Draft Introduction" – Institute for Social History (IISH), Amsterdam, Socialist International Archive (SI), 293.
6 Fonseca, «*É Preciso Regar os Cravos!*».
7 Odd Arne Westad and Paul Villaume, eds., *Perforating the Iron Curtain. European Détente, Transatlantic Relations and the Cold War, 1965–1985* (Copenhagen: Museum Tusculanum Press, 2010); Matthew Evangelista, "Transnational Organizations and the Cold War", in *The Cambridge History of Cold War. Vol. 3 Endings*, edited by Melvyn Leffler and Odd Arne Westad (Cambridge: Cambridge University Press, 2010), 400–421.
8 "Party Leaders' Conference, Paris", January 13–14, 1973, Confidential Summary – Institute for Social History (IISH), Amsterdam, Socialist International Archive (SI), 347.
9 Ulrich Lappenküpper, *Die Aussenpolitik der Bundesrepublik Deutschland, 1949 bis 1990* (Munich: Oldenburg Verlag, 2008).
10 Patrick von zur Mühlen, *Die internationale Arbeit der Friedrich-Ebert-Stiftung. Von den Anfängen bis zum Ende des Ost-West – Konflikt* (Bonn: Dietz Verlag, 2007).
11 Bernd Rother and Wolfgang Schmidt, "Einleitung", in *Berliner Ausgabe. Vol. 8, Über Europa Hinaus. Dritte Welt und Sozialistische Internationale*, edited by Willy Brandt (Bonn: Dietz Verlag, 2006), 15–109.
12 Marcelo Caetano was a law professor and had been minister of colonies (1945–1947) and head of the National Union (from 1947 onwards), the single party of the Estado Novo. He was also rector of University of Lisbon between 1959 and 1962, when he resigned because of the clashes between the political police and the students. Caetano was seen as a possible but not a perfect successor to Salazar. In September 1968, following Salazar's deteriorating health, Caetano was named prime minister. See Filipe Ribeiro Menezes, *Salazar. A Political Biography* (New York: Enigma Books, 2009), 598–610.
13 Mário Soares was the lawyer that had represented, among other opponents of the regime, the family of General Humberto Delgado after his assassination in 1965. Soares had been, since 1964, the leader of the Acção Socialista Portuguesa, Portuguese Socialist Action (ASP) and was, since 1968, exiled in São Tomé and Príncipe. See Pedro Oliveira, "A Sense of Hopelessness? Portuguese Oppositionists Abroad in the Final Years of the Estado Novo, 1968–1974", *Contemporary European History* 26, no. 3 (2017): 465–486, https://doi.org/10.1017/S0960777317000248 and Fernando Rosas,

A Transição Falhada. O Marcelismo e o Final do Estado Novo (1968–1974) (Lisbon: Editorial Notícias, 2004), 16.
14 Norrie MacQueen and Pedro Aires Oliveira, "'Grocer meets Butcher': Marcello Caetano's London Visit of 1973 and the Last Days of Portugal's Estado Novo", *Cold War History* 10, no. 1 (2010): 29–50, https://doi.org/10.1080/14682740902764551; António Costa Pinto, "Twentieth Century Portugal: An Introduction", in *Contemporary Portugal: Politics, Society and Culture*, edited by António C. Pinto (New York: Columbia University Press, 2003), 1–46.
15 "Procès-verbal de la première réunion du Comité du Portugal de l'Internationale Socialiste", Circulaire n° p.5/72, 06.04.1972 – IISH, SI, 779.
16 "Statement by the Commission of the Socialist International", 24.10.1969 – Institute for Social History (IISH), Amsterdam, Socialist International Arquive (SI), 778.
17 Letter from Hans Janitschek to Marcelo Caetano, 21.10.1969 – IISH, SI, 778.
18 Cable from the Socialist International to Marcelo Caetano, 24.10.1969 – IISH, SI, 778.
19 Letter from Hans-Eberhard Dingels to Hans Janitschek, 09.10.1969 – IISH, SI, 778.
20 According to the former head of the PS's International Department, Rui Mateus, the Friedrich Ebert Foundation paid for the travel expenses of the participants but had no direct intervention in the process. Rui Mateus, *Contos Proibidos. Memorias de Um PS Desconhecido* (Lisbon: D. Quixote, 1996), 42–44. The same was confirmed by Elke Esters (Sabiel), former delegate of the Friedrich Ebert Foundation for Portugal during the 1970s, in interviews with the author in July 2014 in Bonn, and in Lisbon in April 2016.
21 Fonseca, *«É Preciso Regar os Cravos!»*, 77.
22 Rui Lopes, *West Germany and the Portuguese Dictatorship, 1968–1974. Between Cold War and Colonialism* (London: Palgrave Macmillan UK, 2014).
23 Fonseca, *«É Preciso Regar os Cravos!»*, 78–79. The first international event of the Portuguese Socialist party was in July 1973, when Soares and others were invited to London by the Labour Party in anticipation of Caetano's visit to the United Kingdom, to celebrate the 600th anniversary of the Anglo-Portuguese Alliance. See MacQueen and Oliveira, "Grocer meets Butcher", 29–50.
24 Ana Monica Fonseca, "From Iberian Peninsula to Latin America: The Socialist International's Initiatives in the First Years of Brandt's Presidency", in *Willy Brandt and International Relations. Europe, the USA and Latin America, 1974–1992*, edited by Bernd Rother and Klaus Larres (London: Bloomsbury Academic, 2019), 179–193.
25 Fonseca, *«É Preciso Regar os Cravos!»*
26 On the international relations during the final years of the Portuguese dictatorship, see: Rui Lopes, "Accommodating and Confronting the Portuguese Dictatorship within NATO, 1970–4", *The International History Review* 30, no. 3 (2016): 1–22, https://doi.org/10.1080/07075332.2015.1046388.
27 António Muñoz Sanchez, "Aportacion al estúdio de la influencia de los factores internacionales en la transicion democrática espanhola", *Memorana*, 3 (1998): 55–67. See also Charles Powell, "International Aspects of Democratization. The Case of Spain", in *The International Dimensions of Democratization. Europe and the Americas*, edited by Lawrence Whitehead (Oxford: Oxford University Press, 1996).
28 Willy Brandt, "Sessão de Abertura da Conferência do Estoril", in *Processos de Democratização na Península Ibérica e na América Latina. Conferência de Lisboa, 30 Setembro a 2 de Outubro de 1978* (Lisbon: Partido Socialista, 1978), 42.
29 Fonseca, *«É Preciso Regar os Cravos!»*
30 Soares' interview with Maria Joao Avillez.
31 "Besprechungen in Caracas und Mexiko ueber möglichkeiten und formen zukünftiger zusammenarbeit auf parteien-ebene", Klaus Lindenberg, 31.05.1976 – AdsD, Klaus Lindenberg Depositum, 91.
32 Notes on the Bureau's meeting in Rom, 2–3 June 1977 – AdsD, 1/WBASI00003.

33 "Informe de la mission de la Internacional Socialsita a la America Latina", 15–25. Marzo. 1978 – IISH, SI Archive, 1127.
34 Author's interview with Klaus Lindenberg, Bonn, 09.04.2014.
35 Author's interview with Klaus Lindenberg, Bonn, 09.04.2014.
36 Declaração de Lisboa, 03.10.1978, in *Processos de Democratização na Península Ibérica e na América Latina. Conferência de Lisboa, 30 Setembro a 2 de Outubro de 1978* (Lisbon: Partido Socialista, 1978).

9 Contribution to the critique of "Social Democracy in One Country"
The case of Sweden

Olle Törnquist

The puzzle

There is something strange with the crisis of Social Democracy in the North. Beyond party labels, Social Democracy is clearly about sustainable development based on socio-economic justice by democratic means. Similarly, adherents seem to agree that the main challenges are neoliberalism and right-wing populism, even if they differ on how to counter them. The left-wing factions emphasise class, domestic spending, welfare and taxation of capital. Those inclined towards green politics add measures against climate change. And those oriented towards the centre favour financially less expansive policies along with restrictions of migration, arguing that this will save national communion and welfare.[1] This can be observed when looking at the various think tanks that have emerged, like the British *Momentum* against *Blue Labour*, and in Sweden *Reformisterna* (along with union think-tank *Katalys*) against the party think-tank *Tiden*. Mysteriously, however, the previously common ground is ignored even by the left wing – that neoliberalism, increasing use of fossil energy and xenophobic counter-movements are all nourished by the capitalist globalisation.

This chapter argues that this amnesia is a result of social democrats having failed to regulate the market-driven globalisation and conceded to it. From a southern historical perspective, this is not just due to the strength of the foes but also the weakness of the social democrats.[2] A critical case in point is the former stronghold of Sweden. Almost like Stalin's turn to "socialism in one country" (by giving priority to Soviet Union's own narrow interests when socialism in other countries faltered), Swedish social democrats have adjusted their national growth pact between capital and labour to the priorities of the internationalised companies, without involving labour and social democracy in other contexts. By implication, the scope for development based on social justice and democracy is reduced in Sweden too, and quests for nationalist protection have gained strength. When refugees from the South reached northern Europe in 2015, Swedish social democrats were even short of an internationalist alternative to national chauvinism, just as Corbyn suffered a humiliating electoral defeat in 2019 for want of an international alternative to Brexit. At the time of writing (spring 2021), it is an open question

DOI: 10.4324/9781003181439-10

whether and how the Swedish labour party will consider the dilemma in a more apt international programme during its November 2021 congress.[3]

To unpack the historical dynamics, it is useful to focus on four junctures. One, why it was so difficult in the 1970s for Olof Palme, Willy Brandt and others to build a social democratic alternative to the market-driven globalisation. Two, how liberal economic perspectives got the upper hand among social democrats in the 1980s, along with Blairist adjustment to the neoliberal globalisation and governance. Three, how moderate social democrats adopted a similar view of the third wave of democracy, while leftists tried to change from the bottom-up – and both lost out. Four, how new party leader Stefan Löfven designed a more union-based internationalism in 2012 but retreated in face of the refugee crisis.

From national internationalism to "new international economic order"

The Swedish post–Second World War model had two international pillars. One was national independence and the ability to decide on one's own priorities. This called for the alliances of like-minded countries and movements to contain imperial powers. Most famously, during the Cold War, this stance included engagement in favour of all countries' – and colonies' – right to national independence based on equal citizenship and chances to develop their own reforms. Sweden, with leaders like Olof Palme, was in the forefront, not being part of the North Atlantic Treaty Organization (NATO).

The other pillar was successful export industries and free trade on equal terms. With access to iron ore and forest products, in high international demand, the industrial competitiveness was firmly based on innovation and high productivity. This stemmed from the growth pact between capital and labour, complemented by strategic public procurements, representation of unions, employer's organisations and other concerned parties in public governance, and productivity-oriented education and welfare.

Export and support for free trade on equal terms was in opposition to colonial and imperial monopolisation. Hence, it did not undermine the first principle of supporting genuine national independence in other countries too – as long as these countries could develop their own policies and withstand negative business pressures. Besides, Swedish export industries were rarely involved in the developing countries where progressive development was at stake. And when they were, as in South Africa, social democrats were often in the vanguard of support to progressive forces, such as supplying a major part of the funds for the African National Congress (ANC) and United Democratic Front. Conversely, where private business stayed out but investments were needed to build political and economic independence, as in North Vietnam, Sweden took the lead, becoming the first western country to recognise North Vietnam's independence. When the United States engaged in terror bombardments, strategic support was given for industrial and social development.

Meanwhile, from the 1960s, first textile and garments, then basic sector industries and shipbuilding were shifted to countries with "firmer governance" and lower wages. Deindustrialisation and internal Swedish migration to "more competitive" cities was extensive and swift. Initially, the troubles could be handled in accordance with the growth and welfare model agreed on between unions, employers and the government – that factories with weak productivity and inability to pay the same wages as in other sectors were closed down, while workers were taken care of, re-educated and shifted to more competitive production and services. Soon enough, however, the preconditions in terms of expanding markets and Keynesian stimulation of demand were at risk.

The disbanding in 1971 of the Bretton Woods agreement on fixed currency exchange rates was a major warning that the space for national economic governance was shrinking. Social democrats had to go beyond their nationally confined models. While friends in previous empires like the United Kingdom and France contemplated economic cooperation with their former colonies, internationalists in search of renewal of Social Democracy progressives like Olof Palme and Willy Brandt tried instead to construct a "new international economic order" (NIEO) and promote a "North-South Program for Survival" (NSPS). This meant, primarily, additional co-operation with countries that were not aligned either to West or to East in the Cold War. According to basic Keynesian thinking, less unfair terms of trade for the developing countries, and better conditions for their poor people, would increase demand for products from the North too.

However, the efforts for promoting NIEO and NSPS failed. The plans received positive attention at the United Nations, but the outcomes of negotiations were inconclusive. Primarily, of course, Washington and its allies resisted NIEO and NSPS, along with the increasingly powerful transnational companies and financial institutions. Yet, an equally important factor was the weakness of the potential southern partners, even though they had blossomed in the struggle against colonialism. Now the leaders in the oil-producing countries increased their prices but catered to their own short-term interests rather than inclusive development, which, according to the advocates of NIEO and NSPS, would have boosted demand for other products than weapons and luxury from the North. Authoritarian developmental states opted for low-cost export-oriented industrialisation. China, on its part, was engulfed in a devastating cultural revolution. Liberation movements were economically fragile. Social democracy in countries such as Sukarno's Indonesia, Nehru's India and Nyerere's Tanzania had failed, or ceased to progress. Popular democratic movements suffered from interventions from the West or the East. In 1973, for example, another US-nurtured coup ousted democratic socialist Salvador Allende in Chile.

Drawbacks of second-generation social democrats

To understand the failure of NIEO and NSPS – which paved the way for neoliberal globalisation and undermined Social Democracy – we must thus ask why the like-minded partners in the South had become so weak. While the first-generation social democrats grew out of the northern industrial revolution, the second generation social democrats were rooted in the emancipatory movements against colonialism. Still, Social Democracy has four universal cornerstones: (1) democratic popular-interest collectivities, (2) democratic links between the state and equal citizens, (3) social rights and welfare and (4) economic growth pacts between the state, primary producers, labour and employers.[4]

In the South, the first two cornerstones were up against colonialism, feudal-like subordination and uneven development, but it was anyway possible to construct the first two pillars. Critical cases such as the Indian state of Kerala and Indonesia until the end of the 1950s show that social democratic policies were not doomed in spite of divisive identities, limited industrialisation and the absence of unifying class interests. In both contexts, the demands for equal citizenship and democracy against colonialism, and representation through ethnic and religious groups, served as unifying frame among scattered classes and movements for interest-based struggles such as for land and welfare reforms.

Elsewhere, however, equal citizenship and democracy were often subordinated to the struggle against landlords, oligarchs and foreign domination. This sequencing spread to Indonesia too. After independence, renewal-oriented communists who essentially advocated broadly defined social democratic policies had built the world's largest peaceful popular movement and advanced in elections.[5] But, in the late 1950s, they responded to threats from adversaries by rallying behind President Sukarno's left-populism. Campaigns against imperialism and landlordism in the context of authoritarian so-called guided democracy were deemed more important than democracy based on equal citizens and their own mediating organisations.

Meanwhile opponents, including Singaporean oriented social-democrats, revised the modernisation theory that social and economic progress would spawn middle-class-driven liberal democracy. The new argument was that, paradoxically, the attainment of democracy also called for firmer political and legal institutions by way of a "politics of order" – in the worst cases through "middle-class coups" supported by the army, backed by the United States. Over the years, this approach, theorised by Samuel Huntington,[6] spread around the South. In Indonesia, "politics of order" was even by reviving the colonial form of despotic indirect rule through communal leaders in the form of army-led massacres of leftists in co-operation with religious and other militia groups. The leftists were helpless, having abandoned the focus on equal citizenship and democracy.[7]

Similarly, Eastern bloc modernisation theorists were for their part worried that workers and "national capitalists" remained weak. The suggestion was therefore that progressive leaders and army officers might promote non-capitalist development from top-down. This approach spread around the South too. An early case was Abdel Nasser in Egypt, but existing democracies were also undermined, such as in India through the cooperation between the pro-Moscow communists and Indira Gandhi and the emergency rule 1975–1977.

The third social democratic cornerstone of social rights and welfare was crucial in terms of movements' self-help, but extensive welfare state programmes have been unfeasible since they have rested with the fourth cornerstone of socio-economic growth pacts – which, in turn, have presupposed effective democratic governance as well as strong unified unions and employers' organisations. The substitute in the South was democratic elections of elitist leaders and their top-down planning through what was referred to as "developmental states", focusing on basic industries, import-substitution and at times nationalisation of foreign companies and reforms. Social rights and deeper democracy would have to wait. Typically, however, these efforts were not economically successful either – while the East Asian "developmental states" were proved more able thanks to authoritarian means and focus on the world market.

More radical struggle against oligarchs and "bureaucratic capitalists" (the Maoist terminology for generals, top bureaucrats and political bosses) focused on their presumed reliance on "landlords" and "imperialists", especially with links to Dutch, British and American companies and governments. But control of land in Indonesia was a complicated matter making it difficult to unite the rural poor against a common enemy. And fighting imperialism was insufficient. For example, most generals even supported the nationalisation of foreign companies and gained control of them when it was pushed through. To weaken the "bureaucratic capitalists", progressives obviously needed to give priority to democratic control of public resources they had captured. But the struggle for democracy was deprioritised. The same dilemma applied to the struggle against oligarchs in countries like the Philippines. For many years, political bosses such as Ferdinand Marcos had used the US-exported electoral system to gain office in local and state governments and bureaucracies in order to accumulate power and wealth for private investments. But not even non-Maoist leftists focused on containing this political accumulation of capital by fighting for democratic control of public office and resources – until, instead, the traditional elite ripped the benefit of the popular power revolution in 1986.

Adapting the Swedish model

Increasing competition from newly industrialising countries and higher oil prices were no problem for Swedish social democrats – as long as there was rising demand for export, investments in new job-creating sectors, and socially responsible structural adjustment to adapt to the new lay of the land. By the late 1970s, however, much of that was unfeasible, given the failure of NIEO and NSPS. Consequently, Swedish aid to the South – which aimed at strengthening political and social rights plus welfare to promote inclusive development, like once at home – turned into a cost rather than an investment in rising markets. Business, and often unions too, deemed the supporters of welfare in the South idealists in need of a "sheltered workshop", arguing it was necessary to focus on expansion and profits within the market-driven globalisation.

In addition, unions asked for better wages, but Keynesian stimulation of demand meant more imports than investments. And deregulation of international finance facilitated tax evasion and capital flight. Blue-collar workers' unions suggested wage earner funds to gain better control and encourage long-term investments, but this caused divisions in the social democratic movement, while the bourgeois parties united and joined hands with business.

In 1983, President Mitterrand of France made a U-turn away from his socialist and Keynesian-oriented programme, yielding to new liberal-priorities and austerity policies. In Sweden, Palme was not as optimistic as one decade earlier. In 1985, he even lost control of the Bank of Sweden and his finance minister, Kjell Olof Feldt, who conceded to international liberalism by deregulating the credit market, paving the way for financial and real estate speculation.

Subsequent governments had to repay huge public debts. Welfare spending was reduced, including the support for those badly affected by structural adjustment. Business-like new public management gained ground, as did privatisation of public welfare and services.[8] Some two-thirds of the population with fitting education and skills, mainly in the big cities, benefitted from good jobs and cheap loans, which facilitated speculation in housing. The 2008 financial crisis hardly affected them. The losses were socialised, i.e. paid by the most vulnerable citizens, including those in run-down suburbs and the "rural rust belts".

After the fall of the Berlin Wall in 1989, the European Union (EU) was often perceived as a viable substitute for the capsized NIEO and NSPS. Business, export sector unions and the bourgeois parties were positive. Sweden joined in 1995, and social democrats supported Tony Blair's "third way" of combining centre-right economic policies with centre-left social policies. National rights and growth pacts were deemphasised in favour of a "social Europe" with fair competition, social cohesion and increasing standards of living. This vision generated some optimism and electoral advances for social democrats in several countries. But just like in the Global South in the 1970s, sympathetic partners in Europe were not strong enough to foster anything like continental Keynesianism or much of a social Europe. Social democratic ideas lost out to ordo-liberal regimes – adding judicial guarantees and strong governance to underpin free and dynamic markets and austerity policies – and then, over the years, to right-wing nationalists too. Back in Sweden, the social democrats were humiliated in the 2006 elections by losing badly to a centre-right alliance, faced internal divisions, were short of alternative policy proposals and did not manage to get back in office until 2014.

Lost in the third wave of democracy

Meanwhile, liberal internationalism gained ground alongside an increasing market-driven globalisation. Beyond the EU, leading social democrats found no other way but trying to adjust to this trend by deregulating finance and supporting exports and investments in the South. The old idea of preventing trade and investments that contradicted local attempts at progressive change was swept under the carpet. In 1996, the Swedish prime minister, Göran Persson, even expressed his admiration for China's stability – only seven years after the massacre in the Tiananmen Square.

The other side of the coin was much more positive. In response to popular protests, the more market than imperial-state-driven globalisation allowed for a third wave of democracy. The new wave arose in the mid-1970s, with the transitions from authoritarian rule in Portugal, Greece and Spain. It then spread to Latin America, other parts of the South and after the fall of the wall to the former Eastern bloc. The major exceptions are where dictatorial regimes with support from hegemonic parties as in China or competing global powers as in the Middle East and North Africa. Elsewhere, however, the third wave was also an opening for a third-generation social democrat to discipline globalisation. While the new generation moderates had much in common with the northern Blairists, the radicals were rooted in the struggle against repression and wanted to build democratic alternatives with popular movements and citizen action.

Like-minded friends provided support. From Sweden, Olof Palme tried to hold on to international cooperation among kindred partners as the alternative, coordinated via the Socialist International and the United Nations. Efforts included support for the anti-dictatorial struggle in Europe and Latin America, and the anti-apartheid struggle in South Africa and meditation in conflicts such as between Iran and Iraq.

The assassination of Palme in 1986 meant that these priorities lost steam in Sweden. With regard to democratisation in the South, liberals and moderate social democrats promoted elitist pacts rather than popular-driven negotiations. Radicals and popular movements were marginalised, with partial exceptions such as Lula's Brazil and Mandela's South Africa. The Swedish liberal and conservative parties – in office 2006 until 2014 – showed even less interest in unions, social movements and their parties. The official development cooperation emphasised mainstream think tanks, elitist reformists and civil society watchdogs – and resisted, with great fanfare, bilateral agreements – including support for human rights – with non-liberal countries like Vietnam.

Over the years, third-wave democratisation petered out. Even the efforts in South Africa, the Philippines and Brazil were not as successful as expected. The admirable centre-leftist regimes and movements did not stand out as a solid footing for any new attempt at the social democratic internationalism of the kind that had been visualised by Palme and others. This brought to mind how weak partners in the South made NIEO and NSPS unfeasible. Once again, we must thus ask why broadly defined Social Democracy did not make more headway in the South.

Stumbling blocks in the South

The studies of Indonesia, India and the Philippines with references to South Africa, Brazil and Scandinavia that I have been involved in since the 1970s point to six main causes for the problems. *First*, democratic popular-interest collectives cannot be based on the working class – as it was in the North – to the same degree as in the South. Labour and democracy activists rarely combine their priorities. Workers themselves are too few, too scattered and often divided by specific interests and demands. Some 90% of India's workforce, for example, is in the informal sector. Unity is difficult on the workplace level and between them; and higher up the system, union leaders tend to develop their own preferences, such as striking deals with dubious politicians. Informal sector labourers are often neglected; as are small farmers and fisher folks.

Second, the radical third generation's focus on democratisation and reformist policies from the bottom-up is necessary but insufficient. Previous emphasis on citizenship and democracy as a framework for common interest-based demands for social rights and land reform has been overlooked. There are few exceptions to the liberal view, fostered by donors, that civil society is little more than a corrective supplement to the mainstream formula for elite-negotiated democracy. Pro-democracy spearheads such as journalists and students are important but at times run ahead of themselves – neglecting organisation and protection of the people they speak for. Local organisers trying to do just that are rarely able to scale up. Cause-oriented groups are typically issue driven, dependent on donors' priorities and mutually competitive. Building broader alliances and wide membership is rarely a priority. Quick, visible results are easier to achieve by actions, media coverage, lobbying and "good connections" in the metropolis. Worst, Civil Society Organisations (CSOs) and unions have problem to engage politically, mainly because of fragmentation and narrow priorities but also their donor's hesitance to be associated with politics. With few exceptions such as the Workers Party in Brazil, and, partially, the Philippine citizen action party *Akbayan*, the attempts to build new parties based on CSOs, social movements and unions have been disappointing.

In the less common cases where leftist parties dominate, the problem is rather top-down party-politicisation of popular-interest and citizen organisations. South Africa is a case in point. Fortunately, the exceptional Kerala civil society activists proved that this can be altered by impressive campaigns for decentralised development. But in the end, they were also stabbed in the back by dominant leaders in the major leftist party who ignored the principles of the campaign as well as the potential candidates having fought for them, accusing these candidates instead of giving in to neoliberal forms of decentralisation and scholars allegedly linked to the US Central Intelligence (CIA).[9] Later on, party leaders came to their senses, cleared the purged activists and sustained most of the benefits of decentralisation. But remaining problems include how to combine representative and direct democracy, participatory and professional governance, development and welfare, and civil society activism with party and interest organisation.

Third, decentralisation is important to counter authoritarian and top-down rule, and foster local democracy. But the celebrated participatory budgeting in Brazil, for one, presupposed that the Workers' Party won mayoral elections and then introduced the popular deliberations from the top down, along with trusted rules and regulations. And local participants were unable to keep an eye on the central-level political corruption that generated so much distrust and lit the flame of right-wing populism. Generally, decentralisation is not a panacea for local democracy as long as progressives in CSOs and popular organisations are not strong enough to make a difference. The shining example is Kerala where local oligarchic rule had been uprooted through land reform and struggle for citizen civil and social rights. In this context, progressives in civil society and government managed to cooperate and introduce both democratic decentralisation and participatory planning. Still, localisation of politics is often unviable. Villages are open economies with outside links. For example, local governments cannot be expected to be responsible for the full welfare of those who work outside the villages. There must also be *state* programmes – as when local responsibility for fighting poverty in Scandinavia was supplemented in conjunction with industrialisation by national welfare schemes.[10] Similarly, local communities are difficult places in which to combine the preoccupations of CSOs and unions that are not confined to the local territories but related to production and national governance.

Fourth, democratic representation remains neglected. For all its promise, the third wave of democratisation turned out to involve the accommodation of elites who adjusted to – and then dominated – elementary democratic rules of the game. While many moderate social democrats contributed to this, radical pro-democrats in CSOs and popular movements rarely gained access to the playground, except as individual subordinates in the elite-teams. This nourished populist reactions, often turning rightist. Dedicated liberals and social democrats worry but lack alternatives. Some of them even return to the old idea from the late 1950s that weak states with poorly enacted rule of law and rampant corruption must be fixed before democratic deficiencies are attended to – an updated version, of the old "politics of order", now spearheaded by Francis Fukuyama.[11]

So far, frustrated progressives have mainly confined themselves to building alternatives within their own ranks, from the bottom-up. But CSOs typically deem politics "dirty", fail to scale up the movements they speak for, and mainly participate in election through leaders' association with mainstream parties. The common man's party (Aam Aadmi Party, AAP) in Delhi was first exceptionally successful by fighting corruption in public services that matter for poor people too. But populism has overshadowed solid democratic practices and broader agendas on inclusive development.

In Indonesia, reform-oriented populist leader Joko "Jokowi" Widodo became successful mayor, governor and even president by agreeing to deal with citizen groups and popular movements. This was an opening for progressives, as long as the agreements were clear-cut and based on comprehensive reforms. Another reason for failure was informal individual negotiations and transactions, in tandem with populist ideas of direct relations between leaders and "the people" – instead of democratic representation in institutionalised collective negotiations. The most promising achievement was the successful alliance in the early 2010s (with some support from social democratic Friedrich Ebert Stiftung) between CSOs, urban poor associations, unions and progressive politicians in favour of a universal public health reform. But there was no forum with democratic representation of the vital partners which could assume the role of negotiating follow up-reforms with the government. Even none of the progressives suggested such a format, rather returning to their own special issues, and transactions with individual politicians. In addition, most international democracy-donors failed to provide CSO and popular movement activists with support to encourage representative democracy. In Aceh, for example, the international community facilitated both the massive post-tsunami reconstruction and "democratic peace" accord. However, even Sweden and Norway neglected a strategy to combine the processes and support pro-democrats rather than the autocratic leaders in the independence movement (GAM).

Fifth, the Blairist combination of market-driven growth and welfare has bifurcated. Social democratic-oriented "developmental state" governments in Brazil, for example, benefitted from the commodity boom and combined global market friendly economic growth with welfare programmes, but stumbled over inequalities and corruption when the boom petered out. In India too, during the centre-left Congress governments of 2004–2014, economic liberalisation was combined with technological advances and impressive rights and welfare reforms, but growth generated more inequality and corruption than new jobs. The reforms were typically supplementary rather than designed to transform the growth model, and the middle classes found little for them in the targeted schemes for the poor. This played into the hands of Hindu nationalist Narendra Modi. The centre-left Philippine government of 2010–2016 could also not renew its mandate. "Good governance", increased productivity and some welfare measures but failed to make much of a dent in the negative effects of market-driven growth, making increasingly many people interested in a "strong man" like Duterte. In President "Jokowi's" Indonesia, reformist populism (with social contracts on decent urban planning and a broad alliance for universal public health) was short of a strategy to continue work for more reforms and negotiate sustainable development. When challenged by conservatives, Jokowi toned down reforms and consultations with labour in favour of compromises with political elites and business, including creating new jobs by less burdensome employment regulations and no significant compensation in terms of rights and welfare.

Generally, moreover, union-based social democrats remain based on the first-generation growth models. According to them, decent jobs and good, collectively negotiated or regulated minimum pay (to "compress the wage level") would stimulate productivity and generate more jobs in expanding economies.[12] In the South, with less strong unions, this was expected to be facilitated by a more democratic edition of the second generation's "developmental states". This may be valid where there are good markets, but it remains insufficient when there is much underemployment and poorly developed production for nearby markets, such as within agriculture, food and clothing where many people must eke out a living. In such sectors, producers and retailers cannot survive immediate global competition and as high minimum wages as in the capital intensive sectors. One example is South Africa, politically aligned with social democratic policy. The example of Sweden, and others, of pacts between capital and labour was not successfully transformed as a policy model to farmers and others in rural areas. The idea about welfare for all, protection to prevent these groups from losing their land and livelihood, and support to create new jobs did not materialise.

Worse, the leftist leaders in West Bengal – in office since 1977 – even gave up on efforts at rural development and welfare-driven development in the 1990s, in favour of East Asian–inspired industrialisation by outside investors and production for markets elsewhere. In 2011, India was democratic enough to allow citizens to resist and vote the communists out of power when their policy was at the expense of small farmers and informal labourers.

Meanwhile the immensely important human rights and democracy activists have had little to say of inclusive development. The decentralised people's planning in Kerala in the 1990s was exceptional. It aimed at *local* growth pacts based on rights and welfare. But the farmers were reluctant to cooperate, the village plans did not extend beyond public investment, there were limited links and coordination beyond the villages, and the middle classes disengaged, as welfare and other measures were for the poor. Yet the local development plans remain crucial for all those who do not but should benefit from the thriving market-driven growth within construction, technology, service, education and health that rest with decades of public action for human development. To kick off a comparatively successful local public action campaign against COVID-19, the Kerala Left is now combining welfare reforms with efforts at knowledge-based development.

Sixth, transformative politics have been overlooked. Social Democracy is not just a counter-movement to make capitalism liveable by regulations and taxation to finance better welfare, as often stated by supportive academicians such as Joseph Stiglitz.[13] Social Democracy is also about transformative strategies of striving for public reforms and civil society agreements that strengthen the capacity of broad collectivities to fight for more advanced reforms, and then even better reforms after that – towards a system where equity, equality and welfare are both investments and outcomes. This, Palme said (1982), is what made him a "democratic socialist". In short, there is a difference between taming a wolf and breeding it into a working dog.

Impasse, restart and collapse

Did northern social democrats study and consider the problems and options in the South? Not really. In Sweden, much of the previous interest in the fate of cognate movements elsewhere was lost. A typical argument was that much of the Global South was now doing well enough to handle its own problems of repression and exploitation of people and nature. Aside from international trade unionism and demands for human rights, plus the signing of International Labour Organization (ILO) conventions in return for free trade agreements to prevent social dumping, there was, in this view, little Sweden, or any Northern nation, could do. International aid should focus on poverty, disasters, supporting elections and civil society watchdogs. Hence, the demand for contextual knowledge of the problems and options for potential partners in the Global South faded away. Higher education and research, for example, fixated, beyond human rights, on free-floating international relations, "global governance" and quantitative indices of growth and democracy – far above the realities and contexts where transformative politics must be rooted and gain strength.

Many social democrats even turned down the troublesome effects of the market-driven globalisation. One reason was the primacy of export and free trade. Another was to resist the claims by employers, bourgeois parties and rightists within their own ranks that the international challenges called for further reduction of taxes and wages for less qualified jobs, the downgrading of public spending and services, and the deregulation of business and employment conditions, in order to defend Sweden's competitiveness. The counter proposal was to revive the Scandinavian model and thus adjust to globalisation in socially responsible ways. One could foster competitiveness based on efficiency, innovation and education as well as relocation and protection of labour.

This proved unviable. Uneven development and inequalities increased in the North too, making it more difficult to build broad popular interest-based collectivities. Privatisation and neoliberal governance shrunk the number of vital issues that could be handled democratically. The international economic concentration of power increased dramatically. The links between state and civil society were weakened, especially the participation of issue and interest groups in public governance. As compared to taxation of wages, it was much more difficult to levy the incomes from capital and speculation, which cause most of the spiralling inequalities, and, thus to also finance the universal public welfare system. The same applied to the difficulties of restructuring the economy and addressing the mounting inequalities and unemployment among migrants and refugees. Several of the conditions for the social pact between capital and labour were also undermined. Its basis within industry had been hollowed out. It is much more difficult to increase productivity in the new low-wage sectors of private and public services and welfare than previously in trade and production; and the services and welfare cannot be closed down – but who shall pay? Most importantly, the major task was no longer to handle a shortage of skilled labour but also unemployment. And much of the growth strategy could no longer be controlled due to the international mobility of capital and labour.

Unsurprisingly, Swedish Social Democracy was thus in a crisis, partly reflected in toothless policy development, internal conflicts and reduced membership. Support plummeted especially among those negatively affected by structural adjustment. Most of these lost voters linked up instead with the chauvinist right-wing party. Meanwhile numerous intellectuals and young people lost interest and trust in politics.[14]

Revival

In trying to regain direction and strength, the Social Democrats opted in 2012 for their first trade union leader, Stefan Löfven, the former chair and international secretary of the Industrial and Metal Workers Union (IF-Metall). After the 2014 elections, the party limped back into office in coalition with the Greens. Löfven called for the reinvention of the old Scandinavian model, at home and globally. The ethos of the "Scandinavian model" would be added to the ILO principles of dialogues between labour, employers, and governments in terms of a "global deal" – "so that the benefits of the global market can be shared by everyone". This was also projected as the major mean to fulfil the UN's 2030 agenda and particularly its eighth goal to promote inclusive and sustainable economic growth, and productive full employment and decent work for all.

The party and related unions were supportive. And even though responsibility for international development cooperation was ceded to the Green coalition partner, social democrats with long experience from the UN, the EU, development cooperation and civil society gained new ground for their ideas. A special minister would direct strategic studies to help coordinate ministerial work and efforts by unions and other progressive organisations.

Promising but stumbling

Löfven gained international reputation for his idea of a global deal. Employers, unions and state representatives were invited to promotional workshops. Unions could complement work in the International Labour Organization (ILO) with engagement in the Organisation for Economic Co-operation and Development (OECD), which is now in charge of fleshing out the concept. Local implementation, however, was up against the same challenges that Palme and Brandt faced in the 1970s and the new generation social democrats suffered from during the third wave of democracy. Firstly, the shortage of strong enough progressive partners in governments, unions and civil society on the ground. Secondly, the absence of several of the preconditions for the iconic social pacts in Scandinavia, including sufficiently expanding economies to absorb unemployment.

Separately, the new minister for foreign affairs (2014–2019), Margot Wallström, added a bold "feminist-oriented" policy for democracy and human rights in favour of Agenda 2030, bilaterally and within international organisations. But the policies met with immediate resistance, including from rulers in the Arab world. Consequently, Swedish businesses and unions with interests in exports to these and similar countries became worried too.[15]

Export versus inclusive development?

Social democrats are eager to promote export and "free trade on equal terms", as former Minister of Trade and now Minister for Foreign Affairs Ann Linde puts it. But what if the terms are not equal?

While paying due respect to democracy and human rights, business and some unions prefer codes of conduct for the concerned companies, in return for freedom to trade and invest in all countries that are not affected by international boycotts. As the social democratic chairman of the Swedish parliament's Committee on Foreign Affairs, Kenneth G. Forslund, put it: "I do not think that the politicians shall decide on each and every Swedish business deal to export arms". Subsequently, Sweden even maintained its commitments to sell arms to Saudi Arabia and the United Arab Emirates in spite of their contribution to the conflicts in the Middle East that people had to flee from – including to Sweden itself.

Potentially, however, there is also a progressive dimension to the interest in exports. In 2014, the blue-collar workers confederation (LO) published a major report arguing that it was necessary to increase wages and investments to foster full employment. This was in stark contrast to the dominant austerity measures and efforts to compete by neglecting work conditions. The analysis focused on Sweden, but the authors, C-M Jonsson and I. Lindberg, said the original argument was expanded to the rest of Europe and the Global South too, given that austerity measures and weak economic demand outside Sweden was not just bad for the other countries but also for Swedish exports. The case of southern Europe was obvious. In the South, moreover, it is insufficient to rely on uneven and environmentally disastrous development and the buying power of the nouveau riche. However, Jonsson explained somewhat sheepishly: the top LO leaders who thereafter negotiated the general report felt that the focus had to be on Sweden, because improvements in other contexts were "too far away".

Beyond provincial minds, however, the fact remains that Sweden's economy is internationally oriented and the demand for its products must be considered beyond Europe and North America. Hence, according to the LO study, Sweden should take steps to raise demand in the South by way of more equitable and sustainable development – while also increasing its own imports of products produced in an environment-friendly way and by decently paid labour. It should also abstain from those aspects of the international trade and investment agreements that generate uneven development and reduce the space for progressive politics.

Such expansion of markets by means of more equitable and sustainable development in the South calls for altered power relations and the representation of a broad popular base and progressive forces. How could the positive vision of Agenda 2030, ILO, and the global deal be implemented in practice? It is true that when local regimes sign international conventions without applying them, this may anyway legitimate external support for unions and CSOs that try to enforce implementation. But, the fundamental factor is whether these progressives are strong enough in their own right.

An early attempt to strengthen partners was made by the Ministry for Enterprise and Innovation (and later the Ministry of Trade). The ministries agreed with business and unions to combine a campaign for exports to unevenly developing and often authoritarian countries with corporate social responsibilities that the unions, and not just the companies themselves, would oversee. One dilemma, however, is that unions and managers tend to prioritise what is good for their own companies and employees. Another is that well-implemented codes only apply to individual Swedish companies and, at best, a local union, not collective action among other labourers.

Similar problems may beset unions' international cooperation. Only a minority of workers in the South have formal employment and are unionised, and many of them do not value the importance of broad alliances with other labourers. Sofia Östmark, leading the Swedish non-political union-to-union organisation until mid 2021, adds, "this is why we support demands for formal employment of many more laborers, efforts at wider and stronger organisation, plus that unions link up with others to, for example, improve employment conditions and minimum wages". However, as already mentioned, the South African experience, for example, shows there must also be policies to compensate for the lack of similar conditions to those that prevailed when social democrats were strong Scandinavia – low levels of underemployment and the steady growth of new jobs in competitive sectors when less productive units cannot pay decent wages and close down.

A supplementary approach is contained in the international framework agreements such as between IF-Metall, the Industri ALL Global Union and the retail-clothing company H&M, ideally affecting some 1.6 million workers. The idea is to strengthen the right to organise and the bargaining power of workers in subcontracted H&M units. Yet, senior union researcher Mats Wingborg says the reality does not live up to the hype: "While H&M benefits from good media attention and the leading unions enjoy the benefits of a profitable 'mother company', the local unions are weak and informal laborers not contracted by H&M's partners remain unaffected". Similar challenges apply to the Swedish backing for the ILO to promote the "global deal" concept by negotiations between unions, employers and governments in countries such as Bangladesh or China. Obviously, the opportunities to include and strengthen weak unions, promote democratic principles and enrol temporary workers and labourers in sweatshops vary with the strength of the unions and the decency of the regime.

Coordination in despair

Löfven also assigned a special minister, Kristina Persson, to identify the strategic challenges and synchronise policies in favour of Agenda 2030. She appointed experts from unions, business, think tanks and the like to three advisory groups. These were tasked to suggest ideas, respectively, about working life, the environment and global cooperation. But the groups consisted of volunteers in the special minister's network and lacked representatives from some crucial ministries and vital organisations such as the Palme Center, as well as some of the best qualified scholars, to review previous insights and experiences. In short, the groups differed from the practice of the old public commissions that – in addition to tripartite negotiations – are crucial elements of participatory governance in the Scandinavian model worshipped by Löfven. This saved time and money, but the outcome was a list of ideas to be followed up – in contrast to a well-anchored and knowledge-based platform for the coordination and implementation of social democratic vision. Instead of correcting this and supporting the special minister, Löfven sacked her in May 2016 – and coordination withered.

The new policy for international development cooperation, for example, was as incoherent as ever. In the policy guideline, the Green party minister in charge produced an extended list of poorly connected priorities, including her own special concern for environmental issues, the foreign minister's feminism, and the prime minister's global deal. These priorities, moreover, did not stress how to fight poverty based on celebrated human and social rights, plus democratisation, but rather emphasised market-driven uneven development, which was credited with having reduced poverty in spite of generating spiralling inequality. Support for poor countries remained a priority but at the expense of the many impoverished people in rapidly growing, though thoroughly unequal economies. Analyses of progressive actors of change in these countries and what reforms they may promote and unite behind were next to absent; and support for progressive unions, civil society groups and parties remained marginal. Agenda 2030 and the treaties to reduce global warming were celebrated, but implementation remained technocratic, skating over power relations and the politics of change.

Collapse

When I stepped off the train in Stockholm in November 2015 to make some of the interviews drawn upon in this chapter, the central station was full of tired refugee families comforting their children – but also numerous social service workers and volunteers helping them out. At the time, Sweden received the most refugees in Europe in proportion to population. Only two weeks later, however, the government imposed restrictions, to give the authorities some "breathing space", but not the refugees. Most other European countries did not share the responsibility for human rights, and there were few safe havens elsewhere. Most remarkably: when nationalist right-wing populists gained votes by xenophobic propaganda against the immigrants, many social democratic and union leaders adjusted.

Migration is not a new dilemma for Swedish social democrats.[16] The welfare state model was inclusive of all citizens but did not consider immigration. After the Second World War, however, import of labour force was deemed as necessary – Swedish industry was intact and its products in great demand for reconstruction elsewhere. This import was organised jointly by the state, employers and unions. As long as the "new labourers" contributed to the welfare state, they were granted the same social and cultural rights as everyone else. The problems appeared as the market-driven globalisation and liberalisation within the EU generated growing numbers of temporary migrant labourers subject to social dumping, as well as to refugees who had difficulty finding work. The principle of equal social rights for all with decent jobs and the payment of taxes became increasingly difficult to combine with equal human rights for all. Refugees from failed attempts at progressive transformation, such as after the coup in Chile, were still welcome, but when numbers increased from first Eastern Europe and then the former Yugoslavia, there were restrictive measures and strict application of the UN refugee convention with regard to asylum seekers plus assistance for them to return, when possible. Meanwhile the root causes of forced migration would be addressed through support for peace and democratisation. But when the "new moderates" (the triangulating followers of the renewed conservative party) and liberals won elections in the early 1990s, they instead combined labour migration supported by business with liberal human rights supported by leftists.

Not just centre-right governments but also social democrats deprioritised over the years the struggle that the latter had initially committed themselves to against the root causes of forced migration and the efforts at a comprehensive refugee policy (first advocated by, among others, the Norwegian UN High Commissioner for refugees, leading social democrat Thorvald Stoltenberg). Subsequently, this retreat made it possible for right-wing nationalists to monopolise, for their own xenophobic purposes, the argument that the refugees should be supported in their own countries. In late 2015, the Social Democrat/Green party coalition government even debited much of the cost for attending to the refugees in Sweden to the budget for international development cooperation, rather than using it to, again, confront the fundamental reasons for why the refugees had to flee in the first place. In short, the mainstream social democrats' turnaround since the 1990s has demonstrated a total inability to develop an alternative international strategy to that of right-wing nationalism.

To numerous social democrats, this was a moral and political tragedy. The top leadership avoided a full-scale electoral disaster only by promising, at the eleventh hour, a new welfare scheme – after which the leaders' stayed in office by negotiating liberal support in return for marginalising the basically social democratic-oriented left party, reducing tax for the better off and committing to deregulate labour policies. The admirable aim was to hold back the right-wing national-populists, but there was still no firm international alternative to their xenophobic priorities. Leftist dissidents suggested Keynesian and more radical welfare policies at home – inspired by Bernie Sanders in the United States, Jeremy Corbyn in Britain, Podemos in Spain and António Costa in Portugal – but avoided what here is identified as the global root causes, the need to internationalise Keynesian policies and the importance and potential of social democracy in the South. In short, the attempt at an internationalist restart collapsed.

Meanwhile, moreover, the new editor of the Social Democratic Party's ideological magazine *Tiden* says international issues will be given less attention, and the party's think-tank suggests the protection of refugees should be subordinated to the capacity to integrate immigrants and defend the welfare for ordinary citizens.

Another attempt?

Simultaneously a new ideological turn seems to be in the making among mainly younger political activists. Committed social democratic cadres try to reinvent the links between, on the one hand, the domestic problems of welfare, climate, employment and integration of migrants, and, on the other, their root causes in global dynamics. The party's new international secretary Johan Hassel points out that the challenge is to communicate these links and suggest feasible policies. International development cooperation, for one, is disconnected from other policy areas. There is not even a social democratic policy for this. The party seems to be in need of a new international program if it was to regain momentum in the sense, it can be seen to have had during most of the Cold War period.

Anna Sundström directing the Palme Center and Mikael Leyi leading the social democratic Solidar Foundation on the EU level concur. Both emphasise the need to strengthen local partners in the South and surmount the insufficient capacity of unions and like-minded popular organisations by building cooperation between them. Support for alliances in the South needs to be negotiated in light of the natural attraction among unions of mainly working with their own counterparts.

What can be done?

Yet, how would it be possible to strengthen social democratic partners in the South? Senior scholar Göran Therborn,[17] for one, argues that the old conditions that shaped forceful Social Democracy in the North are not likely to develop in the South. But, while this is plausible, the obstacles identified in my research on efforts at new social democracy also point to new opportunities. They suggest four priorities.

The first is to focus on *broad alliances*. Historically it has been possible to overcome the dearth of broad class-based collective actors with campaigns for equal civic, political and social citizen rights. They served as a unifying frame for diverse interests among classes and social movements. Such an approach remains vital, including as an alternative to ethnic, religious and other forms of communal identity politics. More recently, it has also been possible to build broad alliances for mutually acceptable urban development, non-corrupt public service delivery and universal public health. This has unified and strengthened formal, as well as informal, labour, professionals, progressive politicians and others. In fact, alliances beyond the core labour organisations for universal welfare and inclusive economic growth were also how social democrats came to prominence in the process when Scandinavia was comprehensively industrialised.

The second focus should be promotion of *democratic partnership governance*. Reforms such as for better welfare, services and urban development call for state and government involvement, and coordination with business. Aside from weak union and employer organising, a major reason why alliances for such reforms have been unviable is popular distrust in the state. How does one get there? Trust is mostly due to impartial institutions. An alternative social democratic approach to top-down "good governance" reforms would be to add equal citizenship and representative partners in local governments as well as in business, labour and civil society organisations.[18] One may also learn from the fact that Scandinavian labour movements only toned down their own self-help in favour of universal welfare state programmes when allowed to participate in public governance, along with business and other social partners. In contrast, the impressive Indonesian alliances for welfare and inclusive development withered when agreements and negotiations were not democratically institutionalised and inclusive of all concerned partners. Left-populist ideas of direct links between leaders and people did not help, quite the contrary. Actors returned to special priorities, transactions and confrontations.

Partnership governance may also be the best way to address the crisis of democratisation. Direct citizen participation is fine when issues can be handled in town hall meetings, but in other cases, trans-regional partnership governance is needed. Parliaments and executive offices are basic, but the domination of elites must be balanced by democratic participation of stronger interest and cause-oriented organisations. This may also boost their capacity to build more representative parties.

The third priority must be *rights and welfare based growth pacts*. The northern social growth pacts based on comprehensive industrialisation are unrealistic in the South. The second-generation social democrats tried state-led industrialisation and land reforms ahead of welfare, but were not very successful. The East Asian Tigers added production for global markets, but were authoritarian. Moderate third-generation social democrats aimed at more democratic "developmental states" that adjusted to the global market-driven growth while adding anti-corruption, capital intensive production, and some welfare measures – but lost their way. Growth generated more inequality than jobs, corruption persisted, democracy stagnated and the welfare measures did not transform these dynamics. Coalition governments such as in Brazil, India and the Philippines fell, and those in Indonesia and South Africa beat a retreat. The studies I have been involved in suggest this may be overcome by re-sequencing the social democratic development. Broad alliances for transformative rights and welfare reforms, along with partnership governance, might serve as precursors to social growth pacts. Firstly, by generating the necessary collective actors among labour and capital plus better governance. Secondly, by calling for reforms that contribute to inclusive growth. Thirdly, by demanding more public redistribution than in the original model, to support survival along with balanced development and decent jobs in sectors that otherwise lose out in globalised markets.

The fourth priority would be *social democratic development cooperation*. This has lost steam since the 1970s. Even the Socialist International has split, and the alternative Progressive Alliance is short of a clear-cut agenda. "National internationalism" after the Second World War was based on support for every nation's capacity to develop its own transformative policy. This was undermined by the rise of the market-driven globalisation and the failure to introduce NIEO. Social democrats found no other option but to adjust. The efforts to tame the negative dynamics under the third wave of democracy have petered out. The centre-left combinations of market-driven growth and rights and welfare did not work well even in initially celebrated cases like Brazil. International agreements, including Agenda 2030, ignore how local progressives will be able to enforce them. Union-driven efforts to export the first-generation social democratic growth and labour market model ignore seminal differences between the North and the South, neglecting contradictions between formal and informal labour, and the need for broad alliances in favour of not just decent but also more jobs and associated rights and welfare.

This record of failure may be altered by international agreement on prioritising support for (i) those CSOs, unions and coalitions that relate their priorities to broad alliances for democratic rights and welfare reforms and partnership governance towards sustainable growth; and (ii) studies of transformative reforms that may facilitate such alliances.

This is not about altruism but actual development cooperation. The revival of Social Democracy calls for the internationalisation of its cornerstones – popular-interest collectivities, democracy and rights and welfare-based sustainable development. Quests in the North for more radical welfare policies and taxation of capital are necessary but insufficient to facilitate global Keynesianism and offer alternatives to populist and xenophobic "defence" against globalisation. This calls for progressives in the South who can overcome the enticing conditions for the super exploitation of nature and people in their countries.

Notes

1 Färm, D., A.-M. Lindgren, M. Rynoson, and L. Stjernkvist, *Ordning och reda i vandringstid. En mer hållbar, rättvis och integrationsdriven asyl och migrationspolitik* (Stockholm: Tankesmedjan Tiden, 2020).
2 Primarily, this chapter draws on results in Törnquist, O., "Implications for Scandinavian Social Democracy and International Cooperation", in O. Törnquist and J. Harriss with N. Chandhoke and F. Engelstad (eds) *Reinventing Social Democratic Development: Insights from Indian and Scandinavian Comparisons* (Copenhagen: Nias Press, 2016); Törnquist, O., "Social Democratic Development", in O. Törnquist and J. Harriss with N. Chandhoke and F. Engelstad op.cit.; Törnquist, O., *In Search of New Social Democracy*. Insights from the South-Options in the North (London: Zed-Bloomsbury, 2021). Interviews cited in the text are detailed in the list of references.
3 There was no progress in this regard during the party congress.
4 Törnquist, O., *In Search of New Social Democracy*. Insights from the South-Options in the North. (London: Zed-Bloomsbury, 2021). Ch. 2.
5 Törnquist 2021: Ch. 4
6 Huntington, S., *Instability at the Non-Strategic Level of Conflict* (Washington, DC: Special Studies Group, Institute for Defense Analyses, 1961); Huntington, S., "Political Development and Political Decay", *World Politics* 17, no. 3 (1965): 386–430.
7 Törnquist 2021: Ch. 4
8 For general reviews of these policies, see, for example: Therborn, G., "Twilight of Swedish Social Democracy", *New Left Review* 113 (2018): 5–26 and Enocksson, M., *Kampen om Sverige: Från socialism till nyliberalism* (Stockholm: Premiss, 2021).
9 Törnquist 2021: Ch. 11.
10 Sandvik, H., "From Local Citizenship to the Politics of Universal Welfare: Scandinavian Insights", in O. Törnquist and J. Harriss with N. Chandhoke and F. Engelstad op.cit. (2016).
11 Fukuyama, F., *Political Order and Political Decay. From the Industrial Revolution to the Globalisation of Democracy* (London: Profile Books, 2014).
12 Moene, K., "Social Equality as a Development Strategy", in O. Törnquist and J. Harriss with N. Chandhoke and F. Engelstad op.cit. (2016).
13 Stiglitz, J., *People, Power, and Profits – Progressive Capitalism for an Age of Discontent* (New York: WW Norton, 2019).
14 Therborn, G., "Twilight of Swedish Social Democracy", *New Left Review* 113 (2018): 5–26; Enocksson, M., *Kampen om Sverige: Från socialism till nyliberalism* (Stockholm: Premiss, 2021).
15 Törnquist, O., "Implications for Scandinavian Social Democracy and International Cooperation", in O. Törnquist and J. Harriss with N. Chandhoke and F. Engelstad op.cit. (2016).
16 Brochmann, G., "From Bounded Universalism to the Trial of Internationalization: Migration and Social Democracy in Scandinavia", in Ø. Bratberg, N. Brandal and D.E. Thorsen, "Social Democracy in the 21st Century" *Comparative Social Research* 35 (Bingley: Emerald, 2020).
17 Therborn, G., "Class in the 21st Century", *New Left Review* 78 (2012): 5–29.

18 Svensson, T., "Strengthened Control of Fostering Trust? Indian Politics and Scandinavian Experiences", in O. Törnquist and J. Harriss with N. Chandhoke and F. Engelstad op.cit. (2016).

Cited statements and interviews

Statement by the Swedish government in 2015 on "breading space" regarding receiving refugees https://www.regeringen.se/artiklar/2015/11/regeringen-foreslar-atgarder-for-att-skapa-andrum-for-svenskt-flyktingmottagande/ (last accessed 08.06.21).
Kenneth G Forslund https://www.svt.se/nyheter/inrikes/sverige-saljer-krigsmateriel-som-kan-anvandas-i-jemenkriget (last accessed 14.04.2019).
Johan Hassel, Stockholm, 16.11.19.
Carl-Mikael Jonsson, Stockholm 10.11.15.
Mikael Leyi, Stockholm 17.11.19.
Ingemar Lindberg, mail 03- and 05.11.15.
Linde, A. (2019) "Murarna reser sig", Tiden, 2.
Moula, P. (2019) "En förnyad inriktning för Tiden", Tiden 2.
Palme, O. (1982) Why I Am a Democratic Socialist https://www.youtube.com/watch?v=7i2Ws1X5DSA (last accessed 08.05.20).
Göran Persson: https://www.svd.se/citat-svenska-ministrarna-om-kina (last accessed 14.04.2019).
Anna Sundström, Stockholm 17.11.19.
Mats Wingborg, phone 19,11.19.
Sofia Östmark, phone 26.11.19.

10 Defining progress in post-war Mediterranean

Communist Movements and their influence in Algeria and Egypt after 1945

Rinna Kullaa

Introduction

The concept of social democracy until the 2010s and the Arab Spring was more tightly connected to the questions of Communism and the life cycle of the Soviet Union as well as decolonisation in the Global South[1] than in Europe. Key European exceptions were Spain and Portugal where giving up of colonial empires and transition to democracy were supported strongly by transformative social democratic parties and movements that played an important role in the 1970s. Across the vast continents of Asia and Africa, Communism was a movement and force which was often faint and resembled a local debate in the interwar period. When the Comintern sent its agents to Syria in 1924, it was able to create only some Communist cells that de facto became the Syrian Communist Party folding in its first year of operation as they gathered no wider agitation or support than some groups of intellectuals. The International Communist Movement in the Middle East was also tied to colonial Europe. Of its second coming Michel Aflaq, a founder of the Ba'th Party in Syria, wrote that he stopped flirting with Communism in 1936, because the Syrian Communist Party became nothing more than an executive tool of its French parent party and of the French government in general. Challenges to Communism were plentiful. Since the interwar period west-south and east-south vectors of colonialism and Communism crossed one another for example in the Mediterranean.

Communism struggled to assert itself more forcefully globally after 1945 and before the 1970s détente between the East and the West. The ideology was always connected to the question of national self-determination, state-building, religious and cultural identity and defining of the new political space in post-colonial countries. There were five countries of the Global South that held significant currents and movements of Communism: Vietnam, Indonesia, Egypt, India and Algeria. Among these five states, questions of Communism were not muted. None of the five became strictly a Soviet modelled Communist state, but all were in some periods from 1945 to 1975 allied with Moscow in one way another, and yet each also defined their own leftist thinking. Indonesia was the host of the important 1955 Bandung Conference of Asian and African states that sought to address the future of the most numerous people in the world after colonialism. Indonesia was

DOI: 10.4324/9781003181439-11

and is the world's largest Muslim country in terms of population. India, together with Egypt and Yugoslavia, took part in coining the Non-Aligned Movement in 1961 in Belgrade, but Delhi with its significant size already then considered itself a greater power in the world facing and competing with China. Moreover, India held a strong ideological basis and force of its own for its democratic republic in the thinking of Mahatma Gandhi's theory of non-violence and the *Sarvodaya* theory of uplifting of peoples from poverty which also Nehru alluded to. Here, in these states with massive populations and goals of industrialisation, Soviet Communism offered some answers but was faced with local ownership over how to think about justice and injustice; freedom and bondage; hegemony and non-hegemony. In the southern part of the globe by and large Communism arrived from the outside and was interpreted according to the national, sometimes local thinkers and the political forces existing on the ground. In some measure and in certain locales, it was the antidote to the colonial West and its history of suppression, but it remained a locally defined small force.

After 1989, the pathways towards social democracy were more often than not taken via Communism particularly in Eastern Europe. Against the experiences with national dictatorships across the southern globe, the experience and practice of Communist one party state is an important difference to observe when considering the north-south axis as this book does. The Arab Spring from 2010 ushered in a new and young generation of activists and citizens across Northern Africa and the Middle East that valued the soft power[2] of states such as the those of the Nordic countries where the provision of citizens' legal rights, education, health care, environmental protection and many other qualities stemming from citizens' rights were foremost in political agenda and budgeting. Lebanese Ali Harb writing about the uprisings that shook the Arab world in succession argues that there was a will by which soft power revolutions in the Arab world should lead to the dismantling of dictatorship and fundamentalism.[3] In Tunisia, Morocco, Libya, Egypt and Syria masses of the younger citizens raised protests for protection on individuals' rights and free speech as organising principles for the state in the future, while others continued to agitate for changes in state structures on religious ground. Harb underlines that the Arab Spring revolutions did not only bring down dictatorship and restore freedom, but would lead to the construction in the future of an Arab world that is different in its values and features. Harb's evidence is that these popular movements did not originate from political parties but from youth groups that came outside of all the political templates of the establishment. In the 2010s as in the 1950s, transformation and religion were not necessary opposite sides of an equation but on the agenda. The elections after the Arab Spring brought to power actually Islamists in Egypt, Tunisia and Morocco. Yet, it was precisely the lack of social democratic currents and citizens' rights in the 1970s and 1980s détente Northern Africa and the Middle East that is important to understanding the current generations' minds today.[4] For those without having the opportunity to enjoy wide individual legal rights and benefits of social democracy could not be dead and soft-powered state was still something to aspire to. The fall of the socialist regimes in Eastern Europe and the end of the Soviet Union had not led to peoples' uprisings and demands for freedom in Northern Africa and the Middle East in 1989 or 1991. Arab regimes remained coherent instead with similar economic and security systems in place as before.[5] The Arab Spring revolutions came much later in the 2010s as the result of repression and injustice and young people in these Arab countries rose up to seek a change of regime, but also to the change the way in which the state deals with rights and freedoms of the population.

It pains me to remember how in 2004 as a graduate student at Oxford University I watched the Finnish foreign minister being confronted repeatedly with questions about why he was advocating and arguing for the Nordic welfare state model as the students in my class declared the model overtly expensive, unsustainable and out of date. I was a student in the Russian and East European Studies programme which next year would become purposely the European Studies programme. One third, if not more of the courses in the programme dealt with political and economic transition from Communism to democracy in Poland, in the Czech Republic, Hungary and elsewhere in the former Eastern bloc in Europe. That year as a consequence of the third wave of democratisation which I studied in my classroom, the Czech Republic, Estonia, Hungary, Latvia, Lithuania, Poland, Slovakia and Slovenia joined the European Union by harmonising their legislations and citizens' rights protections with that of the EU. As formerly Communist states of Eastern Europe became democracies and integrated into the largely social democratic governance system of the European Union, there was at the same time also a tremendous need to declare social democracy as socialist dead and buried that reached even into academic debates. The paradox becomes more obvious when we see that further in the time between 2004 and 2021 also Bulgaria, Romania, and Croatia became EU member states and the Nordic social welfare remains alive and in power today. In Finland, Sweden, Denmark, Norway and Iceland, it has not been possible for the best organised conservative or right-wing parties to come to power without strongly advocating for the welfare state and its economic model that is so closely connected to social democracy. The place where the fourth wave of democratisation did not produce social welfare state is post-colonial Northern Africa and the Middle East. Many of the young generations in the 2010s' Mediterranean were protesting against their reality since the connection between soft power, social democracy and citizens' equal rights was and is widely understood by the generation. Thinkers writing about the Arab Spring such as Harb stress the importance of dialogue, synergy and communication between different components of the society because "every fundamentalist though is monolithic and every title is treated as absolute and the final truth within a fundamentalist mind, every project is based on the monopoly of truth and power".[6] The best way to challenge is individual's right, the rule of law and wide societal equality.

From the basis of something that was not, this chapter as a part of a volume on social democracy addresses the influence and position of Communism and Communist currents in two states in Northern Africa where leftist forces were influential. Egypt and Algeria are defining states and examples for the region of

Africa and the Middle East and populous strong powers at the revolutionary vanguard after 1945. The chapter is divided into five parts, the first of which discusses the history of Communism and the Soviet Union in the Middle East and secondly some examples of Soviet oriental imagination of Northern Africa in Russian popular culture. It was on the basis of this imagery that the Soviet leadership approached the spreading of Communism in the area, in addition to military calculations. Third, the chapter describes the Soviet Union's approaches to Egypt and how geopolitical and international relations initiatives took over the importance of Communist ideology. This explains in part the tenuous position of Communist ideology which in Egypt was sometimes tolerated more than at other times and often seen both in Egypt and in Algeria as an antidote to Islamism and Islamic politics. This relationship was however particularly complex as it was also argued simultaneously in the post-colonial time that Algeria in particular did not need another prophet in the form of Communism. Fourth, the chapter discusses the example of the Democratic and Social Movement of Algeria in the 1960s which was an outgrowth of the Communist Party of Algeria.[7] Fifth, the article returns to the geopolitical intentions of the Soviet Union and the influence of events such as the Six-Day War in determining Soviet-African relations rather than Communist ideological precedent. The various elements introduced here describe the landscape of progressive political movements and give some clues as to why they did not emerge to power. In understanding the challenges, directional influences and historical pressures young generations face today in Northern Africa, we can start to see why Finland, Sweden and Norway are close in their minds but politically far apart from North Africa and the Middle East today.

Marxism approaching the Middle East and Africa

The majority of the writings of Karl Marx did not focus on the topic of the Middle East and North Africa in particular, although in 1882 at the end of his life, Marx himself lived for several months in Algiers.[8] Marx expected capitalism to form in developed countries in Europe through which Communism would rise. One of the references one can find is his mentioning the idea of creating "officer patriots" referring to the patriotic role the native army played during the Sepoy Revolt in India.[9] In *The Accumulation of Capital*, another defining thinker of Communism, Rosa Luxemburg developed a theory by which capitalism could develop historically amidst a non-capitalist society expanding on Marx's earliest writings on an Asiatic mode of production.[10] Vladimir Lenin was influenced by Luxemburg's thinking while creating his concept of the revolutionary vanguard with which Lenin came to seize power in Petrograd in 1917. In this roundabout way, the Asiatic model entered the pantheon of Communism. However, in the Middle East, neither argument for the Asiatic model nor the military vanguard fitted particularly well at the turn of the 20th century. In many examples, such as that of Syria, most graduates of the Homs Military Academy came from poor families and did not resemble an elite force. The works of Lenin provided little additional specific perspective on the possible progress of Communism among the

Muslims, Arabs or the area. National liberation was the topic Lenin addressed in his theory of imperialism and declared it should be accomplished through a socialist revolution.

The original early Soviet thinker on Islam and revolution was Sultan-Galiyev, member of the People's Commissariat for the Nation, while the topic of Islam appeared at the time of the Russian Revolution in conjunction with the October Revolution in the Appeal to the Moslems of Russia and the East on 7 December 1917. Lenin together with Josef Stalin addressed the "great events that are taking place in Russia" explaining that

> under the blows of the Russian Revolution, the old world of serfdom and slavery is crumbling ... A new world is being born, a world of workers and free men. At the head of this revolution stands the Workers' and Peasants' Government of Russia, the Soviet of People's Commissars. All Russia is sown with revolutionary Soviets of Workers', Soldiers', and Peasants' Deputies. The power in the country is in the hands of the people. The laboring people of Russia have but one burning desire-to achieve an honorable peace and to aid the oppressed peoples of the earth to fight for their freedom. [11]

Lenin and Stalin continued in their address inserting religious words in their appeal to Muslims:

> In this holy task Russia is not alone. The call to liberty sounded by the Russian Revolution is reaching all workers of the East and the West. The exhausted, warring peoples of Europe already stretch out their hands to us, who are making peace. The workers and soldiers of the West already gather under the banner of socialism, storming the stronghold of imperialism. And far-off India, which for centuries has been oppressed by the "enlightened" plunderers of Europe, is already raising the banner of revolt, organizing its Soviets of Deputies, casting the hated slavery from its shoulders, and summoning the peoples of the East to the struggle of liberation ...In the face of these great events we turn to you, toiling and disinherited Moslems of Russia and the East. Moslems of Russia, Tartars of the Volga and the Crimea, Kirghiz, and Sarts of Siberia and Turkestan, Turks and Tartars of Transcaucasia, Chechens and Mountaineers of the Caucasus – all those whose mosques and chapels have been destroyed, whose beliefs and customs have been trampled underfoot by the tsars and oppressors of Russia! ... Not at the hands of Russia and her revolutionary government does slavery await you, but at the hands of the marauders of European imperialism, of those who converted our fatherland into their ravished and plundered "colony".

The revolutionary thinking of Lenin inferred that since almost all classes in Muslim society have been oppressed formerly by colonialists, all were entitled to be called proletarian. The reality, however, was that the Bolsheviks who took power in Russia neither knew nor understood the Middle East and its history or politics very well and had only some peripheral experience with Muslim communities of the Volga and Transcaucasus. Following the revolution, in 1920, at the Second Comintern Congress, Lenin called for a close alliance of all national and colonial liberation movements with Soviet Russia and referred to a "revolutionary liberation movement". At the meeting, Gregory Zinoviev also called for a holy war against British imperialism. Eventually, a *Colonial International* was to be established, merging the "oppressed" peoples of the Third World but was replaced by the Third International and the third congress in the form of the Baku Congress of the Peoples of the East in 1920 in Baku.[12] Here Algerian Communists carried an important role and also it was significant that Baku itself was a Muslim city. At the same time, to put the developments into perspective from among more than 1900 delegates at the meeting, there were only three Arabs. In the interwar period, Britain and France were still powerful in the Middle East leaving little room for the Soviet Union's influence. Moreover, Mustafa Kemal was opposed to the Bolshevik regime and his revolution cut Moscow's influence over the region. Understanding of the Arab world was made even less when in the 1930s Stalin's purges took away the life of Galiyev. He was accused by Stalin of pan-Turkism and pan-Islamism, a bad combination, but in contact with anti-Soviet guerrillas in Turkestan in the Caucasus. The draw of Communism also in the interwar period suffered from a lack of appreciation for the creation of nation state from under colonialism. Egyptian Communists called upon the workers to remove themselves from any national movement, and the Egyptian Communist Party was doomed to inactivity. At the same time, Communism was attractive to the colonised world as well since it offered an erasure of the past, which for many in the Global South was imperialism. This became easier in the 1960s, as new states were formed from former colonial entities and Arab Communist, for example, gathered in Vienna in 1964.

Concept of the Orient in the Soviet Union after 1945

The second Communist world had a large and important impact on the Third World in the early decades of decolonisation. Much has been written about the extent and significance of this encounter.[13] While the Soviet Union's academia and university did house experts on the Middle East and Africa after the Second World War, the two regions did not occupy the centre stage of public imagination of the world beyond the extensive Soviet Union. Yet, popular imagining in the communist vanguard state of the Soviet Union already from the late 1960s reflected the state's policies and not only coloured but also justified the state leadership's relationship with North Africa and the Middle East. One of the places where we find images of the Middle East together with Islam is in the Soviet cinema. One such example is the movie *The White Sun of the Desert* directed by Vladimir Motyl and filmed in 1969 which is representative of the historical-revolutionary genre reflecting the main ideas of Communism, including the liberation of the working people of the entire world. The film also presents idea of Soviet orientalism[14] – the civilising mission of the East in the south that appears to be backward, dangerous and uncontrollable. The film takes place during the time of the Civil War at the beginning of 1920 and tells the story of a Red Army soldier Fyodor Sukhov who is crossing the sands of Central Asia[15] while returning home from the War. On his way back to Moscow Sukhov meets a harem of local Muslim bandit nicknamed Black Abdullah and proceeds to take his harem under his protection.

Sukhov the Russian hero in the Soviet film fights villains who are the White Army soldiers and the native Black Abdullah against the background of the desert frontier of the Soviet Union. He saves the nine women in distress in the harem. The film contains a kind of double setting. Where it refers to the Muslims of the North Africa and the Middle East by extension, it is showing the Caucasus and the Far East as the orient of the Soviet Union itself. The links build into the Leninist thinking between the Far East and the Middle East are here in popular lens. This is clear from the language of the film referring to the Soviet Union's mission to lift the people at the periphery from backwards living. Thus, although addressing Communisms and the Soviet Union's role in the world, the film represents clearly also the idea of the civilising mission in the East that appears to be backward, dangerous and uncontrollable. In the film appear slogans, for example, such as "Down with prejudice! A woman is human as well".

The women of the harem in the film are thusly re-educated. First, they wonder about how could a man ever do with only one woman as they are used to a system where one wife loves the man, another one mends his clothes, third on cooks his dinner and so on. In the course of the film, the women learn to appreciate being the only one, the only wife and the full person – a Comrade.

Sukhov states "Comrade women! The Revolution has set you free. You don't have a master now. And call me simply comrade Sukhov. Forget your accursed past. You'll work freely with us, and each of you will have a separate husband".

The White Sun of the Desert expresses stereotypes of Orientalised desert and transmits important social and political meanings through cinematographic images. It remains one of the well-cited and popular movies engaging the topic of the orient in the domestic popular imagination in the Moscow-led Soviet Union. In another example, typical of the 1960s' declarations of African culture incompatible with Communism, Professor Potikhine, a specialist in African Affairs, denounced with vigour and passion the ideology of Pan-Africanism as "a development of racism in reverse and leads to the flowering of so-called African socialisms which have nothing in common with scientific socialism" in the *Kommunist* journal of the *Pravda* newspaper[16]

The Soviet Union's relationship with the Middle East and Africa was not as simple as orientalist conception of a Communist civilising mission or the spread of international Communist movement, but it was part of the outlook of spreading its ideology and its inner contradictions. When we next look at the Soviet Union's relations with both Egypt and Algeria, we discover another important perspective of geopolitical thinking that often superseded or worked side by side with Communist ideology.

Challenging Soviet Communism while Socialist: Arabic, African and Islamic Egypt

The Soviet Union's political approach to Africa after the Second World War was largely set by two factors: the politics of Josef Stalin and geography. Whereas Lenin had set out the early approaches to national liberation and colonialism, Stalin continued to personify the political impact to post-colonial Africa. In the early years after the war, Stalin sought to divide the globe with the Western allies. After the death of Stalin in 1953, with Khrushchev, Soviet foreign policy became increasingly interested in the geography of the Mediterranean, the Red Sea and the Indian Ocean beginning from the straights from Ukraine where he was born to the open seas. The Soviet approach to the Global South when the Middle East and North Africa were concerned was pragmatic, thinking about communication sea routes, the position of the United States and accommodating to the life in the global world accord to other entities such as the United States and China.[17] Soviet foreign policy initiatives in Egypt display much of this approach beginning with the importance Moscow placed from Khrushchev's leadership in 1955 onwards on acquiring naval bases in Egypt and the investments the Soviet Union would make in the country.

In the 1960s, decisive decade, half of all Soviet Union's funding towards Africa went to the Aswan Dam in Egypt. The Soviet Union granted credits between 1958 and 1961 alone to the Egyptian part of the United Arab Republic in 2000 million robles in total – 1100 million were delivered between 1958 and 1959 and another 900 million arrived by 1960.[18] The funds were primarily to be used for the construction of the Aswan High Dam but were also purposed for other projects such as steelworks, mechanical engineering, oil refineries, chemicals and shipbuilding as parts of a Soviet style five-year plan format. By the end of 1961, Egypt had received some 2238 million robles and Egypt represented the significant target of Soviet actions. In comparison, Syria, another part of the UAR federation on the Mediterranean, received 737 million from Moscow in the same period of time.[19] This funding was possible for the Egyptian leader Gamal Abdel Nasser to receive despite the fact the Communist movement itself in Egypt remained illegal and many Communists were residing behind bars.[20] Nasser moreover acted to a high degree independently of his relations with other African states without much coordination from Moscow. Money in those years did not buy that yet as in many ways the collaboration with Moscow was forced by Nasser facing the Western allies and Israel in the Suez Crises. According to many foreign relations, historians of Egypt in fact Nasser had before the late 1950s rather sought collaboration with the United States instead of the Soviet Union. The Soviets arrived to the country as its second choice.

A closer working relationship with Moscow begun rather later in 1961 after Syria left the UAR and the interests for a wider regional importance for Nasser and the direction of the Soviet Union's influence from the East to the South met. From around that year, Moscow designed Egypt to be used as a destination relay point in Africa from where to extend its influence over the continent.[21]

The construction of the Aswan Dam was the strategic vantage point for operations. The Soviet Union's traffic across the Suez Canal tripled between 1958 and 1966 from 572 ships to 1469 ships.[22] Moscow via its traffic across Egypt was also on course to building relations with Ethiopia and Somalia. Ethiopia's Haile Selassie had visited Moscow in 1959 and in the autumn of 1961 Leonid Brezhnev as the Chairman of the Presidium of the USSR visited Khartoum on the Nile in neighbouring Sudan. The principal steps to the enterprise-led penetration of the Soviet Union to the African continent begun with Cairo, Khartoum, Mogadishu in Eastern Africa and the Soviet Union's politics followed certainly a penetrative and geographic direction from the north to the south in order to gain influence and monetary transactions.

> This long-standing predilection and this continuity may at first glance be surprising: the Egyptian and, to a certain extent, the Sudanese regimes prohibit and prosecute Communism within their borders. Sudan and Somalia offer certain characteristics of moderate countries [between the Cold War east and the west]. The explanation of [Moscow's] attitude therefore seems to be found elsewhere than in a short-term ambition: the Soviets are interested in the Nile region for its intrinsic geographic value (base of radiation towards the whole of the continent and towards the English East Africa) and more over above all because Egypt, better than any other third world country, lent itself to one of the fundamental enterprises of Soviet diplomacy; the expansion of positive neutralism.[23]

The analysis of France's Ambassador in Moscow in 1961 over the meaning and purpose of the Soviet approach to Africa and lack of Communist of socialist ideology were weighed against one another. The analysis pointed to a complicit agreement established between Nasser and Moscow according to which, Egypt would quickly succeed in increasing its influence in the Afro-Asian and African political groups which came to power after 1957. In the course of decolonisation, Moscow unable to gain direct influence would do so radiating ideologically and in transport of materials down from Cairo.[24] Bellying such an understanding of Moscow's approach were facts such as that the conferences of former colonial states, the 1957 African Asian Peoples' Solidarity Conference in Cairo in 1957, and the All-African Peoples Conference in Tunis in 1960, and in Cairo in 1961 again, aroused satisfaction and notice among the Soviet commentators in the Moscow press, pointing to support and ownership from the Soviet Union to their political power and agenda as well. Simultaneously, and in reality, "the Russian and Chinese Communist [parties and foreign policy establishments] were overwhelmed by the de-colonizing solidarity movement" which by and large was able to avoid controls the organisational penetration otherwise. Nasser's Ba'athist movement their own definitions of socialism and Communism. In many instances, the voices in the conferences echoed attitudes favourable to the political positions of the USSR and its allies even when not controlled by Moscow's direct intervention. African, Middle Eastern and Asian leaders agitated against redemands of colonialism, spoke of national liberation and discussed elimination of foreign bases.[25] Moreover, in addition to compatibility with the decolonial agenda Egypt with the Aswan High Dam project in fact gave a decade-long vehicle to the Soviet Union through which access increasingly marked influence to the continent of Africa which often translated fitted also to the agenda and events of the United Nations which was one of the main forums where decolonisation was discussed and debated.

The Soviet Union could not of course operate from Cairo across Africa without challenges

> like those of Yugoslavia or India which also penetrate there. But overall and depending on the fact that one seeks above all to orient towards gestures of foreign policy, it provides a sufficient facade for a kind of political predominance of the Soviets to constantly increase.... The collaboration of the USSR with countries which, like Egypt that themselves to play a role of transmission belt, remains, for this reason accepted, advocated and used.[26]

To illustrate this, belt's influence is to look at the Casablanca Group of countries which enjoyed the support of the USSR. It contained four countries from North Africa (Algeria, Egypt, Libya and Morocco), three countries from Sub-Saharan Africa (Ghana, Guinea and Mali), three countries under British influence and three countries under French influence. Soviet Union's support and close development aid to Egypt was not only about Egypt or about spreading Communist thinking. The bilateral relations of the Soviet Union enjoyed with Egypt, Guinea and Ghana made it possible to send on the spot many specialists who initiate Africans to Soviet political methods. More than books of ideology and building up Communist parties which could have in time become socialist and then social democratic parties that was often the case in Europe, Moscow sent experts and trainers that helped to maintain one political force regimes much of the 1960s whenever possible.

The Soviet Union's relationship with Nasser and Egypt despite the large investment made and the focal point it created around Cairo was not an easy one. Nasser like many leaders of newly independent former colonial states of the Global South sought to define his own space, ideology, political speech and rhythm in time. Nasser was plainly spoken, handsome and young leader with a military background and defined the kind of appeal and rhetoric still emulated today by many leaders in the Middle East in particular. He was not defined by Moscow central time.

Nasser identified three circles to which the new Egypt led by him and the Ba'thist movement belonged. These were: the *Arab* world; the *African* continent and the *Islamic* civilisation, all three of which Nasser, Egypt and the Aswan High Dam stood inside of. Nasser's theory of the three circles sought to make the new Mediterranean order a geopolitical one which took into account the place of Egypt in the geography of Africa and the world. Not only was Egypt and the Sinai the connecting point between the Mediterranean, the Red Sea and the Indian Ocean which had already been also recognised by leaders in Moscow. Nasser's Egypt was also a very large strategically located country encircled by Arab countries not only historically but also geographically on the continent of Africa and religiously encircled by Islam. Nasser laid out his vision of pan-Arab nationalism as a political argument for his reign. Pan-Arabism which had begun as a cultural and political movement already in the last decades of the 1800s and grown in the interwar period was a foreign policy vision for his new regime.[27] It would be inconceivable to not consider mutual interests of Arabs and Africans in the world after colonialism. Centring Egypt as Arabic, African and Islamic challenged Stalinist and even post-Stalinist Soviet Communist doctrine that had divided the world between the Eastern and Western allies from the direction of the north to the south.

Even as late as in 1969, the Soviet Union's approach to North Africa remained focused on naval facilities and durable influence the Suez Canal secured. French Navy captain wrote "beyond the zone of the Suez Canal, the reopening of which appears to be desired by Moscow, the policy of seeking fulcrums may extend towards the Red Sea and the Indian Ocean".[28] Looking to the east, he continued to observe:

> Algeria constitutes on the other side of the Mediterranean the center of a multifaceted presence which allows the USSR to develop its influence in a dual Maghreb and African direction. The Soviet grip on the equipment of the Algerian army compromises the relative autonomy of this latter, in particular in terms of technical control of aerodromes and military ports. This action is extended by the development of trade and technical cooperation in certain vital sectors of the Algerian economy.[29]

The next part of this chapter looks at the relationship of the Soviet Union and Communism in Algeria as well as at the formation of the Democratic and Social Movement of Algeria.

Algerian Socialist and Democratic Movement

In Algeria leftist and Communist forces had a significant role in Northern Africa in the post-1945 circumstances.[30] Algeria's proximity to Europe and to France had made it subject to the Second World War. The French Communist leader Maurice Thorez in his nation en formation theory had implied that the Algerian nation could not be formed fully without all its components including the support of the French settlers. Yet, the country's relationship to Communism perhaps more than that of any other's was defined by domestic circumstances of the Algeria War 1954–1962. In the course of the extended and violent struggle, the Provisional Government of the Algerian Republic (GPRA) in exile first in Cairo 1958–1960 and in Tunis 1960–1962 asked for support to it from all political factions in Algeria, including the leftists. The National Liberation Front (FLN) demanded that all political movements in Algeria end themselves and cease to exist by the year 1956. This was a difficult demand for Algerian Communists to meet and none of the Communist movements in the country extinguished themselves but seized to exist in the circumstances of the war 1956–1957. Adding to difficult relations between Algerian Communists and the GPRA was that the Soviet Union did not recognise it until the very end of the war and the Evian Accords.[31]

The Soviet-Algerian relationship like the one Moscow enjoyed with Cairo begun in rather financial terms when on 27 December 1963, trade and payment agreements between the two countries were signed in Moscow. Cultural and scientific agreement followed three years later 22 March 1966, with the economic and technical exchange agreement renewed in 1967. The important events took place in 1968 in conjunction with the Soviet Minister of Defence Andrei Grechko visiting Algiers on 16 July 1968, and on 6 March 1969 as Algerian Foreign Affairs Minister Bouteflika visited, Moscow created the permanent commission for economic, scientific and technical cooperation. The FLN vanguard from Algiers did not see the Soviet Union as its main point of reference but rather sought to communicate its own interpretation of revolutionary struggle to the decolonising world from the outset of coming to power.[32] In 1964, in conversation with Khrushchev, Ben Bella reiterated that "Algerian regime will retain a 'specific Algerian Marxism' and Muslim religion could not be left out of it to adopt Marxism socialism". When Houari Boumedienne overthrew Ben Bella in 1965, he declared more forcefully that Algeria under him chooses the path of socialism and the FLN declared it now followed the socialist ideology.

After Boumedienne's definition of socialist direction and a new not officially recognised Algerian Democratic and Social Movement political party appeared in 1966. It was allowed to attend Moscow's invitation officially for the meeting of the Communist parties in Budapest in 1968 as the official voice of Algerian Communists.[33] This otherwise minor issue was a significant sign of support. The Party went on to have a long-lasting life even through existing in clandestine penetrations as a kind of trade union movement apart from the government at times.

In the period of the 1960s after Ben Bella's departure, the distrust which had been there since the Algerian War in the Algerian-Soviet relations was aggravated by the attitude of the USSR in the crisis in the Middle East. While the Algerians considered themselves entitled to expect an unreserved commitment from Moscow of support to the Arabs in the Six-Day War, they observed that during the armed conflict as after the ceasefire, the Soviet Union put peaceful coexistence with the United States largely before solidarity with the peoples of the Third World. This attitude was to arouse renewed bitterness in Algiers. On 10 June 1967, Boumediene asked in urgent terms to socialist governments "to take their full responsibilities, without reservations and without detours" and in June went to Moscow to ask the Soviet leaders for clarification on their attitude.

The cooling of the Algerian-Soviet relations could be observed in terms the energy and commercial exchanges. The Algerian government was irritated by the offers to sell gas made by the Soviets to buyers in Central and Southern Europe who were at the same time in talks with Algeria's company Sonatrach. The bad mood of the Algerians resulted in breakdown of the negotiations undertaken with the possible European customers, by the postponement indefinitely of the visit that Brezhnev to Algiers and by controversies in the press this caused.[34] These episodes show how in many ways the commercial relations between socialist countries in the late 1960s here functioned like those between capitalist countries when it came to resources such as gas. Communist ideology or sympathies were no deterrent here. The lack of Communist allegiance or influence could here also be explained also by certain other bad accounts of cooperation. The Algerians complained, on several occasions, to Western diplomats that Russian aid, both in the economic field and in the military or technical field, was not adapted to their needs. Steel mills, for example, were not built in the way that they could function well in Algeria. For the Soviet Union, such inconveniences as a steel mill built not working properly were less of a concern. Moscow was able to gain domestic propaganda from newspaper stories such as those of Soviet students as labour to Algeria in 1964 to participate in the reconstruction of villages Tesi-Mlaf, Tadjouit Ait Arjeu, Aranov Fanon and Timeroune which had been destroyed in the course of the Algerian War.[35] The students were in Algeria to work with the youth organisation wing of the FLN for six months. The two groups of students were accompanied by 12 specialists and the journal Komsomolskaya Pravda, the official youth wing newspaper of the Soviet Communist Party reported on the activities in Moscow. Such actions added to the orientalist way in which North Africa and the Middle East was portrayed in the Soviet popular culture as a kind of a Communist Party antidote and had domestic and regional propaganda value for Soviet Communism.

Communist directions but no social democracy

In the words of the declaration of the Soviet Union's Communist Party on the occasion of the 49th anniversary of the October Revolution in 1966, the people of the United Arab Republic cited in the lead were to be commended for "fighting, no longer for the socialist development of the country, but for the socialist path of the development of their country".[36] The declaration published in the *Pravda* a few weeks before the 7th November celebration saluted "Algeria, Syria and Burma for continuing to fight for social progress" together with Guinea, Congo-Brazzaville and Mali, always mentioned together as a regional group imagined and brought to life by Soviet Communism.[37] Socialist path and development were wider concepts in the Soviet imagination socialism when imagined far away from the borders of the Soviet Union. The path could contain variations if it also allowed for Moscow's political and economic influence outside its borders. This adjustment allowed for the more strained relationships which Moscow had with Algiers or the uneven measure of development aid to Cairo rather than to Damascus. By the second half of the 1960s, Soviet Union's influence was radiating from Cairo and southern Yemen towards Muscat as for the other countries. The only notable innovation in the declaration belonged to the people of Oman who, in Moscow's phrasing, were "waging a just struggle against imperialism, for freedom and independence".[38] Five years after the birth of the Non-Aligned Movement and the building of the Aswan High Dam begun, African states such as Ghana and Algeria had moved on in coining their conceptions of what Pan-Africanism would mean in the future. Moreover, by the middle of the decade-long construction period of the Dam, it had "also become a necessity to oppose the influence of China which together with other factors brought the USSR to nuance its attitude towards Africa. The politics of direct pressure aiming at assuring certain points of strong support among progressive states in Africa, and to use of crises situation to accentuate cleavages between these states and to diminish the group of moderate states, amount to an effort to establish the presence and the influence nearby all African governments including the moderates" were by then the established arsenal of Moscow. According to many Western eyes in Africa, the USSR was "showing a tenacious and discreet activity, aimed both at undermining western influence everywhere where possible, and at opposing Chinese companies while continuing to give a privileged place to Egypt" among its allies.[39] Despite whatever the Soviet intentions and calculations were, by 1966, many of the post-colonial countries had made strides already in their self-definition of domestic and continental politics. An additional factor causing separation from the Soviet Union for the Arab world was the Six-Day War. At the outset of the conflict, the Soviet Union and its Warsaw Pact partner states withdrew and left their embassies in Tel Aviv for care takers chosen from among European neutral states. Moscow took the stand that Israel was the causing party to the conflict and Moscow delivered arms to the Arab States preferring to fight a proxy war, but its support was interpreted as less than of full measure. Moscow's relations with the Magreb thereafter "suffered the repercussions of the Middle East crisis. Algeria s remained a privileged partner" together with Egypt for Moscow but exchanges were focused on economic substance mostly.[40]

In Egypt and Algeria, as well as in many other places of the Global South Communist, and there after socialist thought was sometimes seen as a balancing force to Islamism and at other times, as in the thinking of Galiyev, as something rather compatible with Islam. This chapter has pointed to several factors which in Northern Africa and the Middle East contributed to the area's relationship to socialism and lack of democratic influences. The region is unified in recent years not only by the rather recent concept of the Global South, but importantly by the Arab Spring. In countries such as Egypt and Algeria autocratic leadership inspired and claiming in part the heritage of Communist and leftist thought came to power after 1945, but no multiparty environment came about and moreover socialist forces were few in between. State-building projects, military leadership and the coining of the state in Algeria under the circumstances of the Algerian war led to republics by marriage – as in terms of until death do us apart with different military leaders. This background however should not confuse us to thinking social democracy or rule by law and citizens' rights are somehow particularly alien to large parts of the younger generations in the countries of the Arab Spring. Today more than perhaps ever, concepts and news sources of social rights can be read through social media and electronic media. When large parts of the population can read and watch videos from across the world, the word no longer necessarily belongs to any government, and soft power such as that of the Nordic model identified with social democracy has an appeal which that of the former colonial power or the Soviet Union's socialist path did not have. Social measures that are equal identify the citizen and the individual as powerful. Against a history of power defend as hegemony, wars and military conflict defining history and existence, soft power stands in contrast and it has to in some ways also define relations between the north and the south even if in the case of the Magreb in this chapter rather influenced via the Russian east.

The Magreb today reminds us of the saying " We are young; We have time!". The history of something that never was does not prevent a generation from not valuing it or considering that there is a relationship to a desired future where citizens' rights are more central to society. The transitions to democracy of Eastern Europe and parts of the Balkans and the integration into the European Union also suggest us to reconsider the relationship of the Magreb to social democracy. In many of those states, social democracy certainly still carries little political force and appreciation although social policies within the EU are to a great extend regulated and harmonised. Even stronger suggestions are the examples of Portugal and Spain, discussed elsewhere in this volume, where after very long dictatorships and colonial traditions, social democracy took central stage. The history of Algeria and Egypt in the period after 1945 is very complex and difficult to analyse masterfully. Yet, when considering north and south relations, complexities should not deter us from thinking about the future from another angle, even if so much of the post-1945 history of the Mediterranean are predicated on the Soviet Union's and also the United States' international relations and influences.

Notes

1 The Global South is a relatively new concept and terminology which refers broadly to the regions of Latin America, Asia, Africa and Oceania. It is ahistorical to use it for the time prior to 1969, when it did not have political definition and even afterwards it lacked wide usage. The contemporaries of historical periods discussed here referred rather to the Third World as signifying developing nations. However, for the purposes of this book's foci on north and south trajectories, the Global South is a more encompassing term which is why it is used here. Northern Africa and the Middle East are grouped together as well in this chapter as they were both the ground of the Arab Spring discussion. Moreover, the United Arab Republic which is discussed here crossed both regions.
2 Nye, Joseph S., *Soft Power: The Means to Success in World Politics* (New York: Public Affairs, 2004).
3 حرب علي: ثورات القوة الناعمة في العالم العربي من المنظومة إلى الشبكة. الدار العربية للعلوم ناشرون
(Harb, Ali, *Soft Power Revolutions in the Arab World: From System to Network* (Beirut: Arab House of Science Publishers, 2014)).
4 Rabah, Makram, *A Campus at War: Student Politics at the American University of Beirut 1967–1975* (Beirut: Nelson Publications, 2009).
5 Op.cit. Harb, p.16.
6 Op.cit. Harb.
7 الحركة الديمقراطية والاجتماعية

8 Pennar, Jaan, "The Arabs, Marxism and Moscow: A Historical Survey", *Middle East Journal* 22, no. 4 (Autumn 1968), pp. 433–447.
9 Also see *Marx, marxisme et Algérie: textes de Marx-Engels; Présentés par René Gallissot avec la collaboration de Gilbert Badia* (Paris: Union Générale d'éditions, 1976).
10 Luxemburg, Rosa, *The Accumulation of Capital* (London: Routledge, 2003). Originally published in 1913.
11 *USSR, Sixty Years of the Union, 1922–1982* (Moscow: Progress Publishers, 1982), p. 35.
12 Young, Robert J. C., *Postcolonialism: An Historical Introduction*, Anniversary Edition. (London: Wiley-Blackwell, 2016), p. 127.
    Drew, Allison, "Bolshevizing Communist Parties: The Algerian and South African Experiences", *International Review of Social History* 48, no. 2 (2003), p. 167.
13 Engermann, David C., "The Second World's Third World", *Kritika: Explorations in Russian and Eurasian History* 12, no. 1 (Winter 2011), pp. 183–211.
14 Concept of Orientalism from Said, Edward, *Orientalism* (New York: Pantheon, 1978).
15 In Turkestan somewhere in Central Asia in a fictitious town Pedzhent, which is located on the eastern shore of the Caspian Sea (Musskij 2005: 239, 241).
16 *Kommunist*. Moskva. Issue 194 printed 1.2.1964.
17 Ch. 1 "Sources of Messianism and Pragmatism", in Vasilev, Alexei, *Russia's Middle East Policy: From Lenin to Putin* (London: Routledge, 2018).
18 Ministère des affaires étrangères de la France (MAE): Direction des affaires politiques: Europe, Série 36; Sous-Série 23; Dossier 1. U.R.S.S.: Politique Exterieure; Ligues Politique. 1961. "A/S accords de "coopération industrielle et technique" entre l'U.R.S.S. et les pays sous-développés d'Afrique et d'Asie". Ambassade de France Moscou 5.1.1961, pp. 5–6.
19 MAE; Drection des affaires politiques: Europe, Série 36; Sous-Série 23; Dossier 1. "A/S Aide des Etats socialistes aux pays sous-développés". L'Ambassadeur de France en Pologne, Varsovie, 12.5.1961, pp. 1–2.
20 See for example, Mahmoud, Hussein, *L'Égypte: lutte de classes et libération nationale 1945–1967* (Paris: Maspéro, Petite collection, 2 vol) (2ème ed. 1945–1973, 1975).
21 MAE; Direction des affaires politiques: Europe, Série 36; Sous-Série 23; Dossier 1. U.R.S.S.: Politique Exterieure; Ligues Politique. 1961. "A/S. L'URSS et l'Afrique". Ambassade de France Moscou 29.11.1961, p. 5.
22 MAE; Direction des affaires politiques: Europe, Série 36; Sous-Série 21; Dossier 21. U.R.S.S.: Politique Exterieure; Ligues Politique. 1967. "A/S Navires soviétiques transitant par Suez". Ambassade de France Moscou 2.08.1967, p. 1.
23 MAE; Direction des affaires politiques: Europe, Série 36; Sous-Série 23; Dossier 1. U.R.S.S.: Politique Exterieure; Ligues Politique. 1961. "A/S. L'URSS et l'Afrique". Ambassade de France Moscou 29.11.1961, p. 5.
24 MAE; Direction des affaires politiques: Europe, Série 36; Sous-Série 23; Dossier 1. U.R.S.S.: Politique Exterieure; Ligues Politique. 1961. "A/S. L'URSS et l'Afrique". Ambassade de France Moscou 29.11.1961, p. 5.
25 MAE; Direction des affaires politiques: Europe, Série 36; Sous-Série 23; Dossier 1. U.R.S.S.: Politique Exterieure; Ligues Politique. 1961. "A/S. L'URSS et l'Afrique". Ambassade de France Moscou 29.11.1961, p. 6.
26 MAE; Direction des affaires politiques: Europe, Série 36; Sous-Série 23; Dossier 1. U.R.S.S.: Politique Exterieure; Ligues Politique. 1961. "A/S. L'URSS et l'Afrique". Ambassade de France Moscou 29.11.1961, p. 6.
27 Melasuo, Tuomo, *Algerian poliittinen kehitys 1800-luvulta vapautussotaan 1954* (Tampere: Tampereen yliopiston paino, 1999).
28 MAE; Direction des affaires politiques: Europe, Série 36; Sous-Série 7; Dossier 6. U.R.S.S: Défense Nationale 1966–1970 "A/S: L'URSS en Méditerranée. 29.9.1969, p. 4.

29 MAE; Direction des affaires politiques: Europe, Série 36; Sous-Série 7; Dossier 6. U.R.S.S: Défense Nationale 1966–1970 "A/S: L´URSS en Méditerranée. 29.9.1969, p. 4.
30 Sivan, Emmanuel, *Communisme et nationalisme en Algérie, 1920–1962* (Presses de la foundation nationale des sciences politiques, 1976).
Alleg, Henri, *The Algerian Memoirs: Days of Hope and Combat*. Translated by Gila Walker (Chicago: University of Chicago Press, 2011).
31 MAE; Direction des affaires politiques: Europe, Série 36; Sous-Série 23; Dossier 16. Relations avec l´Afrique 1962. "A/S. L´URSS et l´Afrique". Ambassade de France Moscou 2.5.1962, p. 1.
32 Byrne, Jeffrey James, *Mecca of Revolution: Algeria, Decolonization and the Third World Order* (London: Oxford University Press, 2016).
33 MAE; Direction des affaires politiques: Europe, Série 36; Sous-Série 23; Dossier 16/1. Relations Afrique du Nord -URSS: URSS-Algerie. 1968. "A/s Communistes algeriens" 15.10.1968.
34 MAE; Direction des affaires politiques: Afrique du Nord: Algérie, Série A14; Sous-Série 8; Dossier 1. 1966-1968. Relations Afrique du Nord -URSS: URSS-Algerie. Politique extérieur; Pays socialistes Européens; URSS. Sous-Direction Algerie " A/s. l´URSS et l´Algerie en 1967. 22.1.1967, p. 2.
35 Komsomolskaya Pravda 1.7.1964.
36 MAE; Direction des affaires politiques: Europe, Série Série 36; Sous-Série 23; Dossier 1. U.R.S.S.: Politique Exterieure; Ligues Politique. 1966. "Moscou No 4748-57 Pravda 18.10.1966", pp. 2–3.
37 MAE; Direction des affaires politiques: Europe, Série Série 36; Sous-Série 23; Dossier 1. U.R.S.S.: Politique Exterieure; Ligues Politique. 1966. "Moscou No 4748-57 Pravda 18.10.1966", pp. 2–3.
38 MAE; Direction des affaires politiques: Europe, Série Série 36; Sous-Série 23; Dossier 1. U.R.S.S.: Politique Exterieure; Ligues Politique. 1966. "Moscou No 4748-57 Pravda 18.10.1966", pp. 2–3.
39 MAE; Direction des affaires politiques: Europe, Série Série 36; Sous-Série 23; Dossier 1.U .R.S.S. 1966-1970: Politique Exterieure; Ligues Politique. 1966. "Les Tendacies Actuelles de la politique exterieure Sovietique" (Memorandum without date.i.e. white paper.), p. 14.
40 MAE; Direction des affaires politiques: Europe, Série Série 36; Sous-Série 23; Dossier 1.U .R.S.S. 1966-1970: Politique Exterieure; Ligues Politique. 1967. "La Politque de L´U.R.S.S". au cours des six derniers mois. B. Doctrine militaire et stratégie: 8.11.1967, p. 28.

References

Allison, Drew, "Bolshevizing Communist Parties: The Algerian and South African Experiences", *International Review of Social History* 48, no. 2 (2003), p. 167.
Byrne, Jeffrey James, *Mecca of Revolution: Algeria, Decolonization and the Third World Order* (London: Oxford University Press, 2016).
Engermann, David C., "The Second World's Third World", *Kritika: Explorations in Russian and Eurasian History* 12, no. 1 (Winter 2011), pp. 183–211.
Gallissot, René with Badia, Gilbert, *Marx, marxisme et Algérie: textes de Marx-Engels* (Paris: Union Générale d´éditions, 1976).
Harb, Ali, *Soft Power Revolutions in the Arab World: From System to Network* (Beirut: Arab House of Science Publishers, 2014).
(ناشرون للعلوم العربية الدار. الشبكة إلى المنظومة من العربي العالم في الناعمة القوة ثورات: حرب علي)
Henri, Alleg, *The Algerian Memoirs: Days of Hope and Combat*. Translated by Gila Walker (Chicago: University of Chicago Press, 2011).

Hussein, Mahmoud, *L'Égypte: lutte de classes et libération nationale 1945–1967* (Paris: Maspéro, Petite collection, 2 vol.) (2ème ed. 1945–1973, 1975).

Luxemburg, Rosa, *The Accumulation of Capital* (London: Routledge, 2003). Originally published in 1913.

Melasuo, Tuomo, *Algerian poliittinen kehitys 1800-luvulta vapautussotaan 1954* (Tampere: Tampereen yliopiston paino, 1999).

Nye, Joseph S., *Soft Power: The Means to Success in World Politics* (New York: Public Affairs, 2004).

Pennar, Jaan, "The Arabs, Marxism and Moscow: A Historical Survey", *Middle East Journal* 22, no. 4 (Autumn 1968), pp. 433–447.

Rabah, Makram, *A Campus at War: Student Politics at the American University of Beirut 1967–1975* (Beirut: Nelson Publications, 2009).

Said, Edward, *Orientalism* (New York: Pantheon, 1978).

Sivan, Emmanuel, *Communisme et nationalisme en Algérie, 1920–1962* (Paris: Presses de la foundation nationale des sciences politiques, 1976).

Vasilev, Alexei, *Russia's Middle East Policy: From Lenin to Putin* (London: Routledge 2018).

Young, Robert J. C., *Postcolonialism: An Historical Introduction*, Anniversary Edition (London: Wiley-Blackwell, 2016).

Archives

-Ministère des affaires étrangères de la France (MAE)

Newspapers

- *Kommunist* (Moscow)
- *Komsomolskaya Pravda* (Moscow)

Epilogue
North-South and Social Democratic transformations in Europe and beyond

Bernd Rother

This book deals with two main topics: the European social democracy's gradual shift from Keynesian to so-called neoliberal economic policies and the importance of the spatial divide into North and South in Europe for the trajectory of the social democratic movement. I will try to put both issues in a larger frame, chronologically as well as geographically. I will shortly go back to the origins of the European workers' movement and I will look beyond Europe.

North and South in the history of the European workers' movement

Industrialisation started in Western Europe (England and Belgium) and then spread to Central Europe (Germany and the Czech Lands). Southern and Eastern Europe were the latecomers. In terms of socio-economic structures, Europe was divided in an industrially developed Northwest and a backward agricultural South and East. In the 19th century, sometimes even until today, inside of many European countries, the North was economically stronger than the South: Germany, France, Italy, the Netherlands, Portugal and Spain are proof of this, and Belgium, Great Britain and Sweden the most prominent counter-examples.

As a stepchild of capitalist industrialisation, the workers' movement adopted this spatial pattern. It began in Western and Central Europe, but rapidly gained a foothold in many other countries (the Portuguese socialists were founded in 1875, the Spanish in 1879). It took considerably different shapes, and here again we find a spatial pattern: Marxists dominated in the Northwest, except for England, whereas Anarchists, Anarcho-Syndicalists or Maximalists (under which I do subsume also the Bolsheviks) had their strongholds in the South and in the East (and – not forget – in Northern Sweden). During the following decades, things did not change drastically except for the slow fading away of anarchism which experienced its last apogee in the first 12 months of the Spanish Civil War. From the 1930s onwards, the Communists took over their place as the main rival of the Social Democrats, and as a result of their important role in the French and Italian national liberation movements against the Nazi occupation, in both countries, the Communists even surpassed the respective socialist parties.

In the 1970s, under the impact of the New Left, the European democratic socialist movement, organised in the Socialist International, fanned out in two currents: the "Socialdemocrats" and the "Socialists". "Socialdemocrats" became the autodenomination of the moderates, Socialists those of the more radicals, although this did not perfectly correspond with the real names of the parties – the moderate Austrian party's name was until 1991 "Socialist Party of Austria/Revolutionary Socialists" – the Norwegian party, as well as the Dutch and the British were "Labour" or "Workers" parties, and only the Danish, Finnish, German and the Swedish parties really called themselves "Socialdemocrats".

In spatial terms, both currents could be easily distinguished: the "Socialdemocrats" were the parties from North and Central Europe, the "Socialists" those from countries neighbouring the Mediterranean Sea plus Portugal and Belgium. Only the British Labour Party did not join any of these groups. In the 1970s and the first years of the 1980s, the "Socialists" criticised the "Social Democrats" for having given up any efforts to overcome capitalism, whereas they themselves would introduce socialism when being in power. The "Socialists" condemned the German model of "co-management" ("Mitbestimmung") as corrupting the workers' representatives; their alternative was "autogestion", i.e. the workers run the factory and elected the bosses.

A third cleavage contributed more to the division among the "Socialists" than to unite them and to differentiate them from the "Socialdemocrats": the question of alliances with the Communists. After all, in the 1970s, it was only an issue for the French socialists. François Mitterrand and his comrades succeeded in changing the SI policy that until then had forbidden such alliances. But he did not succeed in convincing other socialist parties to follow his example, not to speak of the "Socialdemocrats". In the latter's countries, the Communists were irrelevant and an alliance out of question. But also in Greece, Italy, Portugal and Spain, the socialist parties rejected any idea of building popular front-style electoral coalitions or forming common governments with the Communists.

The split between northern "Socialdemocrats" versus southern "Socialists", discussed in this book by Paolo Borioni with respect to Italy, never reached the level of fixed organisations, despite some meetings arranged by Mitterrand in the mid-1970s and despite the loosely organised discussion circles of Scandilux and Eurosud which in the 1980s served for the Northern resp. the Southern parties to discuss international security problems. But this happened at a time when most of the previously "radical" southern parties had practised a U-turn in the field of economic policies, adopting austerity measures, and emerged as strong backers of the NATO double-track decision unlike the northern "Socialdemocrats" which now suddenly stood to the "left" of the "Socialists". These changes should invite historians to reflect on the importance of studying programmatic party documents.

Is there a socialist economic policy?

Until the 1930s, no proper social democratic policies on employment and to manage the business cycles ("Konjunkturpolitik") existed. With regard to economic theories, Marxism was an heir to the classical liberal economy: as long as capitalism survived, there was – according to Marx – no chance to influence the business cycles. The workers' movement could reduce the workday (Marx called the 10-hours-bill a victory for the "proletarian political economy", opposed to the "bourgeois political economy"), child labour could be forbidden, but the cyclical business crashes were kind of a natural law. The only way to end the repeating crises was to substitute capitalism for socialism, mainly via socialisation of the means of production and the planning of production by the society.

This programmatic deficit did not create any political problem as long as the workers' movement did not enter any government, i.e. until the end of the Great War 1918/19. But it became pressing when the world economic crisis broke out in 1929 and mass unemployment became the most urgent problem. Whereas Social Democracies in Scandinavia and the Democrats in the United States resorted to Keynesian recipes, and thus won elections, brought people back into work and established the welfare states, the German SPD in its vast majority ignored Keynes' recommendations. The result was that by promising job creation, the Nazi movement attracted more and more voters, even from the workers' class, and in 1933 took over power in Germany. The heritage of Marxism combined with the SPD's intellectual weakness and political timidity in the field of economics contributed to the rise of the Nazis with all its devastating results.

After 1945, the European Social Democrats had learned their lessons, and not only them. The Christian Democrats, the Gaullists or the British Conservatives also embraced a Keynesian strategy to combat crises and participated in building welfare states.

This explains why it took time for important Social Democratic parties to govern their countries. Here also we see a North-South pattern: Scandinavia had become a social-democratic stronghold already in the 1930s, followed by Great Britain in 1945 (until 1951). Only in the 1970s, the Social Democrats succeeded in expanding their command over more European countries: Austria, Germany and the Netherlands. Southern Europe with Portugal, Greece, France and Spain came next, between 1976 and 1982. But this wave of electoral triumphs happened when the era of the "boom", the Golden Age of spectacularly growing economies, rising salaries and expanding social services came to an end in the midst of the 1970s, exactly when the left parties (Social Democrats and Communists) gained the biggest share of power ever.

From the second half of the 1970s onwards, Social Democrats seemingly had to make a tough choice: either to protect the international competitivity of their national economies or to protect the share of the national income (salaries, social services) the workers had achieved in the last decades. The latter possibility would have meant to abandon the principle of free-trade, enshrined in the history of the workers' movement from the beginning when it fought against the corn bills that would have made bread more expensive, and to prefer a national way to socialism, as the British Labour Party did in the 1980s. But most other parties choose the former alternative.

At this moment, Social Democracy lost its programmatic hegemony in economics. The fact that it conserved its cultural hegemony did not outweigh this backlash; on the contrary, it laid the seeds of the current problems to combine the cultural and the economic left, or in other words: intellectuals and workers.

The first steps to embrace a neo-liberalist strategy were taken already in the 1980s, e.g. among the SPD economists, and even before; as the chapters in this book by Sami Outinen, Ilkka Kärrylä and Alan Granadino and by Michele di Donato show, there were clear signs pointing in this direction already in the mid-1970s. The result could be seen in the late 1990s and the following decades: the turn from social democracy to progressive neoliberalism in the version of Bill Clinton, Tony Blair and Barack Obama. In many countries, right-wing populist movements could now play the role of defenders of the welfare system, albeit in an ethnocentric version. The East European ex-communists, now converted into Social Democrats, followed the footsteps of their Western comrades, thus opening the way for the Kaczynski brothers and for Orbán.

But for some time, it seemed that Social Democrats could escape from the deadly alternative described above by helping to establish a New Economic World Order inspired by Keynes' theories. This leads us to the second main topic of the book, explored in closer detail from a French perspective by Mathieu Fulla.

The Socialists and the Global South

When the Second International (1889–1914) discussed imperialism and colonialism, it did so from a Northern standpoint, even if this was a critical one. Born as an adversary to nationalism and as herald of internationalism, it was hard for it to relate to national liberation movements. The adoption of Marxist thoughts did not make things easier as Marx and Engels taught their followers that history and socio-economic evolution would take place in stages, capitalism following feudalism and socialism following capitalism. For 19th-century Marxism, the imperialist powers brought progress to India and other countries by pushing the traditional societies into capitalism. Whereas the Communist International, founded in 1919, partially overcame this dogmatic thinking and for some years propagated national liberation as supporting the advance of a socialist revolution, European Social Democrats in the interwar period hesitated to fight for rapid independence of their respective national colonies. The few members of the International from outside Europe mostly represented the "emigrated Europe"; they were parties from countries such as Argentina organising the white workers who had left Italy etc.

After 1945, the European parties of Democratic Socialism did not act as a vanguard of decolonisation. The British Labour government accepted the independence of India, Pakistan (including what we know today as Bangladesh), Ceylon/Sri Lanka and Burma/Myanmar in 1947, but left the African part of the Empire untouched. The Dutch Labour Party PvdA supported the war against Indonesia's independence in 1946/47. The French socialists fought, when in government in the 1950s, against the Algerian liberation movement FLN and participated in the 1956 Anglo-French Suez Canal intervention. It was during the rule of the Conservatives in France and Great Britain that Africa was decolonised.

Not surprisingly, the Socialist International had a bad reputation in the so-called Third World. The first to break with this sombre past were the Swedish SAP, the renewed PvdA and the German SPD. In the second half of the 1960s, they started to reach out to liberation movements, but outside the SI framework.

As a paradox, the expansion of Social Democracy, embodied by the Socialist International (SI), beyond the "old continent" began in Europe, more precisely in Portugal, and outside the organisational framework of the SI. In 1974/75, Portugal was the scenario for the last experiment of a classical socialist revolution worldwide, but already with some non-classical ingredients, i.e. the military origin. For the first time in history, the social democrats gained the upper hand against the communists in a non-electoral way, Mário Soares being not the revenant of Alexander Kerensky, as Henry Kissinger had predicted, but the herald of a bright future for democratic socialism.

The Socialist Party's triumph in Portugal and a few years later the successful and peaceful transition from dictatorship to democracy in Spain bringing the PSOE to power in 1982 were one of three motifs for Latin American reformists to approach Europe's Social Democrats. The second motive was the admired example of the European welfare state. Latin American oligarchs always argued that social reforms had to be postponed until economic success had happened. In Europe, Social Democrats (and Christian Democrats) had proved that both goals could be reached at the same time. The third motive was the search of the Latin Americans for allies on a global scale to weaken the US hegemony over their subcontinent.

The three motifs brought Europeans and Latin Americans together, starting with the Caracas conference in May 1976. It is important to emphasise that the initiative for the cooperation often came from the Latin Americans. On the European side, as the chapter by Ana Monica Fonseca in this book shows, there was growing interest within the European social-democratic parties towards Latin America in the early 1970s. There had also been some discussions between Willy Brandt, Bruno Kreisky and Olof Palme about a collaborative project, but until 1975/76 with no practical results. At this moment, the Latin Americans took the lead.

The Caracas conference was not a SI project. Brandt and his fellows regarded the International as a sclerotic organisation. The Latin Americans wanted to avoid appearing in a context labelled "socialist". The final document of the Caracas conference where nearly 30 party leaders from Europe and Latin America had gathered vaguely spoke of "like-minded" participants. As to contents, it followed more or less the Bad Godesberg version of Social Democracy.

Only in November 1976, with Willy Brandt being elected president of the Socialist International, the Caracas project was integrated into the SI framework. Brandt, who for months had hesitated to accept the SI presidency, finally gave in under the heavy pressure by nearly the totality of his fellow party chairmen, led by Kreisky and Palme. One of his conditions to accept the new office was that the SI should show programmatic flexibility when looking for new partners outside Europe. He dreamed of bringing together European Social Democrats and Socialists with US Democrats, India's Congress Party, Latin American populist reformists like the PRI in Mexico and the Venezuelan Acción Democrática, the ruling African parties from Kenya, Senegal, Tanzania, and – last but not least – liberation movements as Angola's MPLA or the ANC. Brandt did not look for social democrat (or socialist) purity but for forces with power that had the potential to ameliorate the fate of their peoples.

Much of this could not be realised. In Africa, as well as in Asia, the expectation of closer contacts did not materialise, despite some hope-generating first contacts. And unexpected problems laid stones in the way of the SI's global expansion. Senegal's Leopold Senghor organised the "Interafricaine socialiste" that brought together reformist, Western-orientated parties from North and West Africa. The liberation movements from southern Africa and Julius Nyerere's Tanzanian party declined to work together with the "Interafricaine" because it was not anti-imperialistic enough. Vice versa, Senghor and the other leaders objected to the liberation movements because of their narrow ties with Moscow and their adherence to Marxism-Leninism. Led by the SPD and the Swedish SAP, but also supported by the Portuguese and French socialists, the SI chose to prefer the liberation movements over the "Interafricaine".

Contrary to Africa and Asia, Latin America became a success story for the SI, although the cooperation that followed the Caracas conference and Brandt's election as SI president proved to be difficult and often asymmetric, with the Europeans trying to preserve the control of the process. What was the reason for the different outcomes? As mentioned, the Latin Americans themselves were searching for new allies. In Africa and Asia, this was not the case or only to a much lesser extent. Second, in terms of programmes, of ideological catchwords, the Latin American reformists were closer to the European social democratic tradition. Third, among the potential partners in Latin America which Brandt et al. had on their list, there was no one-party-state. Mexico, which came closest to this model widespread in Africa, was nominally a pluralist democracy. Fourth, the cleavage between traditional Cold War orientation towards the US-led West and preference for anti-imperialist alliances was not as important in Latin America as in Africa. With the exception of Costa Rica, all SI members from the region professed a more or less aggressive anti-US rhetoric.

Much of this was not new. New and decisive was that under the impact of decolonisation, of the New Left, of the global "1968", and also of a generational change inside the parties (both on the level of membership and of leadership), the SI and most of its European member parties from the early 1970s on embraced anti-imperialism. Time and again, Latin American SI leaders stressed that until then, the SI had been regarded in their countries as faithful allies of the United States. Only when the Europeans began to distance themselves from US activities in Vietnam, Chile and other places, doors were opened and the SI was welcomed in Latin America.

What did this anti-imperialism mean programmatically? Until the late 1960s, the SI regarded an unequivocal commitment to a multi-party democracy and the alignment with the United States led bloc as indispensable for membership. But what did multi-party democracy have to do with real freedom of choice when oligarchs controlled the election process, when their puppet parties alternated in government without changing anything regarding illiteracy, poor health services, poverty and social inequalities? Or to put it the other way round: How should the SI evaluate the Cuban system, where political democracy was absent but in terms of education and health people lived much better than in most other Latin American countries? In the early 1970s, Cuba became a touchstone for European-Latin American relations. Many left and centre-left forces in Latin America admired Cuba for having successfully challenged the United States and for having introduced state-of-the-art social services. Even if those forces did not want to emulate Cuba's political system, in any conflict between the island and the United States, they stood side-by-side with Castro. During Willy Brandt's presidency, the SI's image in Latin America changed drastically and very quickly from that of a US vassal to an anti-imperialist force.

What the Latin Americans aimed at when joining the SI, were two things: the larger countries and parties were looking for allies to improve the terms of trade of their national economy vis-à-vis the OECD countries; the smaller countries and parties looked for solidarity in their struggle to overcome oligarchic structures. And we should not forget personal ambitions: Carlos Andrés Pérez, twice President of Venezuela, wanted to enter the international stage and become a globally respected leader; as a black man with Haitian roots José Francisco Pena Gómez, secretary general of the Dominican Republic's PRD party, had no chance to be elected president of his country, and so he began an international career; Luis Echeverría from Mexico strove for the Nobel peace prize and the best way to succeed seemed to become a (political) friend of the 1971 Nobel Peace Prize winner.

But political, not personal motifs were dominant. To improve the terms of trade implied two aspects that were rarely mentioned. First, Latin American countries strove for an increasing integration into the global economy which was (and is) dominated by capitalist structures; what perhaps could be changed was the geographic breakdown of the major export/import partners, i.e. to substitute (partially) the United States for the EC/EU. Second, it implied forgetting about South-South cooperation. Taken together, for the South, this strategy meant more, not less Eurocentrism.

For ten years, the SI – and especially Jamaica's Michael Manley – tried to elaborate a Socialist Economic Program. An important contribution to this discussion was the so-called Brandt report, published in early 1980 resuming the discussions of the Independent North-South commission headed by the SI president. This body did not have any direct links to the SI, but with Willy Brandt as chairman and Olof Palme as member of the commission, it did not come as a surprise that the ideas of the report were interpreted by many observers as SI thinking. Manley built upon the report's findings. He shared the neo-Keynesian proposal of large financial transfers from the North to the South that should stimulate the economies there. The idea was that growing "Southern" economies would order goods in the "North" and thereby contribute to job creation in the European and North American industries. A mutual win-win situation seemed reachable. Manley was also looking for a solution to the debt crisis that shook the Third World in the 1980s, a solution that would be different from the IMF's and World Bank's austerity programmes. He hoped to build a social democratic bloc in the governing bodies of both institutions and – beyond these finance institutions – to organise a system of mutual help between governments led by SI parties. Nothing of this became reality. With first Margaret Thatcher's and then Ronald Reagan's victory, the neoliberal agenda dominated the World Economic Summits. And among Social Democrats, national interests often stood in the way of inter-governmental solidarity.

Whereas efforts to synchronise the economic policies of SI members in the North and the South were to no avail, the solidarity with local anti-oligarchic movements was much more successful. In the Dominican Republic, the European SI party's solidarity with their PRD comrades was important to secure in 1978 the victory in the presidential elections against the long-time conservative office-holder who tried to falsify the results. In Nicaragua, governments led by SI members, especially Costa Rica and Venezuela, channelled more arms and other supplies to the Sandinista guerrilla movement than Cuba. After the FSLN's victory over Anastasio Somoza, European social democratic governments were among the largest contributors of aid to the new rulers. In El Salvador, the tiny MNR party had influence in the political wing of the local liberation movement against oligarchic rule only because it belonged to the SI network. For the guerrilla, the MNR was the gateway via the SI to the international public arena.

El Salvador and Nicaragua proved to be difficult partners. The MNR was too weak to steer the guerrillas' political course; time and again, the SI was faced with actions it could not tolerate, such as attacks on voters or politically motivated kidnapping. In Nicaragua, the Sandinistas tried for some years to establish a Marxist-Leninist one-party rule. The United States under the Reagan administration led a covered war against Nicaragua. The SI tried to tame both, the United States and the government of Nicaragua. What happened in Central America and the Caribbean was not only a conflict over values such as democracy and social development but also a geopolitical challenge for the Europeans and some Latin American SI members such as Costa Rica's PLN. On the one hand, they sympathised with the cause of the liberation movements, on the other hand, their countries were allies of the United States, and to appear as anti-American weakened the position in elections. To the credit of the SI and its member parties, especially Acción Democrática (Venezuela), PLN Costa Rica, SPD, the Swedish SAP, the French PS and the Spanish PSOE, it can be said that they contributed decisively to avoiding a full-scale US military intervention in the region and, at the same time, convinced Nicaragua's Sandinistas to accept the result of democratic elections, ousting them from power in 1990. But looking at El Salvador and Nicaragua today, nothing reminds us of these glorious times.

Index

Agenda 2030 167–170, 173
Amsterdam Treaty 50, 61
autogestión (self-management) 5, 31, 40, 195

Bretton-Woods 6, 29, 71, 157
British Labour Party (BLP) 4, 13–14, 35, 51, 75, 84, 111, 143, 195–196

Caetano, Marcelo 87, 93, 143–144
Caracas conference 148–149, 198–199
carnations 145; coup 87; revolution 30–32, 151
Cold War 1, 15, 29, 50, 67–70, 111, 124, 142, 156, 171, 184, 199
communism 9, 29, 67, 91, 142, 176
Communist International 12, 197
constructivism 10, 112
Council of Europe 16–17, 21, 89–91, 144
cultural affinity 124–125, 127–128, 130, 134
cultural diplomacy 127, 130

decolonisation 15, 34, 67, 93, 124, 176, 181, 197
Delors, Jacques 49–52, 57–61
democratic socialism 3, 11, 29, 48, 93, 107, 134, 148, 197
democratisation 2, 40, 84–87, 142, 151, 161, 178
détente 32, 68, 94, 127, 143, 176
development aid 124–125, 127, 132, 185

employment policy 39, 48
Estoril conference 147–150
Eurocentrism 148, 200
European Community (EC) 3, 5–6, 17–18, 20, 38, 50, 69, 74–75, 79, 95

European Economic Community (EEC) 13, 17–21, 34–35, 37, 52, 88–91, 108, 131, 143–144
European Employment Initiative (EEI) 50–52
European Free Trade Area (EFTA) 18
Europeanisation 51–54, 57, 67–68, 72, 74, 77–78
European Monetary System (EMS) 53

Fascism 12, 36, 111, 142
Frankfurt declaration 13–14
Fredrick Ebert Foundation (FES) 31, 90, 144–145, 147–151, 163
full employment 29, 39, 42, 48–49, 54–56, 61–62, 166–167
Future studies 125, 131–132

geopolitical 77, 179, 182, 185, 201
Ghent system 5, 105, 108
globalisation 1, 29, 67, 133, 155–157, 160
Global South 1, 124–126, 130–133, 165, 176, 181, 197
Godesberg programme 2, 14, 37, 198
González, Felipe 6, 48, 52, 147, 151

Iberian: countries 150; democracy 97; democratisation 147; dictatorship 142–143; experiences 147; parties 4, 84; peninsula 3, 20, 85, 87, 146; processes of democratisation 47, 85; transitions to democracy 84–85, 87, 97, 142
international cooperation 6, 69, 161, 168
internationalisation 40, 126, 173
International Labour Organization (ILO) 165, 167
international solidarity 11–12, 126

Keynesian: demand 109; demand management 70; economic policies 2, 11, 39, 48, 106, 118, 171, 194; Euro- 61; full employment policy 42; post- 76; principles 61; public borrowing 57; stimulation of demand 159; strategy 196; thought 117
Keynesianism 160; Neo- 200; *see also* Keynesian
Kissinger, Henry 71–77, 198
Kreisky, Bruno 2, 35, 62, 142, 148, 198

Latin America 6, 14, 142, 147–151, 161, 198–200
Latin Europe 76, 147
Lenin, Vladimir 179–183

Mediterranean 32, 73, 129, 176–179, 181, 183, 185–187, 189–190
methodological nationalism 1
Middle East 7, 148, 161, 167, 176–185, 187–189
Mitbestimmung 106, 108, 110, 119, 195
modernisation 70, 105, 115, 127, 130, 134, 158

nationalism 12, 16, 171
Nazism 12, 106, 108
neoliberal economic policies 2, 194
neoliberalism 31, 37, 39, 49, 155, 197
New International Economic Order 2, 39, 73, 125, 156–157
non-aligned 6, 131, 177, 188
Nordic balance 124
Nordicisation 48, 50–51, 53, 56, 61–62
Nordic model 53, 58, 190
Nordic social democratic: parties 27, 50, 54, 124; political reforms 7; societies 7
norm entrepreneurship 124–125
North Atlantic Treaty Organization (NATO) 16, 32, 67, 89–90, 124, 156, 195
Northern Africa 177–179, 186, 189
Northern Europe 3–5, 29, 155
North-South Program for Survival (NSPS) 157

Opinion formation 133
ordo liberal 50, 62, 106–107, 121
Ordo liberalism 106
Ostpolitik 72, 143

Palme, Olof 2, 35, 48, 71, 88, 125, 142, 156, 198

Pan-Africanism 182, 189
Party of European Socialists (PES) 4, 49, 52
periphery 19, 134, 182
political economy 2, 30, 131
political history 1, 29, 117
populism 3, 155, 158, 162–164
Portuguese Socialist Party (PSP) 29, 31, 35, 93, 144, 146, 150
public diplomacy 125–126, 129–130

radicalism 105–106
Reagan, Ronald 4, 39, 48, 201
reformism 9, 12, 105, 111–113, 118

Schröder, Gehard 30, 52, 62
small state: doctrine 131–132; solidarity 6, 124–125, 130–131, 134
Soares, Mário 6, 31, 35, 49, 89, 143–151, 198
social democracy: end of 2; European 1, 9, 30, 50, 70, 105, 145; Nordic 126
socialisation 9–11, 15, 21–23, 54, 68, 70, 86, 196
Socialist international 5, 9, 69, 84, 142, 161, 195
Southern Europe 1, 6, 29–30, 48–49, 67, 73–75, 84, 97, 106, 142, 168, 196
Soviet orientalism 181
Soviet Union 88, 145, 155, 176
Spanish Socialist Party (PSOE) 53, 57, 90–92, 94–96, 147, 198, 201
Stalin, Joseph 155, 180–181, 183, 186
Suez Canal 184, 186, 198
Swedish Institute 125–127, 129
Swedish Social Democratic Party (SAP) 51, 92, 132

Thatcher, Margaret 4, 39, 48, 201
third way 1–4, 30, 52, 61–62, 160
Third World 3, 73, 124–126, 128–134, 181, 198
transatlantic relations 69, 71, 73
transnational networks 1, 9–11, 21–22, 68

United Nations (UN) 3, 39, 125, 157, 161, 185

Washington Consensus 4
welfare state 2, 9, 38, 107, 124, 158, 178, 198
Willy Brandt 2, 35, 62, 71, 88, 106, 142, 156, 167, 198–200
Wilson, Harold 35, 88, 91, 143
working class 3, 29, 31, 36, 105, 161

Printed in the United States
by Baker & Taylor Publisher Services